Teaching Compassion

On Behalf of the Animals

Robert Sebastian Everett Caine, Ph.D.

WH
WATERHILL
PUBLISHING

ISBN: 978-0-9939938-2-4

DEDICATION

During the final stages of completing this book, I tragically
lost seven of my children,
Woody, Sir Maximillion, Sterling Silver, Chester,
Stella, Noah Bunny and Maya. They all were and continue to
be eternal loves of my life.

In Loving Memory

My little girl Anna 'Bunny' Caine
who was taken from this life far too soon. How I miss holding her and cuddling
with her on the sofa. She was the first bunny I adopted into my home and Anna will
always be remembered as a matriarch of my extended family.
She emanated pure innocence and unconditional love. Her gift to me was peace,
tranquillity, and unrelenting acceptance.

Anna remains forever in my heart.

In Loving Memory

Woody was and will always be the patriarch of my family.

Woody was a beautiful grey cockatiel whose personality surpassed any human I have ever known. I adopted Woody when he was five years old; he lived to a ripe age of more than 24 years.

A faithful and loving companion, a best friend, a true teacher of compassion and love, Woody exuded the purest form of unconditional acceptance and love; he brought so much positive energy into my life; if not for him, I probably would not have adopted the dozen more animals that became my family.

I will always remember Woody as my hero, my most loyal friend, and my eternal love.

Woody remains forever in my heart.

In Loving Memory

Sir Maximillion was my constant companion. An adorable pug with more love than I thought existed in this world, he was at my side as a fellow educator of kindness and compassion for animals, he accompanied me to many events in several cities, and he and I gained notoriety as a travelling pair.

There really are no words to do justice to the deep and intense love I had and will always have for my little companion.

I have included the dedication I wrote for Sir Maximillion in Chapter 2 of this book; I wrote this memorial following his passing on April 2, 2013.

I miss my little pug immensely and I hope to be reunited with him in the not too distant future so I can hug him again and mend my broken heart.

Sir Maximillion remains forever in my heart.

In Loving Memory

Sterling Silver served as one of the family patriarchs. He was a true, loyal, and loving companion to Woody and later, to Chester as well. He trusted my care and love for him and he was an irreplaceable friend and companion.

Sterling overcame extensive illness from his early years due to the persistent and loving care of our former vet in San Francisco. He continued on to live for more than 17 years as an unforgettable and most loved family member. His absence has created a traumatic void and we continue to mourn terribly for the loss of our beloved cockatiel.

Sterling is remembered for his charisma, for his beauty, and for his ever-present love which remains with us eternally.

Sterling remains forever in my heart.

In Loving Memory

Chester was a timid cockatiel whom I rescued from a shelter because I knew that he would make a most welcome addition to our family.   While visiting him at the shelter, Chester called to me with song and whistles.
I happily answered his call and welcomed him into our family.

Chester took an immediate liking to Sterling and tirelessly made the effort to capture Sterling's heart. Later, after Sterling passed away, Chester bonded with Woody.

Eventually, Chester demonstrated his trust and love of me.

His beautiful voice and his pure innocence added so much love to our home and to our family. He will always be remembered as a cherished friend and companion.

Chester remains forever in my heart.

In Loving Memory

Stella was one of the sweetest little bunnies I ever met. I rescued her from a shelter where I volunteered to help care for bunnies and small critters. Stella was the picture of pure innocence, gentleness and unquestionable love. Sadly, her life was very brief.

Rest peacefully, Stella, knowing that you were and are very much loved.

Stella remains forever in my heart.

In Loving Memory

Noah bestowed much love and positive energy into my life and into the life of her companion, Sonoma. She emanated motherhood, companionship, friendship, mentorship, and purity.

Her demise has affected us profoundly as we continue to mourn for the loss of our little bunny. Noah is remembered for her lively energy, for her beauty, for her love, and for her giving presence which remains with us eternally.

Noah remains forever in my heart.

In Loving Memory

Maya was a beautiful milk chocolate brown bunny who befriended Sonoma and evolved as his companion.

I remember rescuing Maya from a shelter; she was full of energy and her eyes spoke to my heart. Always a bit shy, Maya slowly learned to trust my unconditional love for her as she slowly but steadily came to me to receive a treat and some attention.

During the final stages of editing my book, Maya became ill and shortly thereafter, she crossed over Rainbow Bridge.

We continue to mourn the loss of our beloved and treasured Maya Bunny.

Maya remains forever in my heart.

In Loving Memory

Mr. Fish and Silky Fish were two beta-fish residing in my home in California. Most people do not think of fish as having personalities; also, most people do not think that fish can communicate with us. These fish were very much aware of my presence. They resided in octagonal shaped aquaria; when I would enter the room, Mr. Fish would swim to the side that was closest to my physical stance; he would actually make eye contact with me. Whether he was asking for food or simply for some attention, I cannot say with certainty; however, he definitely communicated with me. Silky Fish also was keenly aware of my presence and seemed to look in my direction when I stood nearby. Sadly, Mr. Fish died during our move from Los Angeles to San Francisco. About a year later, Silky Fish quickly became ill and crossed over within a few days; I assume that he was elderly and died from advanced age.

I miss seeing my two fish when entering my home. I truly felt a connection with them. I sensed real communication, a sense of family, and whether or not fish can feel love, I did experience unconditional love from and for these beautiful betas.

Mr. Fish and Silky Fish remain forever in my heart.

All my other companions,

Sonoma, Berkeley, Forest,

you continue to be my motivation for teaching compassion towards animals.

You are my family.

My heart will always belong to you and my love for you sustains eternally.

Further Dedications

This book and the loving messages herein are whole-heartedly dedicated to all the animals who have suffered and fallen victim to the ignorance and cruelty of my species.

It is my greatest hope that one day soon, humans will wake up to the most monumental holocaust they have created on Earth: the holocaust of my animal friends.

Contents

ABOUT THE AUTHOR

Acknowledgments

Writing this book has been a truly emotional and spiritual journey. My unconditional love for animals and my dedication to bringing greater compassion into their lives is what motivates me to carry on from day to day. My heart-felt dedications serve not only as a vehicle for me to convey my deep and absolute love for my companion animals, my family -- or as I refer to them: my children -- but the foregoing dedications are also intended to convey to my readers the magnitude of compassion and unrelenting love that we can possess and express for the other-than-human. Many people possess the capacity for such passion and devotion, and it is my hope that my book assists my readers in bringing such feelings, attentiveness and commitment to the forefront of their conscience. For many of us, our companion animals are not "pets," but rather, cherished members of our family.

To list all the names of individuals for whom I feel gratitude would fill up several pages; also, I do not wish to exclude any individual person or organisation that I feel deserves recognition. However, I do wish to express my deepest gratitude to everyone who has accepted our non-human counterparts as our fellow earthlings -- to those people who see animals as our friends, our family, and our loved ones, to those people who choose *not* to participate in the cultural 'norms' that cause so much exploitation, pain and suffering to our innocent and defenceless fellow beings, and to those who have worked so tirelessly to defend the rights, the dignity, and the freedom of animals throughout the globe.

In particular, I am extremely grateful to the people on the front line who engage in protests against animal cruelty, who participate in vigils outside of slaughterhouses, laboratories, animal entertainment centres, and all other venues where cruelty towards animals sustains as a function of 'doing business.' I am also profoundly grateful to those individuals who have established safe havens, farm animal sanctuaries, and protective forever loving homes for animals desperately in need of a safe and caring place to reside and thrive.

I am humbled and honoured to know so many vegetarians and vegans who have evolved their lives to a higher level of understanding and empathy towards animals. Our vegetarian/vegan community continues to grow and expand on a global scale. Even the word 'veganism' is quickly becoming a household word. I cannot express my gratitude enough to those of you who have opened your minds and your hearts to the plight of animals to the extent that you have engaged in positive, life-affirming lifestyle changes that abstain from activities that cause needless pain and suffering of our animal friends and I thank you for your courage and motivation to live a compassionate life.

Further, and stemming from the spirit of this book, I wish to acknowledge all those educators who demonstrate the critical significance in teaching your students to thrive as Earth citizens, rather than Earth exploiters -- those educators who understand and convey education not only as learning reading, writing, mathematics, science and history -- but as viewing education as an irreplaceable opportunity to instil humane values within the classroom and beyond. Humane educators know the messages of compassion, empathy, reverence for life, respect, kindness, integrity, truth, cognitive and emotional transitions of both humans and non-human animals, and of course, love. I whole-heartedly acknowledge those educators who have dedicated their career and their life to bringing a greater sense of hope for all the animals in the world who are counting on us to encourage others to literally save countless lives of these truly deserving and loving beings.

And finally, although I could never complete the list of all the acknowledgements in my heart, I wish to acknowledge every person out there who has rescued an animal and provided them a caring and forever loving home. Whether you have taken in a dog, a cat, a bird, a rabbit, a hamster, a cow, a pig, a goat, a sheep, a chicken or any other of the Universe's gentle beings, I am forever grateful to you, as I am sure that animal is forever grateful that you saved their life.

Preface

The primary goal of this book is to wake up society to the realities of our exploitative relationships with animals and nature insofar as our day to day activities and lifestyles that infringe on the rights, needs, and desires of the other-than-human; literally, my hope is to ignite and encourage critical discussions about how we view our fellow non-human earthlings and bring these realities to the forefront of social consciousness as a vehicle for motivating and advancing a more compassionate and loving Earth community.

A broad and diverse audience will find value in the reality of knowing how every person on Earth may be subconsciously contributing to massive pain and suffering of innocent and defenceless animals on a day to day basis; to that extent, every person on Earth has the power and ability to adapt more humane ways of co-existing with our fellow earthlings; hence, everyone is capable of creating more peaceful and loving energy in our world, and in turn, evolving towards a life of compassionate living.

Teaching For Compassion: On Behalf of the Animals tenders a foundation for non-anthropocentric thinking for the whole of society as well as integration of anti-speciesist paradigms within scholastic and academic communities. Broad fields of philosophy – animal liberationist ideology, bio-centric environmentalism, eco-feminist perspectives, and veganism – are explored and integrated for fomenting strong advocacy for non-anthropocentric humane environmental education.

The educational goal of this book is to put forth a framework for humane environmentalism which is able to:

> (1) bring to social consciousness the pain and suffering meted out to non-human animals by humankind;

(2) recognise and acknowledge non-human animals as fellow earthlings with very similar needs and desires as humans; and,

(3) visualise and assert alternative ways of knowing, of thinking, of learning, and of living in relation to our non-human neighbours.

This leading-edge framework delves deeper into non-anthropocentric philosophy whereby humane values are introduced and discussed as means for altering social and individual attitudes, behaviours and lifestyle choices shifting from human-centeredness towards a relatedness of peaceful living with and among all species of Earth.

1

Humane Education as a Foundation for Learning Compassion towards All Living Beings

1.1 Experiential Humane Education: Woody – An Infallible Educator

> *Until he extends the circle of his compassion to all living things, man will not find peace* – Albert Schweitzer.

Nature prevails as an amazing educator. If we open our minds and our hearts to the inherent teachings of nature, we allow ourselves opportunity to experience the many wonders of the natural world. More specifically, animals are often the most effective teachers and are capable of conveying and influencing lessons of humane and loving ways of relating and living.

When I was a child, our family had a dog: Pumpkin. Pumpkin was a cross between a silky and a poodle – a little white dog full of energy and gusto; he was the most loving, adorable and sensitive being one could imagine. Pumpkin would wait by the front door every school day, my mother told me, starting about fifteen minutes before my imminent arrival. He always greeted me with great enthusiasm as I entered the door, jumping at my feet and begging for my attention.

He slept on my bed every night, sat by my side in front of the television, and lay himself under my desk while I completed my homework. The family referred to him as "Rob's dog." We shared a magnificent bond – I held absolute and unconditional love for Pumpkin – I like to think he felt the same way about me. His death devastated me – literally. I felt as though a part of me died with him. He passed away over twenty-five years ago, and to this day, when I think about my best childhood friend, I feel guilty that I did not spend more time with him, take him for more walks, or do anything possible to let him know that he was valued, revered and loved as much as anyone can love anyone. Following his demise, for years, I felt the deep loss and grief over my friend. I swore that I would never get another companion animal – the experienced pain following their demise can be overwhelming.

I met Woody about twenty years ago. Woody was a grey cockatiel with beautiful yellow feathers on his head, bright orange cheeks, and a personality more alive than most people I have met in my more than fifty years of life. Little did I know at the time, Woody was about to change my life in a momentous way. Woody's caretaker was unable to keep him; he offered Woody to me. A ménage of mixed emotions washed over me: scared, sceptical, nervous, excited, thrilled, happy and anxious to accept the responsibility of this vivacious and beautiful animal. I went with the latter emotions and gleefully took Woody into my home. This quick adoption was a pivotal point in my life – a transformative event.

Woody taught me that I could love again. He allowed me to look beyond my selfish need to protect myself from the pain of loss and to give my abundance of love to another. Although Pumpkin had died several years previously, I still experienced the sense of loss from the death of a loved one; Woody allowed me to heal further – I will never feel completely at peace with the loss of my childhood friend, Pumpkin – I do not know if we ever heal completely from losing someone we love; nevertheless, I have learned that I possess unlimited love to give to others. Woody taught me – yes, *he taught me* – that I need to have animals in my life, to share my living space with animals I can care for, and that it is better to provide happiness, care and love for an animal, even if only for a short time, than to never experience such a gift.

It is difficult to describe how an animal *teaches* us. Perhaps the lessons derive from their pure energy, their spiritual essence, their innocence. Or maybe the learning stems from their ability to give so much and ask for so little. I could feel the love emanating from Woody, just as I sense love from my other companion animals. A priori, if not for Woody, I would not have received other animals into my home. He opened that door. He allowed me to open my heart to others and realise my greatest gift is the gift of caring and love.

From living with several animals (three birds, six rabbits, two dogs, two cats, two fish), I have experienced innocence, beauty, magic and pure love of the universe. I have been able to celebrate life in the midst of continuous tragedy aired on the media. I have been able to rejoice daily because I am surrounded by love. I have learned that I gain pleasure, joy, elation and love by giving those very same gifts to my companion animals. Furthermore, I am focussing my entire life on caring ethics – for animals, environment, community, planet – somehow, in my heart, I know that I owe enormous gratitude and saving grace to Woody, a rather influential little bird.

*   *   *

The field of Humane Education presents an opportunity to reflect upon values indicative of a more peaceful and less oppressive society – namely, values of compassion, empathy, respect, reverence for life, kindness and love – moreover, humane education embraces human and non-human Earth residents as well as the whole of the biosphere. Humane education discourse is about making connections among all life forms, invoking a deep sense of compassion for other beings, and promoting a sense of peace and tranquillity throughout the biosphere. This field endeavours to facilitate students in realising their essential and integral role as planetary citizens; it delivers messages of responsibility, conviviality, and nurturance of other beings and of Earth. Humane education accomplishes these tasks through non-anthropocentric critical analysis as well as highly interactive and participatory group work whereby students are provided an array of activities to rethink their relatedness and connections with nature, with other species, and with one another. Some of the main topics covered in humane education include human/animal relationships (similarities and differences between the species), responsible pet care, issues surrounding farm animals (including lifestyle options of vegetarianism and veganism), wild animals and the natural environment, wild animals in captivity (embodying ethical argumentation for and against holding animals in captive and controlled settings), and animal experimentation/biomedical research/school dissection. But humane education is so much more than the sub-topics comprising the field of study; the overarching philosophy embarks on critical reflection of one's lifestyle, one's daily decision making, and how one relates to the natural world and all who abide within this world.

It is certainly a daring adventure to challenge the majority of society that sees fit to exploit other species and the natural environment for human gain; however, that is one of the paramount undertakings that I believe humane education endeavours to promote through critical thinking. Humane educators, as advocates of humaneness and humane values, need to challenge inhumane activities, behaviours and attitudes; the objectives of humane education embrace creating a more convivial and less violent world – no less can be acceptable in the process of educating children and adults alike to embrace compassion as a foundation for relating to nature, to other species, to each other. This book explores the need for humane education stemming from a non-anthropocentric foundation and an eco-spiritual relatedness to nature, to the *other-than-human* and to the whole of the biosphere. That notwithstanding, this book is not limited to an audience of educators/teachers; all human residents of Earth can benefit from the mindset philosophy embedded within the core messages of the forthcoming contents. Further, my intent in composing this book is hopefully to encourage educators and non-educators alike to ponder the issues of interconnectedness among species, including our human interactions with other species insofar as our affectation on their lives and vice versa. It is truly my hope that my readers will engage their critical thinking skills when delving the following pages, and really reflect upon daily activities, seemingly benign actions, that carry significant and life-altering impact on our fellow earthlings and on ourselves.

1.1.1 Inherent Hypocrisy of Anthropocentrism

Anthropocentrism is a dangerous run-away train of social order – the environment, non-human species, the planet itself are regarded as resources for human consumption and exploitation – such humanocentric ways of knowing are handed down from one generation to the next. Whether in the home, the classroom, the community centre, the media, industry, government, or a multitude of other outlets, children are taught to relate to nature from a human-centred bias that permeates all aspects of human society. Anthropocentrism is the root foundation of enormous pain and suffering caused by humans towards non-human species and the natural environment.

If we assert inherent value in every living being, as I do, why is it criminal to kill a cat or a dog, but not a cow or a pig? I am not suggesting that we ought to be allowed to torture and kill cats and dogs as we do to cows and pigs – obviously, I do not condone the killing of cows and pigs any more than I would of cats and dogs. I abhor any actions that bring pain and suffering to non-human animals or their natural environment – I most sincerely love all non-human animals and consider them my fellow earthlings, the extended family to which I belong. By adhering to the paradigm that all living beings possess inherent value, how can we subjectively, through our humanocentric valuation, decree one species as having a life of great *value* while diminishing the *value* of another species? Is there a moral justification for valuing specific life forms and condemning other life forms based on our subjective opinions of who or what possesses value? By exploiting some species while embracing and protecting other species, are we not teaching mixed and conflicting messages to our children reflecting our incongruent relationships with nature? And even if we do not categorise the act of killing an animal as criminal, what about the moral implications of such an action? My foregoing rhetorical questions merely point out a social hypocrisy – albeit a monumental hypocrisy and contextual conflict of moral and ethical reasoning. How *can* we condemn some species to torment and death while revering other species as our fellow companions and family? Selected species are awarded, sometimes, with kindness, companionship and a higher place in the so-called animal kingdom hierarchy (e.g., domestic dogs) while other species are destined to endure agony, torture and horrific suffering (e.g., pigs). How can we justify such hypocrisy in the disparate ways we treat other species?

In the case of dogs and cats versus cows and pigs: all four of these species are capable of experiencing pain and of suffering; all are capable of forming bonding relationships with parents, children, siblings, community members – even with humans; all are able to distinguish the difference between joy and pleasure versus agony and misery. A pig feels no less pain than a dog when stabbed with a knife, clubbed on the head, or kicked by a farmer's boot. Anatomically and psychologically, as well as psycho-emotionally, the dog and the pig are very similar in the light of their shared experience of pain and suffering. Nevertheless, society has managed to delude itself into ignoring the evidence that these two species do experience the same quality of sensory capacity. Or at least, we deny the commonality among species as regards their capacities for experiencing pain and suffering.

The perceived valuation between species, as subjected through anthropocentric hierarchicalisation, invokes irrational and illogical compartmentalisation of animals into divergent species categories of greater value or lesser value. Hence, humans decree hierarchical valuation of various species insofar as those species serve as means to human ends. For example, dogs are often viewed in Western society as companion animals, as family members, and even as adjuncts to our ego – fellow comrades who provide us with unconditional love and faithful devotion enabling our emotional, psychological, and familial needs. Especially in Westernised cultures, dogs are received into our homes as welcome friends, playmates, and even confidants. Contrarily, pigs, cows and chickens, for the most part in Western society, do not play an integral part in our lives – at least not when they are alive; so-called farm animals are usually kept far away from urban areas and out of sight from our witnessing their fatal destiny. This geographical distancing permits us to maintain a psychological distancing from these doomed animals; we do not want to see the faces, hear the voices, acquaint ourselves with the personalities, or witness the family and community dynamics of animals whom we are going to devour as food. Many of us remain in denial of the parallel similarities between what we term companion animals and what we think of as agricultural or farm animals (we also make the distinction, although subconsciously, between 'companion animals' and wild or free roaming animals). We justify protecting and nurturing companion animals – even though so many of these domesticated animals end up in shelters and abandoned along roadways, near farms, or on our city streets. We are abhorred upon hearing about a dog who is abused or a cat who is mutilated by some psychopath in our community; however, we do not feel this same repulsion or rage at the abuse, torture, and killing of millions of animals trapped and confined in factory farms, scientific and medical laboratories, circuses, zoos and marine parks, and military and governmental research facilities. This is a monumental hypocrisy of our cognitive dissonance pertaining to our inconsistent relatedness to various species: some animals are worthy of our protection, of our respect, of sharing our home and our space, and of receiving our love; other animals' lives are easily extinguished as pests, as human-end resources, as potential food products, and as objects lacking capacity for emotional, psychological, physical or even spiritual transitions. The whole notion of teaching children about 'happy farm animals' is ludicrous in light of the sheer agony these animals experience in factory farms and slaughterhouses; moreover, such convoluted messages whereby animals are 'happy' to be confined until slaughtered (although these words are never spoken in the classroom) invokes a curriculum that is nothing short of madness.

1.2 The Crux of Humane Education

Humane education advocates and encourages compassion, empathy, respect, kindness and positive regard towards all living beings – human and non-human alike. Humane education comprises a wealth of knowledge for transforming our society from a state of violence, chaos, and fragmentation towards a society of peace, tranquillity, egalitarianism, non-anthropocentrism, conviviality and harmony between the human and non-human beings of planet Earth (Selby, 1995; Weil & Sikora, 1999). Humane education truly engages a transformative paradigm (Pike, 2000; Pike & Selby, 2001; Selby, 2000) and pedagogy striving to connect humans with one another (and with non-human animals/nature) in more co-operative and convivial ways. Humane education encourages the acknowledgement and recognition of inherent value in each other and in other species; hence, each living being is viewed as possessing value unto itself for the sheer fact of its existence (Rowlands, 2002).

Unfortunately, most people are unaware of the field of humane education insofar as its far-reaching implications are concerned – they may oversimplify this area of study to confine its teaching to responsible pet care and spaying/neutering of domestic pets (Weil, 1999). This misperception may stem from the common usage of the term 'humane' in that it is usually associated with a 'humane society' or animal shelter. The responsibility of humane educators extends far beyond *pets* – moreover, responsible care of domestic animals is only a tiny fraction of the whole tapestry of humane education and all the topics and issues inhered in the field. Humane education essentially encourages students to view nature, other species and each other from a perspective of the values of compassion and empathy inherent of the field. This is an opportunity to teach young people (and older) not only the importance of respecting all of life, but also the connections that we, humans, share with our fellow earthlings. Just as students need to be taught history, geography, how to calculate mathematical problems, and how to write an effective and well organised essay, they also need to be taught about *kindness*; people need to understand and acknowledge the needs and desires of all living beings *a priori* to fully appreciate the very fact that the other-than-human carries the potential for suffering, for experiencing pain, for feeling the love and companionship of family and fellow community members. This field endeavours to facilitate what many people would think of as good sense – *being kind to others*; nevertheless, humane education is essential in that it addresses the needs, challenges and rights of non-human animals as well as of humans. As a member of the teaching profession, I do believe that children need to be taught how to be kind, respectful, and compassionate towards their fellow beings. Humane education serves as a launch pad for such erudition.

A foundation for humane living needs to begin with capacity for compassion. Ryder (1998) has faith in the human race for extending compassion for the *other-than-human*.

> All people are born with the potential for compassion. How far that compassion is extended and nurtured is dependent on culture and experience. We no longer perceive an unbridgeable gulf between ourselves and those of other species who share with us this short interlude of consciousness and pain that we call *life*. Instead, we all feel

> part of the same community of pain; we view nonhumans now as fellow sufferers in the cosmic game. With even greater clarity we can see that pain, in the broadest sense, is the common enemy and the best focus for a new morality. The concern for the welfare of nonhumans is a truly moral quest in what is often seen as an increasingly amoral world (Ryder, 1998, p. 126).

Ryder expresses elevated optimism in the human capacity for demonstrating and invoking compassion; however, speciesism, or prejudice and discrimination based on species, has far reaching implications throughout society on local, national, bio-regional, international and global scales. Humanity has indoctrinated speciesism through normalised and systemic assent (Taylor, 1999). The multiple ways in which humans discriminate against the other-than-human are too numerous to discuss within the confines of this book; however, some of the more prevalent attitudes, behaviours and lifestyle choices include our relatedness to the other-than-human as food products, tools for medical/scientific experimentation, targets for sport hunting, entertainment in zoos, circuses, marine parks, and many other recreational environments where non-human animals are deemed performers for human pleasure. My hope is literally to bring to social consciousness the abundance of cruelty perpetrated upon non-human animals and nature by humanocentric narcissism:

> Animals have been, and still are, treated with hideous cruelty around the world. Most human beings look upon animals as things to be eaten. Historically, animals have been defined as little more than things: resources, tools, units of production, objects of entertainment, and simply as means to human ends. Our use of animals has only just begun to receive the ethical attention it deserves (Linzey, 1998, p. 87).

Further, I endeavour to invoke critical thinking of our habitual anthropocentrism; we need to investigate and critique our human-centred lifestyles that contribute to massive pain and suffering of non-human living beings. My predominant focus stems from a position of sympathy and compassion *for* the other-than-human. To this end, I will show how a non-anthropocentric humane perspective can integrate contemporary educational agendas in ways that promote more compassionate ways of relating to the natural world – specifically, to the other-than-human.

My philosophical stance is founded upon utmost respect for nature, for other species, for natural geographies, for planet Earth. More succinctly, it is my intention not only to bring about greater discourse of *need* but of *desire* – i.e., bringing to social consciousness a deep and heartfelt desire to *want* to live humanely, to minimise or eliminate to the greatest extent the pain and suffering meted out to our non-human neighbours, to the environment, to nature and ultimately to ourselves. If we can understand our unavoidable connections with nature and with other species, we can begin to realise the significance of engaging a transformative movement (O'Sullivan, 2001) away from habitual anthropocentrism and towards non-speciesist, non-anthropocentric, non-hierarchical biospheric justice.

1.3 The Need for Introducing Humane Education to Children

It is especially crucial to facilitate our younger students (of elementary school age) in learning about our interconnectivity with nature. Opinions, beliefs, daily decision-making and character are formed at a very young age. Although anyone at any age can learn more humane ways of living, young children are far more flexible, open to new ideas, and less set in their ways – they have not yet become rigid (usually), at least not to the degree of their adult counterparts, in their habits, attitudes and behaviours (Vander Zanden, 1989). Specifically, for these younger students, teaching about our relatedness, interconnectivity and interdependence with nature and the natural world provides them a chance to critically examine how they can relate to nature.

> It is astonishing that humane education finds no place in the national curriculum of British schools, nor of most schools in the United States and Europe [and Canada]. Whether pupils gain any sense of the need to respect other life forms or are encouraged in compassionate behaviour towards them is wholly dependent on enlightened teachers or animal-friendly parents. In the light of this lamentable lack, it is surprising that people are not crueller than they actually are. Finding formal space within the curriculum for some expression of

the need for humaneness is an urgent task if institutionalising animal protection is to become a reality (Linzey, 2009, p. 67).

That notwithstanding, many children display apathy, aggression and violence towards the other-than-human (Arkow, 1997; Gredley, 1999; Rigdon & Tapia, 1977; Tapia, 1971; Wax & Haddox, 1974; Weil, 1999). This is the runaway train of habitual speciesism that needs attention and correction if we are to instil humane values necessary for living peaceably with nature (and each other). Regan (1998) acknowledges the less than innocent intentions of children in how they treat non-human animals. Locke (1905) rendered this same observation:

> One thing I have frequently observed in Children, that when they have got possession of any poor Creature, they are apt to use it ill: They often *torment*, and treat very roughly, young Birds, Butterflies, and such other poor Animals, which fall into their Hands, and that with a seeming kind of Pleasure... (Locke, 1905, In Regan (1998), p. 42).

As educators, we need to remain alert to the fact that the family alone carries an overwhelming degree of influence (Arkow, 1997) over a child's capacity for humane living. Children reflect their environments in multiple ways. If a child is physically, emotionally, psychologically and/or sexually abused, s/he will in all likelihood suffer negative repercussions in her/his own development and in the ways s/he relates to the world around her/him (Arkow, 1997; Gredley, 1999; Hellman & Blackman, 1966; Ressler, Burgess & Douglas, 1988).

Research and literature in psychology reveal a strong connection between family violence/child abuse and children's behaviour towards their peers, nature, non-human animals and other forms of antisocial behaviour (Arkow, 1997). Hellman and Blackman (1966) found a positive correlation between children's cruel behaviour towards non-human animals and a greater propensity for future criminal activity. Rigdon and Tapia (1977) studied children who had committed acts of cruelty towards non-human animals. These same children displayed further antisocial behaviours including bullying, rage, lying, stealing, hyperactivity and other destructive tendencies. In an earlier study, Tapia (1971) found that boys who were raised in abusive environments – homes where brutality, neglect and hostility were prevalent – also showed extensive antisocial behaviours including cruelty to animals. Wax and Haddox (1974) studied institutionalised male delinquents and found that all had derived from homes where abuse was endemic in their family dynamics – these boys had all committed acts of cruelty to animals. Other studies (Ascione, 1993; Felthous, 1980; Felthous and Kellert, 1986; Geddes, 1977; Hickey, 1991; Kellert and Felthous, 1985; Ressler, Burgess, and Douglas, 1988) confirmed the foregoing in showing direct relationships and links of experienced abuse in childhood with overt cruelty towards non-human animals. The American Psychiatric Association (1994), upon revising their criterion for behavioural disorders, cited physical cruelty to animals as a diagnostic criterion for *conduct disorder* (I raise the inherent hypocrisy of conduct disorder later; namely, the inconsistency of naming one form of animal abuse as a criterion for psychological disorder(s) while condoning other forms of animal abuse as normalised and socially accepted behaviours).

Given the aforementioned studies indicating links between child abuse and repercussions of that abuse including cruelty to animals, it becomes apparent that perhaps speciesism stems from much inhumane treatment thwarted upon the child early in life. A deeper and more critical look at the multiple forms of structural and familial violence may find such dysfunctional experiences to serve as precursors for future maladjusted behaviours. Perhaps recognising and understanding that violence has no boundaries may help us to realise a domino effect of oppressor to oppressed: an oppressor victimises an oppressed; the oppressed feels helpless and out of control; in turn, the oppressed needing to gain control and feel less victimised may become an oppressor; the cycle continues from person to person, generation to generation, and often proceeds to target non-human animals (Arkow, 1997; Ascione, 1993; Felthous, 1980; Felthous & Kellert, 1986; Kellert & Felthous, 1985; Ressler, Burgess & Douglas, 1988; Rigdon & Tapia, 1977). The monumental task of humane education is to stop this cycle of abuse, oppression and violence through teaching and encouraging humane values of compassion, empathy, kindness, respect, and love. The humane educator has a unique opportunity to serve as a positive role model for demonstrating many and multiple ways for living more humanely.

1.4 Motivation(s) and Values of Humane Education

Elizabeth Gredley (1999) is a strong proponent of humane education. She recognises the need to integrate humane education throughout the learning journey, across the curriculum, and encompassing the learning environment in any and all ways that bring about humane objectives. Her assertion that children who are kinder toward animals tend to be kinder toward fellow humans may someday be recognised as universal truth.

> Research clearly shows the transference and escalation of aggression from animals to people. It also shows what causes that aggression – and some of those causes can be prevented with humane education. Furthermore, there is research that shows that improved attitudes toward animals generalize to people. If children learn to treat animals well, they're more likely to treat people well too. If children are allowed to vent their aggression on animals, they will learn to vent it on other people as well…Humane education not only provides knowledge about animals and their care but develops empathy, respect, sensitivity, responsibility, self control and self esteem. Including humane education as part of the regular school curriculum would make sure all children learn appropriate behaviours… (Gredley, 1999, p. 1).

Advocacy of kindness toward non-human animals needs to invoke a value laden message of the intrinsic value of non-human animals, of nature – the other-than-human deserves respect and our moral duty of compassion (Adams, 1996; Donovan, 1996; Rowlands, 2002; Taylor, 1999) for *their* sake.

Arkow (1992) acknowledges the dual need of humane education for invoking such values towards both humans and the other-than-human. Several values, what he terms the "Five Rs" (Ibid. p. 3) encompass basic foundational values needed in humane education curriculum. These values (Kaufmann, 1992) are summarised in **Figure 1-1** on the next page. I will elaborate somewhat on the first three of the five Rs.

Respect is the very foundation of humane education. Without respect for life – whether human or the other-than-human – all subsequent messages conveyed through humane education are lost. One needs to recognise and understand what it means to respect another living being. It means acknowledging the other's right to thrive, to endure its purpose and motivations, to attain her/his own enjoyment of life. Existentially, respect means allowing one to exist for its own sake and trusting the universe that this being exists because it has a reason/purpose/value for existing (Rowlands, 2002). Awareness and conveyance of respect extends to all living beings whether in our homes, our communities, or in greater bioregional geographies. From respect, we learn to appreciate the other, to celebrate the existence of the other, and even to love the other. This 'other' is a fellow earthling, a part of us. By protecting the 'other', by refraining from infringing upon the rights/needs of the 'other', we invoke a deep sense of affirming our common bonds with the other life – common in that we perceive our shared needs for life, for nurturing, desires and continuance of our very existence.

Mnemonic Definition of Humane Education: The Five Rs
Respect – for the other animals that share our homes, our cities, and our planet
Reverence – for the life force of which we are but a small part
Responsibility – toward those other animals that we have chosen to domesticate and bring under our dominion
Realistic – awareness of animals for what they are and are not
Relevance – fellow and accessible creatures with which we are intimately familiar, but who are worlds apart, whose "us-ness" and "other-ness" may teach us much about ourselves as we study their uniqueness

Figure 1-1: Kaufmann, 1992.

Reverence for life translates to mean a deep respect and honouring the celebration of life. When we convey a reverence for life, we assert our heartfelt appreciation and connection to the sacredness of life. Although Arkow does not allow for the possibility or probability that non-human animals experience a sense of awe and wonder, that they may very well experience enchantment and utter tranquillity, we cannot dismiss the existence of such experiences by the other-than-human. I have personally witnessed animals – namely, my companion animals and animals I have worked with in shelters and sanctuaries – experiencing enchantment, excitement, peace, and curiosity (wonder). Such experiences – I believe that non-human animals do have these experiences – are natural events in the lives of others; these *others* are entitled to their experiences as much as we (humans) are entitled (or not) to our own.

Responsibility means that we consciously accept our abilities to affect the quality of life for an *other*. Whether we are talking about domesticated animals or free roaming animals, we have a responsibility – moral, ethical, even spiritual insofar as not interfering with nature's creation (Linzey, 1998) – for not bringing harm to the other. Also, this means that we take on the responsibility – in the case of domesticated animals – of caring for those unable to care for themselves. There are not only survival needs (i.e., water, food, shelter, medical care, etc.) but also psychological and emotional needs. Non-human animals share the human capacity for forming relationships with others (Masson & McCarthy, 1995; Rowlands, 2002). Non-human animals experience loneliness and camaraderie, pleasure and joy, pain and suffering, depression and despair, happiness and love (Adams, 1998; Donovan, 1996; Luke, 1996; Regan, 1983; Robbins, 1987; Rowlands, 2002; Singer, 1998; Hill, 1996; Marcus, 1998). When we adopt an animal into our home, we take on a responsibility that is just as serious and maternal as caring for a human infant. They are completely relying upon our responsible behaviour, our sound judgement, and our unconditional love. These notions of needs and desires remind us of the realistic component of other-than-human animals; quite literally, we need to remember that our non-human counterparts are living beings and require many of the same survival needs that we humans require.

Being responsible for the caring of an *other* translates to providing basic needs of that dependent other; however, we need to be aware that being responsible is not synonymous with *being responsive* to that other. If I provide fresh food and water for my companion animals, clean my birds' cages and my rabbits' enclosure, walk my dog, and bring my animals to a veterinarian whenever necessary, I may be acting as a responsible caretaker; nevertheless, am I also being *responsive* to my animals? Am I aware of their moods, their emotions, their desires at any given time? Am I in tune with my animals on a level that extends beyond the basic necessities of survival?

I understand and experience responsiveness toward my companion animals on a continuous basis. My dog clearly communicates to me when he wants to go outside, desires a cookie, or craves my attention. My birds, particularly Woody, communicates to me when he wants me to pick him up or massage his head and face. My bunnies let me know when they want more of my attention by leaning up against their fencing and looking towards me. However, this communication moves in multiple directions: they communicate with me and I respond to their communications; also, I communicate with them and they respond (or not) to my efforts. When my dog Maximillion lets me know that he desires a cookie, I do not ignore his actions; rather, I respond to his clear message of want. If he seems bored and lonely because I am spending too much time at the computer, I become aware of his experience by observing his body language, his attempts at getting my attention, and even his facial expressions. Paying attention to my dog or any of my other animals is not merely being responsible; I am *responding* to their needs and desires – I am being *responsive* to them. In summary, when I am responsive to my companion animals, it means that I relate to them as my family, my loved ones; I continuously empathise with my animals' feelings by placing myself in their position and imagining how I would feel or think if I were them and they were me. I am then able to imagine what they want or desire; in turn, not only can I respond to them, but also I am able to be responsive to their wishes.

1.5 Making Distinctions for Humane Values

People are capable of becoming educated in humane values, attaining awareness of how their daily lifestyle decisions and choices effect non-humans in negative ways, and of learning alternative ways of living that avert the systemic cruelty of their current anthropocentric practises. Humans' capacity for learning humane living is evident through observation of animal rights activists, animal compassionists, vegetarians and vegans who choose this lifestyle for the sake of compassion for animals, and other individuals who advocate against animal cruelty and in favour of living more convivially with the other-than-human.

With regard to acknowledging the ability of animals to experience pain and suffering, many people do discriminate between domesticated animals (i.e., their pet cat, dog, hamster, etc.) and wild, farm and other non-domestics; the same people who treat their dog as a member of the family and treat her/him with love and compassion may also deny the very fact that non-domestic animals (and those animals not normally thought of as *pets*), also carry the same capacity as their domesticated counterparts as far as experiencing pain and suffering. The unbelievable misconception is the fact that species not embraced by this realm of moral consideration (Regan, 1983) (e.g., pigs, cows, sheep, fish, etc.) experience pain, suffering, emotional, psychological and physical transitions in the same ways as *domestic* animals (Robbins, 1987) and therefore, based on their very real experiences, these animals deserve our moral consideration (Regan, 1983; Rowlands, 2002). Furthermore, too many people fail to consciously acknowledge the parallel experience of pain between humans and non-humans (Ryder, 1998); for if they did, more people would oppose the systemic oppression towards non-human animals – case in point, the sheer numbers of animals terrorised, brutalised and murdered each day for the human desire to ingest animal flesh (*meat*) sustains a very real holocaust for these beings.

> [We] should treat equal suffering equally. In the case of nonhumans, we see them mercilessly exploited in factory farms, in laboratories and in the wild. A whale may take twenty minutes to die after being harpooned. A lynx may suffer for a week with her broken leg held in a steel-toothed trap. A battery hen lives all her life unable even to stretch her wings. An animal in a toxicity test, poisoned with a household product, may linger in agony for hours or days before dying. These are major abuses causing great suffering…[Y]et people still try to justify these torments on the grounds that those who are suffering are not of the same species as ourselves. It is almost as if some people had not heard of Darwin! According to Charles Darwin we are related through evolution to the other animals. We are all

animals. Yet we treat the others not as relatives but as unfeeling objects (Ryder, 1998, pp. 48-49).

Rollin (1992) reaffirms the parallel capacities between humans and non-human animals as proffered by Darwin:

> [In] the *Descent of Man*, Darwin affirmed that 'there is no fundamental difference between man and the higher animals in their mental faculties,' and that 'the lower animals, like man, manifestly feel pleasure and pain, happiness, and misery' (p. 56).

Humane educators may ponder, Why is the teaching of peace and respect for all living beings so threatening for the masses? Similarly, Why is it more socially acceptable to protect gun ownership rights than to accept the notion that other living beings have rights and that depriving those beings of their rights is, in and of itself, inhumane and globally destructive? – I am specifically addressing the desires of avid hunters who find joy in killing innocent animals just for sport. Likewise, and on a much grander scale, Why are most people so resistant to the idea of vegetarianism? I can recall mentor teachers warning me about the dangers of mentioning the "v" word in an elementary classroom – vegetarianism and certainly veganism are viewed by many as too controversial to introduce to young students; the fear is often that irate parents will angrily confront school administrators with the usual, "My child refuses to eat her dinner because an animal was killed for it." Furthermore, How can so many people who claim a desire for peace and non-violence contribute to massive violence, torture and killing of billions of innocent animals?

Additionally, and even more fundamental to the causes and foundations of our cruelty meted out to non-human animals, we need to address the social, political and global structures and systems that create and sustain anthropocentrism at its very core. The fact that it is socially condoned (worldwide) to ingest animal flesh goes back thousands of years in human history; educating people about vegetarianism and why such a choice is optimal for compassionate living is a most challenging task. Economically and politically, animal cruelty is sustained. Agribusiness generates billions of dollars globally (Robbins, 1987) and the notion of ceasing all activities inherent of this industry engenders a monumental transformation unheard of thus far in human society; humans would have to rethink their entire relationships with the other-than-human.   The task(s) at hand sound near impossible, yet there are those of us who continue our endeavours to save animals from harm's way. Perhaps education, although a slow process, is the optimal way of reaching people. This is the endless task of humane education.

1.6 Humane Education as Transformative Education

The essence of current pedagogy and curricular design throughout scholastic and academic environments is based upon anthropocentric and human-centred paradigms (Orr, 1994). Students are taught about the world from a perspective of *how that world can serve their needs*.

> ...[Much] of what has gone wrong with the world is the result of education that alienates us from life in the name of human domination, fragments instead of unifies, overemphasizes success and careers, separates feeling from intellect and the practical from the theoretical, and unleashes on the world minds ignorant of their own ignorance (Orr, 1994, p. 17).

Economics, career building and monetary success are stressed as motivations for studying hard, staying in school and persisting to establish oneself as a productive member of the community (O'Sullivan, 2001). Throughout curricula, references to the natural world, other species' needs and humans' role as *caretakers* of the environment and the ecosystem are practically non-existent; rather than invoking standards of caring for nature, environmental education often prescribes stewarding, managing and controlling nature (Leopold, 1968, [1949]).

Ralph Metzner (1995) reminds us of our neglect of the natural world:

> [We] as a species are suffering from a kind of *collective amnesia*. We have forgotten something our ancestors once knew and [practised] – certain attitudes and kinds of perception, an ability to [empathise] and identify with nonhuman life, respect for the mysterious, and humility in relationship to the infinite complexities of the natural world.

> It may be that at several crucial turning points in the history
> of human consciousness we chose a particular line of
> development and thereby forgot and neglected something –
> with fateful consequences (p. 61).

We need to remember that such a transformation is slow for obvious reasons: (1) we are educating people about viable alternatives to current habituation whereby animals are exploited, harmed and killed – this point in itself connotes an enormous amount of lifestyle changes, behavioural and attitudinal changes, and massive overhaul of systems currently relying upon non-human animals for manufacturing, product development, medical science, entertainment, and a wide array of other activities involving the use of animals; (2) generations of people over thousands of years have lived in ways that have exploited nature and non-human animals without much thought to the negative consequences meted out to those animals – such habituation and normalisation of the use of animals seems seriously arduous to interrupt; and (3) the radical animal liberationist agenda requires the whole of the global society to rethink their entire mindset regarding their relationship with animals. On this third reprisal, one only needs to imagine the entire world community altering their dietary intake to a vegan (no animal flesh, no dairy, no eggs or other animal derived products) diet.

> Education needs to give people the chance to think and
> imagine differently, to conceive of other, better worlds for
> humans and animals. There should be courses, centres,
> institutes, degrees, even universities dedicated to new
> perspectives on animals. The challenge, then, is to find ways
> of institutionalising, embodying, and incarnating new
> perceptions of animals so that, as a matter of course, all
> students -- at all levels -- are encouraged to rethink the
> dominant intellectual paradigm (Linzey, 2009, p. 68).

Nevertheless, humane educators need not panic over the prospect of changing the entire world from current ways of knowing to more compassionate and empathic ways of relating to nature and non-human animals overnight. Humane education, as with other anti-oppression paradigms: women's rights, civil rights, gay and lesbian rights – will take time to catch on and become part of mainstream society's household ideas; in other words, the process of change can be excruciatingly prolonged, but that is no reason to give up on such ideals. As we have seen in other movements, persistence and perseverance are part of the territory for accepting the challenge of creating a more humane world. If we are to begin facilitating students in the learning of humane values, we need to introduce an integrated programme throughout curricula that allows both educators and learners to become acquainted with more humane ways of thinking and relating.

2

A Personal Journey: Compassionate Living

2.1 Introduction: Radical Animal Liberation and Eco-Spiritualism

I do not pretend nor intend to hide my subjectivity towards issues of humane education or animal liberationist philosophy. Naming myself as a *radical animal liberationist* comprises multiple attributes and lifestyle choices – the following premises each elaborate my position:

> (1) Humans are not superior to non-human animals – humans may think they possess a presumed superior intellectual capacity; however, this is only assumed from a purely anthropocentric worldview. Concretely, we do not know how or what other species are thinking – there is no objective evidence or proof of our cognitive superiority (from a purely objective and non-anthropocentric perspective). In other words, cognitive ability or intelligence is normally defined based on *humanocentric* evidence stemming from psychological and cognitive testing designed to pigeonhole and compartmentalise people into fragmented categories of intellectual capacity, ability and levels of IQ. This need to

place humans at a superior level of intellect over the other-than-human, however, is one of the more minor concerns of my philosophy – to focus too deeply on intellectual capacity only confirms and hones in on human-centred criterion for mental capabilities; hence, for moral consideration (Rowlands, 2002).

(2) We do not have the right to oppress other species and utilise them as means to our human ends. Causing non-human animals pain, distress, emotional and psychological torment, and physical suffering is without question immoral and figures amongst the most inhumane and evil deeds of humankind.

(3) Following from premise (2), I believe that it is morally and existentially wrong to imprison[1], control and torture non-human animals for humanocentric gain; hence, deeming animals as food products, clothing materials, research equipment, learning tools or any other activity that denies their freedom from physical, psychological or emotional well-being is morally reprehensible.

(4) I adhere to *vegan ethics* as a conscious lifestyle choice – this entails the following: abstaining from ingesting any animal flesh or animal derived by-products (e.g., dairy, eggs, flesh, muscle, organs, etc.), refusing to purchase products containing animal derived ingredients or products tested on laboratory animals (this includes boycotting all companies that engage in animal testing), minimising my negative impact on non-human animals and the environment (i.e., consciously avoiding intentional harm to any living beings),

---

[1] For domesticated animals born in captivity and for animals not able to care for themselves in the wild due to injury or disease or lack of experience in free-roaming environments, it is preferable to have these animals in sanctuaries (i.e., for injured animals) or in nurturing homes. Releasing such animals into the wild is morally irresponsible, especially for those animals born in captivity and the repercussions of their release would result in further injury or death. For example, my cockatiels have never lived in the wild; also, these birds are of a warm weather species; living in Canada, to release them into the wild would surely force them to meet an early demise.

and a merging of attitudinal, behavioural, and spiritual awareness and connectivity to non-human animals and to nature (i.e., acknowledging my shared place and space of planet with the other-than-human, invoking and practising nurturing and non-violent attitudes and actions regarding the other-than-human, serving as a positive role model for practising kindness and compassion toward nature, non-human animals and planet Earth).

(5) Transformative learning should be recognised as central to environmental and humane discourse. Prescribing to humane values, we are attempting to transform society and the world towards a more peaceful and less violent mode of sustainability (O'Sullivan, 2001; Pike & Selby, 1999, 2000; Selby, 1995; 1998; A. Taylor, 1999).

(6) Humane paradigms need to embrace participatory and emancipatory learning (Dewey, 1997 [1938]). Students need to realise their role in creating change and their impact on the environment, on the world. Often, anti-oppression education only addresses human suffering and needs for acquiring equality, freedom and emancipation from unjust systems (Freire, 2002 [1970]); however, I uncompromisingly encompass the other-than-human within anti-oppression discourse.

The foregoing list summarising my views of humane living is not exhaustive, nor is it meant to be. As a human being, I am continuously evolving and expanding my consciousness of humane, non-anthropocentric ways of relating, knowing and living in the world.

I also call myself an *Eco-Spiritualist*. I do not adhere to any organised religion nor do I pray to a god. Nevertheless, I do experience what I deem highly spiritual essences. This sense of spiritual enlightenment occurs throughout my interactions with nature, with non-human animals. Although difficult to put into words, the feelings I get when engaging one of my companion animals or experiencing the beauty and purity of nature are feelings of inner peace, compassion, empathy and intense love.

2.2 Connected through Love

When I look into the eyes of my dog, Sir Maximillion[2], I sense the deepest level of love and compassion imaginable (for me). My love for my companion animals (as well as other animals) runs so deep that the thought of losing that love hurts – physically, psychologically, emotionally; however, I retain a spiritual connection to my loved ones, in hopes of rejoining them upon my own physical demise from this life – these embedded feelings nurture my spiritual connection to non-human animals and the natural environment.

I experienced such an immense loss of love and wholeness upon the demise of my *daughter*[3], Anna Bunny. When Anna Bunny passed on March 23, 2001, I felt the most crippling loss of my life (parallel to the loss I experienced when my childhood dog, Pumpkin, passed). Anna was a beautiful chocolate brown bunny, possessing profound gentleness and a great ability to share her positive energy with me. When she died, I felt as though a part of me died with her. I experienced the degree of loss often expressed by people who lose a child to death. From the first day I brought Anna home from the shelter, I felt spiritually connected to her and maintained that connection each and every day.

My spiritual connection to Anna remains ongoing even though she is no longer with me physically. As a symbol of physically keeping her *with* the family I have had her ashes placed in an urn – a small shrine I maintain in my home in her honour. This, for me, is a symbolic display of spiritual essence; I believe (or need to believe) that her spirit is in some way still with me; perhaps to further this notion of eternal love, I do not dismiss the potentiality that Anna is waiting for me to join her in some non-physical existence upon my own demise from

---

[2] Prior to completing this book, my loving pug, Sir Maximillion, passed away. Although he is no longer with me physically, he will always remain in my heart on a spiritual level and with feelings of unconditional and eternal love.

[3] I frequently refer to my non-human animal companions as my children; hence, my sons and daughters. I do so with the greatest sincerity that I love these animals in a way comparable to how people love their human children.

this physical life. It is in honour of Anna and many other animals whom I have loved, that I dedicate this book[4].

My experiential love and compassion for non-human animals is deeply ingrained in my actualised *self* – in other words, these feelings are an integral part of who I am. I am able to model these feelings, thoughts or values simply by living a humane lifestyle on a daily basis. It is my hope that others – namely, my students, colleagues and fellow community members – will attend to my attitudes and behaviours just enough to open their minds and their hearts toward a journey of contributing to and creating a more humane world.

2.2.1 Noah Bunny

I remember the first time I met Noah. I was frequenting the local pet supply store to purchase items for my companion animals – at the time, I had three birds and one bunny. I approached the store entrance and just outside the door, the local humane society had set up an adoption centre in hopes of finding homes for several animals. I paused to view the animals and immediately noticed a beautiful and adorable white bunny in a cage; she was with another bunny, but she approached me upon noticing my presence at her cage door. She came right up to my face and looked directly at me, twitching her nose and making eye contact. I spoke with her briefly and then proceeded into the store. On my way out, I stopped again and visited the white bunny for a couple of minutes before heading home.

I could not get the thought of the bunny out of my head or my heart. Something about the way she looked at me told me that she was consciously aware of my presence and that she somehow knew that she wanted to be placed in a loving home. I continued thinking about this small animal and the way she communicated with me with her eyes and her body language.

I must admit, at the time, I was interested in finding a playmate for my other bunny, Anna. I waited a few days before making a

---

[4] Since the commencement of writing this book, I have lost several other companion animals including Sir Maximillion (pug), Noah (bunny), Woody (cockatiel), Sterling (cockatiel), Chester (cockatiel), Stella (bunny), and Maya (bunny); this book is also dedicated to my loving memories of the aforementioned as well as all animals who have suffered in this world because of humanocentric ignorance, greed, and apathy.

decision – adopting another animal, I was well aware, warranted a big commitment – one more adoption would bring my total up to five animals (three birds and two bunnies) in my home. Still, I could not forget the white bunny. I thought that maybe the humane society had found a home for her by now. Nevertheless, I headed to the animal shelter – the facility that had set up the animals for adoption outside the store. Upon entering the 'bunny room,' I immediately noticed the white bunny still residing in the shelter. Many white bunnies look quite similar, but I knew this was the same one I had visited a few days prior to this search; she responded in a very similar way as in our previous meeting – also, I had memorised her posted name on the cage – she was the bunny I had met a few days earlier.

A volunteer at the shelter was kind enough to let me hold Noah. Upon taking her into my arms, I knew that she was going home with me. It was love at first sight. I was so taken by her personality, her beauty, and her responsiveness to me, that tears came to my eyes as I hugged her close to my body. But there was another reason why I cried at the sight and touch of Noah. She looks very much like the white rabbits used all too frequently in medical research, product testing and other tortuous and painful experimentation procedures. I learned that Noah had already been at the shelter for four months, a long time for any animal to reside in such a detached and isolating environment. I thought of the possibility of her being sold to a research facility, although I have no proof that this shelter sells animals to researchers, and then I thought of all the other bunnies (and other animals suffering at the hands of mad scientists). I instantly recalled seeing many pictures in psychology books of white rabbits undergoing painful and inhumane experimentation procedures. Not that I hesitated — I did not pause for a moment — but I knew that I was going to save Noah's life. I promised her, right there in the shelter, that I would provide for her the best possible home free from isolation, suffering, hunger, lack of companionship and free from monotonous confinement, and of course, a home filled with love.

Noah became a cherished member of my family. While in the final months of completing my doctoral programme, Noah passed away at the age of 11 years. She will always be very special to me – perhaps because she reminds me of the innumerable bunnies used in scientific research and the very reason why I have chosen to make animal liberation central to my career and my lifestyle. Noah had been a great teacher, friend and companion. She let me know when she wanted to come out of her house by leaning against her door with both her front paws and looking directly at me. She would lie on the floor next to the chesterfield and let me massage her face and body, often for an hour or longer; if I stopped before she had had enough, she would look at me as if to say, "Why did you stop? I was enjoying that." She came to me when I called her name (if she felt like it). When I brought her breakfast, she jumped around with excitement and looked at me as if with grateful thanks for the gourmet meal she was about to receive. She was aware when it was bedtime – by my closing lights, drawing shades, covering the bird houses – and waited for her bedtime snack of a carrot slice or apple wedge. No one can ever tell me that non-human animals do not communicate with us – we only have to open our eyes, our ears and our hearts. I believe, in my heart, that Noah knew she was and will always be with me: she *is* my family, she *is* my daughter, she *is* the essence of pure love that motivates me in my life's work.

Arkow (1992) suggests that non-human animals may teach us (humans) about ourselves; we may be able to relate to their behaviours as similar to or different from our own. However, we need to be careful about assigning relevance to other species only insofar as they may serve as teaching tools for our further understanding of our own species. Remember that scientists continue to exploit animals in laboratories for the sake of medical research; rats, monkeys, dogs, cats, and a multitude of other species undergo inhumane and unspeakable torture in the name of science. Utilising a rat or a monkey for the purpose of finding a cure for a human disease is not a humane understanding of relevance. That said, we can observe other species in their interactions with each other: family members, same-species interaction, other-species interaction, and of course, their interaction with us. On a level of non-exploitation, we can learn a great deal from non-human animals about both them and us. My most effective teachers have been non-human animals: they have taught me about love, dependency, respect, companionship, and compassion. Even though an "us-ness" and "other-ness" may exist in terms of species identification (Arkow, Ibid.), there is a shared togetherness of all species. We all share the same planet, we all experience relationships with others – whether family, friends, enemies, or fellow community members, we all have basic needs for survival, and I further believe that we all have capacity for emotional and psychological experiences. On this latter assertion, relevance is basic. If I am similar to a chimpanzee or an orang-utan, then how can I bring harm to them? Would I not also be harming myself?

In delivering humane education, the most crucial reality of non-human animals is that they are living beings with needs, desires and physical, psychological, emotional, and relational conceptualisation (Caine, 2001; Robbins, 1987; Rowlands, 2002). Too many people, upon adopting a dog or cat for example, do not take the responsibility seriously (Caine, 2000). They bring this living being into their home as if they have purchased a new toy. After the children grow tired or bored with the animal, the amount of attention and care diminishes. Such ill treatment of any animal results in physical, psychological and emotional trauma. The people who had a moral obligation / responsibility to the animal failed miserably in their inability to see the animal realistically – literally, as a real life.

2.2.2 Norman and Ashli

Several years ago, I discovered the farm animal sanctuary, Snooters, in southern Ontario, Canada. This was a beautiful paradise run by very kind and giving people who rescued mostly pigs, sheep, chickens, horses, a donkey, even cats, and of course two steer that I became acquainted with: Norman and Ashli. After getting to know the founders of Snooters, I would occasionally visit their sanctuary and volunteer to help out with the animals. I immediately fell in love with every resident of Snooters; how could I not? I quickly became emotionally attached to very playful pigs such as Edgar, Valentine, Belle, Penny, Snoots, Guinness, Johnny, Roy, Easter, Earl, Forrest, Flossy and Poppy; I also felt love and camaraderie with Josie, an adorable donkey, Julie, a mini horse, Dolly, a larger horse, as well as other sanctuary residents consisting of several chickens, a few cats, dogs, sheep, a flock of beautiful peacocks, and of course, two steer named Norman and Ashli. These animals have so much personality, character, and they exude an aura of peace, tranquillity and unconditional love. I came to think of these animals as my extended family.

I spent time getting to know Norman and Ashli; I would talk to them, give them soothing facial massages, and spend quality time with them on my visits. When they would see me approaching, they would draw near the fence with their expectation of my attention and, of course, a massage. I would look into their huge soulful eyes and see them, really see them as individuals with feelings, with thoughts, individual lives deserving a safe, nurturing and loving home. Norman and Ashli are part of the very lucky, very few rescues from among millions of hell-bound victims of the death camps also known as factory farms or slaughterhouses.

Spending time at farm animal sanctuaries reminds me of how many countless victims suffer the agony and inescapable pain and suffering stemming from humanocentric ignorance -- the ignorance of a meat-eating society, people who do not identify these animals as individual beings with unique lives comprising feelings, thoughts, desires, family and friends. People continue to ingest animal flesh as if the animals from which the flesh is torn are not in fact living beings, but simply food products. Most people are unaware of the terror, the horrific atrocities committed against these gentle and peaceful beings, acts of brutality that cause unspeakable horror in these torture chambers; the animals, I believe knowing their fate, smell the blood, hear the screams and cries of their friends and family, awaiting their turn to be bolted in the head or hung by their feet while psychopathic murderers slice into their throats while the animals are fully conscious, without pain killers, without anaesthesia, without any chance of escape from being cut open, with sheer fright so horrifying that many of these victims relieve their bowels, urinate on themselves, and even suffer heart attacks from the terror of their worst imaginable nightmare that will end their lives without mercy. Any person should be able to imagine what this event would feel like, the fear, of knowing that you are moving down a one-way line, unable to turn back, with no one to save you, knowing that you are about to be inflicted with a blade of death; I have no reason to believe that the ghastliness of this experience is no different for the animal victims of the meat industry than it would be for any human subjected to such an atrocity. I will never understand, to my dying day, how people who have knowledge of this killing industry, people who are consciously aware of the monumental pain and suffering thwarted at millions of innocent animals every day, can remain so apathetic. I am shocked that even when I have described the events of the slaughterhouses to some people, their response is often, "but I like the taste of meat." The fact that the majority of our population places their taste buds above such massive anguish of literally millions upon millions of lives is profoundly disturbing; this, for me, marks our species, the human species, as psychopathic in terms of our indifference and denial of such epic misery we are perpetrating upon our fellow earthlings.

When Snooters' owners decided to sell their property, Norman and Ashli were moved to a nearby sanctuary, Wishing Well; there, they would reside with a herd of other cattle already established in this safe haven. I was present on the day of their move. I wanted to be there to provide comfort and stability to Norman and Ashli; after all, moving can be a challenge and even scary for animals not familiar with their new surroundings; I felt that since they knew me, they would realise that they still had loved ones around them and that they only moved physical locations. On the day of their introduction to Wishing Well, I greeted them, along with a small crowd of other concerned fellow animal lovers of our community. Once my two steer friends were off-loaded from the truck, and safely placed into a fenced pen, I remember giving both my friends big hugs and words of comfort. This was an emotional experience for me, as I am sure it was for them as well; I am often highly attuned to my sense of empathy with animals; I wanted to convey my love and compassion for Norman and Ashli, and let them know that they were safe, protected, and that they would always have a loving home. I somehow hoped that my unconditional loving energy transmitted to my friends and perhaps gave them a sense of comfort and peace, and the knowledge that they were in no danger, but that they were so loved by so many people.

I would return to Wishing Well several times, always hurrying to greet Norman and Ashli in the back pasture. I hoped that they would remember me and that we could continue our interactions of massages and enjoying quality time together. One time, I arrived at the sanctuary, and spotted my friends at one of the hay feeders on one end of the field. I approached the fence and got as close to their position as possible. I stood there, and called out "Norman, Ashli, Norman, Ashli, come here." They were busy enjoying their afternoon snack of hay; however, all of the sudden, Norman looked in my direction, and I swear he gently nudged Ashli with his head and pointed his head towards my locale, as if to say, "look who's here." Right then, Ashli, who had his back to me, turned his head around to face me, then immediately turned his whole body around 180 degrees, and started slowly walking towards me. Norman followed him. My friends slowly but steadily moved towards the fence and placed their heads right up to my waiting hands. I felt honoured and very emotional, not only by their remembering me, but by their action of interrupting their meal and coming over to visit with me. This was truly a magical and spiritual experience for me; I felt a bond of friendship, a sense of unconditional trust and love that I have rarely experienced in my life.

I have since visited Norman and Ashli a few more times; they have integrated themselves into the herd of their own kind. I am happy and relieved that they have a safe and protective environment, a loving forever home.

2.2.3 A Vegan Thanksgiving

I visited Animal Acres Sanctuary in Acton, California, a few times, as a volunteer and simply to spend time with the animals at this safe haven. A wide variety of rescued animals call this place home: pigs, chickens, goats, deer, elk, horses, cows, turkeys. Having become acquainted with the sanctuary staff, I received an invitation to attend a vegan Thanksgiving; this event was given for all the volunteers and people associated with the sanctuary. I will never forget my very favourite Thanksgiving dinner; it was truly a beautiful and spiritual event.

Prior to commencing the vegan feast, I helped attend to some of the animals, cleaning their areas and providing them with hay, fresh water, and as much attention as they would tolerate from me. This was the first time I had ever been so close to so-called wild animals such as deer and elk. I had no fear in approaching them; in fact, I was most conscientious about not wanting to scare these timid critters. I was cautious in not infringing on their space, but remaining at a respectable distance and allowing them to approach me once they decided that I was not a threat. Whenever I am in the company of such animals, I feel at peace, I forget about my own problems and stresses of my life, and I become centred, almost entranced by the loving energy of these animals whom I consider my extended family.

When it was time to serve a most delectable vegan Thanksgiving dinner -- all the dishes traditionally enjoyed on this holiday prepared from one-hundred percent plant-based ingredients -- those of us in attendance gathered in the centre courtyard where tables had been set for our celebration. The organisers of the event even prepared scrumptious dishes to feed to the turkeys nearby; this was our humane and compassionate way of denouncing the systemic cruelty meted out to turkeys at this time of year, and celebrating Thanksgiving by serving a feast to the turkeys as our fellow diners. The turkeys seemed most appreciative while gobbling up plates of sweet potatoes, rice, cranberries and vegetables. I recall people calling me over to join them at a table; however, I preferred joining the turkeys strolling the nearby grassy area, while savouring their specially prepared meal. I gratefully took my plate, and rather than joining the people at the table, I proceeded to the lawn and sat down in order to be closer to the turkeys. Within a few minutes, I was surrounded by five or six curious turkeys; a couple of them even allowed me to pet them as I offered a few morsels from my plate. Although the turkeys seemed quite skittish, they slowly approached me, one by one, sensing that I was not a danger, but a friend. This was the closest I had ever been to turkeys and I immediately experienced them not as *things* to be cooked and eaten, but as fellow beings, as my friends, and as loving birds capable of displaying natural behaviours of flocking, of exploring their environment, and of forming relationships with each other and even with their human caretakers. I felt ashamed and disturbed that I had ever devoured such birds as food rather than relate to them as my fellow earthlings; simultaneously, I felt a sense of elation, a heightened sense of spiritual connection with the turkeys, and I knew that I had evolved immensely as a human being; I had somehow matured and cultivated a newly found way of relating to animals that may be comparable to the evolutionary spiritual essence described by so many religious people who claim to "know God," except as a non-believer of religious doctrine, I had discovered a spiritual essence of nature, of animals, and of my deep compassion and unrelenting love for my non-human animal friends. I further pondered how anyone could claim to love God, to love the Universe, but still engage in harming God's creatures, in causing such horrific pain, torment and suffering to billions of God's children. I had found my reason for being, my purpose for living, and my passion for speaking out on behalf of my loving fellow beings. This, by far, was the most wonderful and enjoyable Thanksgiving dinner of my life. This, I thought then and continue to think now, is how everyone should celebrate the holidays; affirming the lives of animals by embracing them into our lives, not as food products, but as fellow community members deserving our compassion, our empathy, our respect, our kindness, and our unconditional love.

2.3 The Journey of a Movement

Humane education reminds us that if we are to invoke peace and tranquillity for humans, we must not forget to include our non-human counterparts, our fellow earthlings. Working towards a more humane world and contributing to the eradication of anthropocentrism will continue to be my life's work.

We live in a time of history manifested by world-wide violence – country against country; culture against culture; religious group against religious group; race against race; even frightened social conservatives desperately fighting against the inevitable liberation of the GLBTQ community – we desperately need to bring *humaneness* into our existence; humane education serves as a light of hope in these dark times. Ideologically, this assertion sounds sane and even negotiable; however, convincing the human culture to embrace non-human animals as they would fellow humans is no easy task. The success of the animal liberation movement – success to the degree of bringing to worldview consciousness the need and desire for kindness towards non-human animals – is an achievement that I would term the *most radical transformation in the history of humankind.* Realistically, and I do not like to admit failure before the endeavour has commenced, I do not foresee such a transformation coming to fruition in my lifetime. However, every movement begins with tiny steps, with incremental progressions towards attaining end goals or objectives. That is my intent – to contribute to a more humane way of knowing, of thinking, of relating, of living – to reach as many people as I can – to convey messages of humane and compassionate living, and to educate people to the fact that they can thrive within their own lives without invoking harm onto the lives of others, including our non-human counterparts.

My motivation for writing this text is extensive and multifaceted; however, I am predominantly concerned with and passionate about educating for compassion – in this case, and more specifically, educating people about compassion towards other species, towards nature, and of course, towards each other.

Discussion of non-human animals as *other* explicates the basic foundation of *speciesism*.

> Speciesism is a form of injustice; *speciesism* means hurting others because they are members of another species. In 1970 [Richard Ryder] invented the concept partly in order to draw the parallel with racism and sexism. All of these forms of discrimination are based entirely upon physical appearances and are irrational. They overlook the great similarity between all races, sexes and animal species, namely our capacity to suffer pain and distress (Ryder, 1989, p. 44).

Eventually, when enough people view the goals of liberation movements as positively contributing to a more just society, the resistance tends to die down – tolerance and even acceptance comes to light. The animal liberationist movement is at its beginning stages of growing pains (Rowlands, 2002); the objectives of this movement – alleviating unjust and unnecessary pain, agony, torment, suffering and death – are of utmost importance to planetary peace. By recognising habitual speciesism (Margulis, 1998) and innumerable ways that such anthropocentric structures (Montgomery, 2000; A. Taylor, 1999) bring about unbearable suffering, we can enlighten our society to empathise and sympathise (Donovan, 1996; Luke, 1996) with the billions of innocent victims of human ignorance. The animal liberationist movement is about ceasing the holocaust of billions of innocent animals. It strives to bring to social consciousness a non-speciesist, non-anthropocentric world where compassion, empathy, respect, and kindness are the most prominent signals of a truly civilised society. The time is long overdue to transcend theory into practise; to speak of a humane society while continuing to oppress, torture and kill our non-human neighbours inheres an unforgivable hypocrisy of the human species. In all good conscience, we cannot advocate for world peace, for cease-fires among and between nations and cultures, and for liberation of all oppressed Earth residents unless we are willing to extend notions of anti-violence and anti-oppression for all of our fellow citizens, and especially, advocate for the liberation of our most innocent and defenceless victims: non-human animals.

2.4 Non-Anthropocentric Eco-Spiritual Essence

Perhaps recognising spirituality of nature is a highly subjective experience not shared by all humans. I remember years ago walking through Muir Woods, just north of San Francisco. This is a dense forest of old growth redwood trees and thousands of other plant species, a beautiful landscape of rock, earth, flora and fauna. Muir Woods is perhaps the most serene environment that I have encountered (along with other parts of the California coast). The trees, some of them thousands of years old, seem to possess an awareness of their majesty and awe. Of course, this observation may be no more than my projected feelings onto the trees. Let us not forget that all experiences are subjective, mine included; nevertheless, this forest conveys a magical quality of age, beauty, protection, nature, and I must add love and spirit. The observer can only imagine the transitions taking place over a period of thousands of years within this great forest. The continuous growth of trees, the birthing and demise of countless animals calling Muir Woods their home, the overgrowth on land and at greater heights, and of course, innumerable humans who have tracked through this enchanted forest. Muir Woods is truly a mystical presence of nature that I hope will continue to thrive long after my demise.

Does my description do any justice to the miracle of this majestic place? Words cannot replace one's sensual experience of Muir Woods anymore than describing the feel of the Pacific Ocean can replace a walk along the coast line, touching the salt water to one's lips, squishing the sand between one's toes and experiencing up-close the life of this enormous body of water full of life, flux and change. That said, we need to recognise the import of these creations of nature as valuable unto themselves (Stone, 2001) for they comprise ecosystems that sustain life and provide ongoing transitions of humans, non-humans, the whole planet. Nature has its own value (Ralston, 2001) – nature does not require human valuation in order to thrive (Ibid.), -- i.e., nature is not valuable merely because we humans deem it so.

Returning to our relatedness to nature, *Can we learn anything from Muir Woods*? There is nothing academic within this great forest. The trees do not provide any rationale for their value. My experiences of Muir Woods are my own. They stem from emotional, intuitive and psychological experiences. They are subjective. Yet they have value.

How can I relate this value to others? Is it possible for me to engage my students in the process of falling in love with nature? Are all humans capable of these feelings? Such inquiries serve as foundations for future inquiry – I do not know if definitive answers can be rendered; however, our relatedness towards nature and the other-than-human proffers a foundation for in-depth critical discussion and ongoing discourse in the fields of humane and environmental education and ethics.

2.5 Who I Am

I feel that it is important that I give my readers a brief background profile of *who* I am. I, like most people, have experienced multiple transitions that I know have had significant influence for my social, philosophical and spiritual development. I live my life on a daily basis with non-anthropocentric values at the forefront of all my behaviours, decision-making and lifestyle choices. My philosophy and ways of thinking about, relating to, and living with non-human animals is most definitely fundamental to all aspects of my life – specifically, in that I always operate to maintain active consciousness regarding any potential positive and/or negative impact upon non-human animals and nature. Such decisions include a vast array of issues and concerns, everything from feeling irritated by smokers who throw their cigarette butts on the ground, to my choosing not to eat animal flesh or wear animal skins (leather). I am aware that my moral values remain on the periphery of social norms; I do not believe that most people are so annoyed by discarded cigarettes and certainly the majority of people choose to eat animal flesh.

I have developed what I believe to be a very real sense of eco-spirituality. I am part of nature and nature is embedded within me. I observe the dangers of prioritising economics and power *over* ecology and individual living beings. I am a pure vegetarian; I am vegan – this means that I make every effort to refrain from utilising products tested on animals, containing animal derived ingredients or produced by companies that engage in animal exploitation.

Day by day, hour by hour, I am fully aware of the horrific suffering endured by billions of non-human animals at the hands of humankind. There is not a day that passes that I do not think and feel for the innocent animals enduring horrific pain and suffering meted out by humans too ignorant to realise the atrocities they cause towards these innocent beings. I am all too aware of the massive degradation of our environment, exploitation of Earth's natural geographies and inherent elements, the slow destruction of the atmosphere, fresh water and relentless contamination of the planet's soil, forests, deserts, oceans, lakes and rivers, and the very air we breathe. Most painful for me is the realisation of a holocaust suffered by our fellow earthlings, our non-human neighbours; this holocaust continues in factory farms, slaughterhouses, medical/scientific laboratories, university science departments, military weapons testing, puppy mills, animal shelters, consumer product testing facilities, and many other organisations, institutions and industries that fail to recognise the immense pain, suffering, alienation, physical, psychological, emotional and spiritual detriment perpetrated upon the other-than-human.

My animal companions are my children. When I was a small child, we had two dogs: 'Fluffy,' a small white multi-mix bread dog, only lived about two years – I was told he had a weak heart; 'Pumpkin,' also a small white/orange mixed breed, lived about seventeen years – he was my closest childhood friend. I remember returning from community college one day and finding Pumpkin lying on the kitchen floor. He was unable to stand up. The vet said that nothing could be done to help him or prolong his life; I was told that the humane thing to do was to "put him to sleep." Standing in the vet's office, hearing this devastating news, I was an emotional wreck; I hugged my dog, but was unable to think clearly. My mother was there with me; she seemed to be pressuring me to allow the vet to "put Pumpkin to sleep." I had mixed feelings at the time: I loved Pumpkin more than anything or anyone else in my life; I also did not want to see him suffer in pain – if I could return to the past, I would have handled the situation differently: I would have taken my dog home to tend to his needs, stay by his side, and allow him as much quality time as nature would permit. Perhaps this would be selfish on my part: not wanting him to leave me. Unfortunately, at that age, I was not equipped emotionally or psychologically to make more sound decisions regarding my little companion. Allowing my mother and the vet to end my dog's life is a thought that haunts me to this day; I feel very guilty and deeply saddened every time I think of Pumpkin's demise. It was the most devastating event of my life up until that time.

I started adopting animals into my home about twenty years ago. First, I attained 'Woody,' a very loving and most personable cockatiel; I swear that Woody had more personality than most people I have encountered. He whistled to me, sang to me, and enjoyed sitting on top my head now and then. His facial and bodily expressions communicated his desires – to be picked up, given a treat, or placed back into his house – he served as one of my greatest teachers throughout my life. A year later, I adopted 'Sterling' as a friend for Woody. Sterling was a silvery grey cockatiel who had charm, character and decided that I am the only human he trusted. Woody and Sterling were best of friends and enjoyed each other's company in favour of mine. In more recent years, I adopted 'Anna,' a chocolate brown bunny with beautiful brown and soulful eyes, 'Noah,' a female New Zealand white bunny with cherries jubilee eyes and full of gusto, 'Chester,' a cockatiel who sang the most beautiful songs but had no interest in anyone other than Sterling, and 'Sir Maximillion,' my pug companion with whom I spent the bulk of my time, day and night. Following Sir Maximillion, I adopted another little animal into our home: 'Sonoma,' an all white New Zealand bunny who befriended Noah; it was shear bliss for me to observe the two bunnies cuddling together, grooming each other, and chasing each other around my home. Later, I rescued three more bunnies: Stella, Maya and Berkeley, and another pug, Forest. When my pug, Sir Maximillion, passed on April 2, 2013, I was devastated; I proclaimed that I would never again adopt another dog; my heart was shattered as he was my shadow, my life companion, my closest relationship. Nevertheless, as people say, time tends to heal a broken heart; I will always feel sad at my pug`s passing; however, I am filled with wonderful memories of all the time we spent together. A short while after Sir Maximillion`s passing, I wrote a eulogy in his memory; the Toronto Vegetarian Association was kind enough to publish this honourarium in one of their monthly newsletters. I share it here so as to convey the connection, the companionship, the unconditional love I held (and will always hold) for my little pug.

Until We Meet Again, The Love of My Life.

Sir Maximillion, My Baby, `Huggy`, My Little Teddy Bear,

There are no words to express the monumental love I feel for you or the immeasurable joy, laughter, and comfort you brought into my life. It seems like a very short time ago I rescued you from a shelter and introduced into my life an intense relationship, friendship, and a bond that will never be broken.

It almost seems redundant to write this final letter of `goodbye` to you; you must know how much my heart is aching because you are not physically with me. However, you will always be with me spiritually and in my loving memories of you forever. And, of course, when it is my time to cross over to the other side, I will anxiously await your greeting and I look forward to seeing you again, wrapping my loving energy around you, and cuddling with you for eternity.

You made a significant impact on this world, My Little Teddy Bear. Since your passing, I have received so many condolences from many people who remember you and love you. These people know how much you and I are connected and they know how much pain I am experiencing over the loss of my pug. Given my spiritual beliefs, although I am suffering from your physical absence, I know that we will be together again -- this thought is what keeps me going.

I could not have asked for a better life partner. All the time we spent together was the greatest gift the Universe could have given me. Our shopping trips, our travelling between Toronto and California, our combined efforts to teach others about kindness and compassion towards animals whether in schools, colleges and even a few visits to universities, our breakfast and dinner times when you begged and won food from my plate, our shared time on the sofa watching our favourite videos, our walks and stroller rides around town, our shared time driving to and from many places, our joyful time at stores that welcomed you and doted over your most charming and ingratiating personality, and the most comforting of all, our `cuddle` time at night -- from the first night I adopted you into my life, you insisted on sharing my bed -- now that you are gone, I wish you were laying beside me again so I could feel your warmth, your soft and squishy body, and just rest my hand on you while falling asleep, as we did night after night for over thirteen years.

My life feels so much emptier and lonelier without your presence, but at the same time, I feel so privileged, fortunate, and blessed to have had your presence in my life. I am truly honoured to have this connection with you, my love. I am a very lucky guy.

Sir Maximillion, Huggy, My Little Teddy Bear, you were, are, and will always be the Love of My Life.

Rest Peacefully, my baby. We will be together again, some day.

Your Daddy

Every time one of my companion animals has passed away, I have felt devastated by my loss of their company. My little brown bunny, Anna, and I were closely bonded and I always think of her as my daughter. Her passing overwhelmed me emotionally, psychologically and even spiritually. It made no sense that such a loving and innocent animal should die at the young age of about four years. I still struggle with her death. Woody, my senor cockatiel, lived a very long life: about twenty-four years. Woody was the patriarch of my family. He was an incredible life force and I enjoyed many years of his incomparable company, his devotion, his love. When Woody became very ill in 2013, I cared for him the best I could; his veterinarian advised euthanasia; however, I wanted Woody to pass naturally and in my hands, the same way that his companions Sterling and Chester passed. I saw he was expiring and I expressed to him my love and gratitude for our relationship; I literally told Woody that it was ok for him to depart, to leave his sick body, and to join Sterling, Chester, Sir Maximillion, and our former companion animals on the other side of Rainbow Bridge, a place that many of us animal lovers believe exists, a place where we will eventually meet our companion animals upon our own demise. I held Woody in the air and slowly moved him, holding him securely, allowing him one more time to fly (Woody had not been able to fly for several months). I then sat us on the sofa, held my little bird in my hands, and told him that his companions were waiting to guide him home and that I would join him in the not too distant future. Woody took his last breath and fell asleep, at home, in my hands.

The love I feel towards all of my children is unconditional, highly spiritual, emotional, and reveres through an essence too powerful for words. This is the essence of my interpretation of eco-spirituality. This is the message I hope to convey to my students and others throughout my teaching career and throughout the remainder of my life.

At present, I have two bunnies, Sonoma and Berkeley, and one pug, Forest; after grieving Sir Maximillion for about seven months, I felt that I needed to adopt another dog into my life. Knowing that the lives of these animals are short, much shorter than my own, such a decision carries with it all the emotional baggage of knowing that someday, I will experience loss again. However, I learned that it would be selfish for me to refrain from adopting homeless animals in that I have so much love to give. As many of my acquaintances have expressed to me over the years, the animals that enter my home are very lucky and guaranteed a forever, loving home. Forest, like all my other animals, is a rescue. He is an adorable pug who had been liberated from a puppy mill in Ontario. I adopted Forest on November 4, 2013, when he was already six years old. He is not a replacement for Sir Maximillion; no animal or loved one can replace the loss of a love; however, he has helped me heal, and he has taught me that I still have so much to offer in terms of providing a safe and loving home for animals in desperate need of such a salvation. Forest is an excellent companion; quite literally, my rescue dog rescued me.

I had already considered myself an animal liberationist and a devout vegetarian prior to graduate school, but I had no idea that a formal field of academia honed in on such issues and concerns. I discovered that I could serve as a voice for the voiceless; literally, I could communicate on behalf of the animals, the pain and suffering doled out to them by our species out of ignorance, stupidity, or mere apathy. Although such a task is a monumental one – realistically, approximately 96% of the human population (of North America) consumes animal flesh (Hill, 1996) as the mainstay of their dietary intake – my heartfelt love and empathy for the animal victims remains diligent and without compromise as I advocate for their liberation from cruelty and inhumane treatment throughout the realms of humanocentric narcissism. I feel empowered to share my perspective of animal suffering, my knowledge of the atrocities committed by factory farms, scientists, and other institutions utilising animals for human ends, and my love and passion towards the well-being and potential peace of the non-human animal communities in a potentially possible absence of continued exploitation of their lives.

2.6 Background of My Work as a Case of Standpoint Research

This book adheres to two distinct perspectives objectified through a standpoint research (Denzin & Lincoln, 2000) method of inquiry: (1) the animal liberationist position, and, at a non-traditional and existentialist point of view, (2) the position of the 'oppressed other,' namely, non-human animals. As a member of the animal liberationist community, I stand within a minority group of compassionists struggling for an oppressed 'other' group – namely, non-human animals. Animal liberationists have a unique and privileged position of an acquired affinity *for* our non-human neighbours; this privilege stems from our perspective of being attuned to the plight, pain and suffering of this non-traditional *other*. Just as a women's feminist perspective gives women a privileged position of situated experience (Ibid.), animal liberationists experience and/or relate to the oppression of the other-than-human with a first-hand knowledge/experience for what the other-than-human experiences. The other position signified through standpoint research stems from the position of the oppressed animals themselves. Obviously, since the animals cannot speak on their own behalf regarding their needs, desires, and experiences, it is the animal liberationists / compassionists who choose to speak for this 'other' group.

"Standpoints are cognitive-emotional-political achievements, crafted out of located social-historical-bodily experience" (Ibid. p. 222). At this juncture, I would like to deconstruct the foregoing phraseology as a method for bringing clarity to my work as a case of standpoint research. Each of the above groupings – cognitive-emotional-political and social-historical-bodily – is easily applied to both standpoint positions: animal liberationist and non-human other. These groupings are taken separately for analysis in order to simplify explanation.

2.6.1 Cognitive-Emotional-Political

Since I cannot speak for all animal liberationists, as variations do exist, I utilise the term liberationist to signify my perspective of animal liberationism as well as how I view applied theorisation for working towards a framework for a non-anthropocentric environmental education model. As a liberationist, I have acquired specific and highly subjective ways of thinking *about* and *for* non-human animals. I see this oppressed other group as my equal(s) or, at times, even superior to my group (humans). Therefore, I have evolved my ways of thinking with regards to the other-than-human; my *cognitive* disposition has continuously altered to embrace the needs and what I interpret as desires of this *other*. My experiences within the animal liberationist community have taught me that people who relate to animals as I do almost always possess a very different cognitive perspective than our non-liberationist counterparts. Our views of how we treat animals, how we believe all of humankind ought to treat animals, and the multifaceted lifestyle choices we embrace in order to achieve our goals of animal liberation vary considerably from the majority of human society – the main of society continues to view non-human animals as food products, tools for research, origins for manufacturing clothing and other consumer goods, and as inferior to humans in terms of rights, needs, and desires.

Animal liberationists also take on an *emotional* level towards non-human animals, a level of empathy, compassion, and understanding not privy to those who do not recognise our non-human neighbours as we liberationists do. There is definitely a strong emotional stance within the standpoint of the liberationist. Speaking from the standpoint of my experience as a liberationist, when I witness pain and suffering of a non-human other, I share in that pain and suffering; the whole experience of empathy evolves and sustains as a highly emotional event. I am able to place myself in the position of the caged laboratory animal, the confined farm animal, or the neglected 'pet' – this is the ultimate essence of true empathy and compassion.

The animal liberationist movement is a *political* movement. Just as we have observed the history of the women's movement, the civil rights movement in America, and the gay rights movement, now we can survey the animal rights movement. Political affiliation translates to action; those who join this political cause may engage in protests, picketing, and boycotts of products and/or industries that permeate discrimination and oppression of non-human animals. Hence, liberationists have a privileged although marginalised position (Ibid.) of experiencing the political struggle and slow advancement of the cause for animal rights.

The cognitive-emotional-political operative also may be applied directly to the non-human animals themselves – *their* standpoint of these achievements. As a liberationist, I assert that these oppressed others possess a *cognitive* standpoint of their experiences; in the absence of our full understanding as to their actual cognitive capacity, they are, in all likelihood, agonising over their state of being and exploitation whether in a science lab, a factory farm, or a slaughterhouse. They may have thoughts about what they are experiencing, what they fear may happen to them and confusion over *why* they are being made to suffer. I suggest that they also experience an *emotional* trauma: physical pain from their ill treatment and emotional pain from the experiences of separation from loved ones, viewing their fellow species being tortured, and a tremendous fear over their own destiny. Although non-human animals may not participate in any *political* agenda, they do depend – whether they are aware or not – on the humans who do fight the political battle to liberate these oppressed beings from their torment. Speaking as one liberationist, I do feel a responsibility to serve as a political and moral voice for these sufferers, a potential saviour of the innocent victims of humanocentric cruelty, and an educator who needs to bring moral consciousness to the ignorant who continue to contribute to the suffering of these victims.

2.6.2 Social-Historical-Bodily

As with the cognitive-emotional-political achievements for standpoint research, the social-historical-bodily experiences also apply to both the animal liberationist position and the 'oppressed non-human other' standpoint. The animal liberationist movement, like other politicised movements, is a *social* movement. The repercussions stemming from the theories, lifestyle choices, and altered behaviours, attitudes, and actions regarding animal liberationism has proven effectual and extensive for at least a portion of our society adhering to a more humane way of living; concretely, social change is possible in the humane direction. There is *history* of this movement. Animal liberationism has existed on the periphery of social consciousness, although the movement seems to be evolving to exist and expand within the main of society.

The bodily experience of the liberationist is somewhat existentialist in that the liberator experiences a bodily event two-fold: (1) when the person evolves as a vegetarian or a vegan, s/he often experiences a heightened sense of physical (as well as spiritual) well-being (Adams, 2001; Linzey, 1998; Randour, 2000); the liberationist often sites a greater awareness of her/his physical body; furthermore, s/he may experience her/his body from a perspective of something to be cared for and nurtured as opposed to the body being used as a receptacle for the remains of animal body parts, and (2) the liberationist may experience the bodily pains of the non-human other, a physio-sensational empathic experience of what the animal victim may be experiencing; this form of pseudo-bodily connection with an 'other' enables the liberationist to recognise the *other's* experiences as though s/he is actually experiencing these events first-hand; this is a very real example of true empathy.

The social-historical-bodily experiences may also apply to the oppressed non-human other; hence, the standpoint of the non-human other is recognised and acknowledged to signify *their* subjectivity of existence. Like humans, non-human animals are *social*; they live, evolve, and thrive in herds, prides, schools, and flocks. Non-human animals have awareness of their family and community members (Masson & McCarthy, 1995). Nature – hence, non-human animals – has an extensive history regardless of which theory of creationism one adheres to. That notwithstanding, individual animals, animal families, and animal communities have *history* of their experiences: births, deaths, extended times of thirst and hunger, times of play and celebration. We humans need to remind ourselves that we are not the only species that has existed for thousands of years, but that other species do in fact carry their own stories of evolution and survival.

The *bodily* experiences of the non-human other parallels those of our own species. As discussed throughout this book, other species share in our ability to experience pain, suffering, joy, elation, sadness, and even love. Just as we may possess an awareness of our physical body, so too can we assert that other species possess a similar awareness; they know when they are in pain, they can experience hunger, and their behaviours can be observed as differing in times of neglect as opposed to times of great care and nurturance. They are not, as Decartes assumed, machines of automata. They are living, breathing, social beings who need recognition and acknowledgement as our fellow earthlings, our fellow community members, and our extended family.

2.7 Grounding the Theoretical Background

While my research includes rationalist theorisation for animal advocacy (Regan, 1983, 1998; Singer, 1985, 1990, 1998, 2001) throughout my argument(s), it is the feminist, rational-emotive and emotionalist theorisations that I predominantly adhere to (Adams, 1996, 1998, 2001; Curtin, 2001; Donovan, 1990, 1996; Luke, 1996; Newkirk, 1992; Robbins, 1987, 2001; Rollin, 1990; Rowlands, 2002). There are many theorists who do not necessarily fall into one of these categories, but adhere to a more central stance (Barnard, 1995; Marcus, 1998; Robbins, 1987; Rowlands, 2002). Rowlands (2002) for example, blends both the rational and non-rational arguments for why we need to morally consider our non-human counterparts as moral equals.

The *rationalists* argue that *sentient* beings, those capable of experiencing pain, suffering, joy and pleasure, ought to be encompassed within our realm of moral consideration; non-human animals' experiences are similar to our own; therefore, we ought not treat sentient non-human animals in ways that we would not treat humans. The *feminists*[5] argue for moral consideration of non-human life not because of sentience or perceived capabilities of having similar experiences as humans, but rather such moral encompassment ought to be considered for the mere sake of affirming the sanctity of life. The feminist animal liberationists follow an *ethic of care* (Gilligan, 1982) – this means that they advocate caring for animals because animals are

---

[5]I use the term feminist as synonymous with emotionalist; as discussed in this book, not all feminists are alike; hence, I adhere to an emotionalist position as well as a rationalist position: a balance of animal rights advocacy.

fellow earthlings, capable of forming family bonds, community relationships, experiencing emotional expressions of sadness, joy, depression, elation. Because of the mere existence of these animals, they deserve to exist. Succinctly, we humans do not have the right to disturb, harm, torture, exploit or kill these innocent beings (Ibid).

The purpose of this book is to address many issues surrounding our relatedness with nature, with the other-than-human, and to attempt to bridge all earthlings through recognising inherent interconnections and shared abilities, capacities and needs and desires for survival. More expansive, I believe that it is critical that we integrate humane values and non-anthropocentric principles throughout our educational institutions as a vehicle for transforming our society from one of violence and oppression to a preferable society of peace, kindness, non-violence, equity for all living beings. Humane educators can contribute to creating a place where we can minimise needless pain and suffering, and where we can optimise positive experiences for all earthlings.

I have chosen three fields of study as foundations for supporting my assertions for non-anthropocentric erudition: (1) Bio-centric Environmentalism, (2) Eco-feminism, and (3) Veganism (Vegan Ethics). My motivation for honing in on these ideological theorisations and premises are based on my personal belief system for advocating an animal liberationist perspective of delivering humane education. After studying many discrete areas of environmentalism, the three aforementioned areas match my own argumentation for advancing a non-anthropocentric paradigm.

Bio-centricity, or "life-centred" environmentalism, addresses concerns of diverse communities, including the other-than-human; eco-feminism parallels my argument that we need to advocate for and protect other species for reasons other than rational premises; and at the core of my advocacy, veganism serves as a compelling transformative model for inculcating humane values and humane living that refrains from harming other species. More concretely, as a vegan myself, I know the power of veganism as well as the spiritual awakening that prevails when one chooses the vegan lifestyle. Together, these areas of academe generate a fervent groundwork for asserting a non-anthropocentric perspective towards humane living for environmental education and environmental ethics.

I am critically driven to study and consider diverse schools of thought for my standpoint. I dichotomise the rationalist and emotionalist schools of thought for animal/environmental advocacy by comparing and contrasting the various theories and learning about the philosophical foundations from which they grew. As a result, I find that the diverse theories can, in fact, be conjoined to create a solid case for advocating humane values and peaceful relatedness towards nature. Both schools of thought – rationalist and emotionalist – can work collaboratively and effectively to form and deliver a stronger case for animal advocacy; hence, it is not necessary nor is it beneficial to fragment these differing ways of approaching the issues at hand, but rather, I strongly advocate for a melding of cognitive/rational *and* emotive methods and assertions towards the liberation of non-human animals (Caine, 2001).

It is essential to include the other-than-human (and nature as a whole) when discussing a futures perspective for peaceful living. From a non-anthropocentric perspective, a preferable future advocates that young students need to be allowed opportunity to include the whole of nature in their vision of an ideal society where violence is abhorred and love and kindness are sought as an end goal (Caine, 2002). Furthermore, I signify an interconnectivity of all species and I proffer the idea that if we fragment ourselves from the other-than-human, we diminish our spiritual essence (Caine, 2003). Concretely, humans and non-human animals share the same place and space of the universe; we are embedded within nature and nature is embedded within us.

2.8 My Personal Motivation

Perhaps the most significant preparation I have had in undertaking this work stems from my own experiences with my non-human animal companions. My animals are also my teachers. Among my birds, rabbits, fish, cats, and dogs, are crucial lessons in compassion, responsibility, and love. I recognise that I am solely responsible for the feeding, cleaning, and necessary care of these living beings. These animals depend upon my time, effort, judgment, and genuine caring for their very survival; I am literally the lifeline for my companion animals.

I can honestly say that my animals have taught me to become a responsible "parent" as well as a more compassionate, empathic, and conscientious person. Through my interactions with my non-human companions, I have also learned about my own ability to nurture and love another being; I have grown emotionally and spiritually and I have gained strength in my ability to cope with loss and grief. When several of my companion animals 'crossed over' from their physical life -- Anna, Noah, Stella, Sir Maximillion, Woody, Sterling, Chester, Maya, Mr. Fish, Silky Fish, Fluffy, and Pumpkin, these were the most devastating events of my adult life. My memories of all of my companions continue to serve as reminders for me to give all my available energy and unconditional love to my now existing[6] animals every day; I do not know how many more days I have with each animal – therefore, every day is precious. I feel honoured to serve as a caretaker and protector for my companion animals. It is from this very passion that I am able to write about animal advocacy. My passion and dedication for animals is evident throughout my writing and I hope that this is what allows me to create powerful and empowering text that will enlighten others to consider and ponder their relatedness to animals and to nature.

---

[6] Here, I refer to "now existing" as my companion animals who are physically still with me. I also believe that my companion animals who have passed away are still with me on a spiritual level; however, for ease of understanding to my readers, I am using the normatively cultural referencing of these terms.

3

Value of Living Beings: Definitions, Values and Theories

3.1 Introduction: Valuation of Living Beings

> [The] essential point [is] that animals do *not* have merely instrumental value for humans, but rather count as ends in themselves; *their* life, liberty and happiness have intrinsic value. This change of perspective requires us to rethink our habitual conception of what an animal is – not a tool but something that has value in itself (Rowlands, 2002, p. xi).

Depending on whom you ask, the term *intrinsic value* is defined in various ways. Rowlands' interpretation, quoted above, is one that effectively conveys a humane message that non-human animals are valuable for the sake of the non-human animals themselves – they are *not instrumentally* valuable existing only for humans' exploitation of them. This means that non-human animals are not tools, at least morally speaking, at the disposal of human use and exploitation; rather, our non-human counterparts have lives of their own with families, communities, and the vast array of physical, psychological and emotional experiences afforded to them by nature. Rowlands contrasts intrinsic value with instrumental value insofar as saying that one who possesses intrinsic value is *valuable unto itself as a subject of a life* while anything deemed to be instrumentally valuable is *valuable only as a means to others* – specifically, as much as it benefits the human.

Paul Taylor (2001) parallels Rowlands' interpretation in that he too distinguishes an individual possessing value for its own sake as one who is intrinsically valuable from the premise that such an individual is a member of the Earth community:

> The principle of intrinsic value states that, regardless of what kind of entity it is in other respects, if it is a member of the Earth's community of life, the realization of its good is something *intrinsically* valuable. This means that its good is prima facie worthy of being preserved or promoted as an end in itself and for the sake of the entity whose good it is (p. 102).

In other words, who are we (humans) to interpret what or who is valuable or what or who possesses intrinsic value – what entities are valuable unto themselves. As Brian Luke (1996) so eloquently expresses, there is no objective proof that we humans are any more valuable as life forms than any other species; hence, our intrinsic value is no greater than that of non-human animals.

Taylor makes the distinction of intrinsic value and inherent worth as stated in the following passage:

> To say that [an entity] possesses inherent worth is to say that its good is deserving of the concern and consideration of all moral agents, and that the realization of its good has intrinsic value, to be pursued as an end in itself and for the sake of the entity whose good it is (Taylor, 2001, p. 102).

Therefore, if an individual possesses inherent worth, then that individual deserves to exist, to live, to pursue its life as a valuable entity not only of an adjoining community (i.e., the Earth community), but as an individual possessing value and worth for its own sake (Rowlands, 2002). Furthermore, this same individual carries intrinsic value for its own sake – because this individual, as we have decided according to its possession of inherent worth, has a life and existence intrinsically valuable unto itself. Such interpretation seems circular: an entity possesses inherent worth; therefore, the individual is intrinsically valuable unto itself; or put more precisely, the individual's life is intrinsically valuable for the individual. This type of circular argumentation and interpretation seems prevalent throughout the intrinsic value/inherent value literature.

Tom Regan (1983) warns us of the multiple interpretations of intrinsic value and how this term is often interpreted in various ways:

> The idea of intrinsic value has been defined in a variety of ways, including "what is desired for its own sake," "what would be good even if it existed in isolation from everything else," "what ought to exist for its own sake," and "what is valued or preferred in itself" (p. 142).

Regan's statements do one of two things: (1) he refers to instrumental value as something's being of positive value *only* as a means to something else and, (2) he parallels inherent value with what he terms *positive intrinsic value* or something's being good *independently* of its being a means to something else. Regan explicates these differences through two theories: a Utilitarian Theory which states that *pleasure and pleasure alone is intrinsically valuable* (also known as value hedonism) and consequently, interprets pain as intrinsically evil; and a Preference Theory which *holds that what has positive intrinsic value is the satisfaction of preferences, understood as desires or goals, while what has negative intrinsic value is their frustration* (Ibid.).

Inherent value stems from the assertion of *"equality of individuals* [which] involves viewing certain individuals as having value in themselves"; hence they possess inherent value (Ibid. p. 235). We need to carefully note that Regan tends to assign inherent value of a living being based on whether it is a sentient being. For example, Regan would not consider an earthworm as possessing inherent value as he would stand on his theory that an earthworm lacks sentience and therefore does not possess the abilities or confines of inherent value; he may, however, say that the earthworm does possess intrinsic value as an entity that is instrumentally valuable for the ecosystem or for other species as a food source or other useful purpose. From this latter divulgence, the earthworm is valuable only as a tool for the soil and for its fellow species that depend upon the earthworm for food and/or sustenance. (Note: Upon studying a wide array of animal rights theorisations, one begins to realise that even within non-anthropocentric theories and assertions lies great diversity for interpreting what is meant by the terms *animal rights* or *animal liberation*).

Before leaving the theories articulated by Regan, we need to address one effective rendering of a significant difference between inherent value and intrinsic value (as he puts forth). Regan distinguishes these terms from one another as follows:

> The inherent value of individual moral agents is to be understood as being conceptually distinct from the intrinsic value that attaches to the experiences they have (e.g., their pleasures or preference satisfactions), as not being reducible to values of this latter kind, and as being incommensurate with these values. To say that inherent value is not reducible to the intrinsic values of an individual's experiences means that we cannot determine the inherent value of the individual moral agents by totalling the intrinsic values of their experiences. Those who have a more pleasant or happier life do not therefore have greater inherent value than those whose lives are less pleasant or happy (pp. 235-236).

Summarising Regan's thoughts on valuation of beings, we note that an entity possessing intrinsic value may simply serve as a "mere receptacle" (Ibid. p. 236) of value for others while an entity possessing inherent value "[has] value in their own right, a value that is distinct from, not reducible to, and incommensurate with the values of those experiences which, as receptacles, they have or undergo" (p. 236).

Peter Singer (1985) also refers to individuals who have independent value or inherent value as entities who are *not* mere receptacles. He further delivers an egalitarian notion whereby all individuals possessing inherent value possess it at an equal level of evaluation. "All who have inherent value have it equally" (p. 21). Singer employs the *subject of a life* credo which states that as long as an individual is regarded as a subject of a life – her/his life has substance, meaning and inherent value unto itself regardless of external valuation – that life is equally deserving of moral consideration with all other inherently valuable lives.

> [We] are each of us the experiencing subject of a life, a conscious creature having an individual welfare that has importance to us whatever our usefulness to others. We want and prefer things, believe and feel things, recall and expect things. And all these dimensions of our life, including our pleasure and pain, our enjoyment and suffering, our satisfaction and frustration, our continued existence or our untimely death – all make a difference to the quality of our life as lived, as experienced, by us as individuals. As the same is true of those animals that concern us (the ones that are eaten and trapped, for example), they too must be viewed as the experiencing subjects of a life, with inherent value of their own (Ibid. p. 22).

As is consistent throughout Singer's animal liberationist theory, claiming that humans have greater inherent value than non-human animals is **irrational** (author's emphasis). Since there is no universal objective proof of such a claim, we need to be careful of the danger of rendering sweeping statements that place humans at the top of some idealistic hierarchy for the deserving of moral consideration and inherent worth.

Mark Rowlands (2002) compares *instrumental value* to *intrinsic value*, naming the former as signifying an entity *valuable only as a means to others* while denoting the latter as naming an entity as being *valuable unto itself as a subject of a life*. Rowlands warns us of the need to reflect upon our relationship with non-human animals in terms of recognising the value of their lives for *them*, not as tools for us. Furthermore, Rowlands asks us to empathise with non-human animals and the experiences they endure at the hands of humankind:

> This is really just a way to put an old moral rule: *ask what you would feel like in the other guy's shoes*. If you wouldn't want it done to you, then how can you justify doing it to someone else? This is a maxim that promotes the recognition of *equality* – in the sense of not discriminating according to morally irrelevant characteristics. The only fair or just way to treat intrinsically valuable beings is equally: that is,

according to their morally relevant characteristics, not
irrelevant ones such as race or sex or species (pp. xi-xii).

Holmes Ralston (2001) asserts that nature does have value aside from
whether humans place any value upon any natural entity. He further
expresses that humans who say that nature only has value when we
give it value are practising "value apartheid" (p. 80). In other words,
nature does not require our subjective evaluation or our committing
any value or worth of existence in order for nature to objectively be
valuable.

> [It] seems absurd to say that there are no values until humans
> arrive. There is no better evidence of non-human values and
> valuers than spontaneous wildlife, born free and on its own.
> Animals hunt and howl; find shelter; seek out their habitats
> and mates; care for their young; flee from threats; grow
> hungry, thirsty, hot, tired, excited, sleepy. They suffer injury
> and lick their wounds. Here we are quite convinced that
> value is nonanthropogenic, to say nothing of anthropocentric
> (Ibid. p. 80).

Ralston further acknowledges the living beings behind the faces of
non-human animals. He reminds us of their capabilities to sense their
world and engage it, often in ways that humans experience sensory
perception of their environment.

> These wild animals defend their own lives because they have
> a good of their own. There is somebody there behind the fur
> or feathers. Our gaze is returned by an animal that itself has a
> concerned outlook. Here is value right before our eyes, right
> behind those eyes. Animals are valuable, able to value things
> in their world (Ibid. p. 80).

Ralston criticises J. Baird Callicott for standing on the philosophy that
"until humans [place value on nature], there simply is no inherent or
intrinsic value in nature" (Ibid. p. 81).

> [The] problem with the "no value without a valuer" axiom is
> that it is too subjectivist; it looks for some centre of value
> located in a subjective self (Ibid. p. 81)…We commit the

subjectivist fallacy if we think all values lie in subjective experience, and, worse still, the anthropocentrist fallacy if we think all values lie in human options and preferences. These plants and animals do not make man the measure of things at all (p. 85).

In terms of value in nature, we need to continuously remind ourselves that our species, humans, were late-comers in the universe. Earth with its plant and animal life existed millions of years before any human evolved. We are not *discovering* value in the world – the value existed long before our conception. Ralston encourages us to remember our historical and psychological relatedness to nature:

> Humans are not so much lighting up value in a merely potentially valuable world, as they are psychologically joining ongoing planetary natural history in which there is value wherever there is positive creativity (Ibid. p. 85)...[There] is something subjective, something philosophically naïve, and even something hazardous in a time of ecological crisis, about living in a reference frame where one species takes itself as absolute and values every thing else in nature relative to its potential to produce value for itself (p. 85).

In Ralston's (1998) essay, "Yes, Value Is Intrinsic in Nature", he reiterates the inherent value of nature apart from and irrelevant to subjective human input and evaluation:

> [*Intrinsic*] *natural* value [recognises] value inherent in some natural occasions, without contributory human reference. The loons ought to continue to call, whether heard by humans or not. But the loon, while nonhuman, is itself a natural subject. There is something it is like to be a loon; its pains and pleasures are expressed in the call. Those who cannot conceive of nonexperienced value may allow nonhuman but not nonsubjective value. Value exists only where a subject has an object of interest (p. 78).

He further elaborates:

> [While] experience is indeed a value, a thing can have values
> that go unexperienced. Just as a human life can have
> meaning of which the individual is unaware…biological
> individuals can play valuable genetic, ecological and
> evolutionary roles of which they are unaware. If the truth
> could be known, not only is much of value taking place in
> nonsentient nature, much of value is going on over our own
> heads as well (Ibid. p. 78).

3.2 Theorisation and Philosophy for the Human/Nature Relationship

John Rawls (1971) suggested a most interesting proposal for consideration regarding all living beings on Earth. He gave rise to the Veil of Ignorance Theory, a profound thought-provoking consideration for critical analysis for all philosophers and laypeople alike. John Lawrence Hill (1996) summarises this theory as follows:

> [We] need a way to determine which social arrangements and
> relationships are fair and which are not. The only way to
> make the determination of what is truly fair, is to attempt to
> find out what [people] *would have agreed to* before they took
> on their social roles, without the benefit of the social and
> political biases inherent in the real world (p. 49).

> [A] veil of ignorance operates basically as follows: imagine
> putting everyone who is to live in a society together in a giant
> cosmic convention hall where they will negotiate the terms of
> the 'social contract' that is to govern all social relationships.
> Everyone possesses general knowledge about the conditions
> of the world – what it takes to live, which living conditions
> are preferable to which, and so on. What the members do not
> know, because of the veil of ignorance, is where in society
> they [will] wind up ... [each] citizen-negotiator is ignorant
> about whether he or she will turn up wealthy or poor, a
> member of a minority group or one of the dominant class,
> heterosexual or homosexual, healthy or weak (Ibid. p. 49).

Within this very interesting hypothetical situation of the veil of ignorance, the destined earthling does not know whether s/he will be human or non-human. Since each being does not know her/his destined species, s/he would opt for maximum fairness and freedom (Hill, 1996). Given the chance that any individual could end up as a non-human animal, meat-eating would ideally remain excluded from social formation as any individual could potentially exist as a non-human animal destined for the roasting pan or deep fryer; the same could be assured for refraining from scientific experimentation using non-human animals or any other exploitative behaviour whereby non-human species are caused pain and suffering (Ibid.). Also, this vast social committee devising the make-up of society would opt to eradicate other exploitative uses of non-human animals such as circuses, zoos, marine animal parks, puppy mills and illegal, long distance trade of exotic animals (e.g., amazon parrots shipped to North America and Europe for the pet trade). Any activity deemed immoral, inhumane and an atrocity to decency would be excluded from the construction of this non-anthropocentric formation of a new world.

Zimmerman (1988) is quick to point out our own inconsistency in how we think of ourselves in relation to nature:

> [Many people subscribe to the theory of] anthropocentric humanism, which holds that humans are the origin of all value, purpose and meaning. When such anthropocentric humanism is combined with naturalism, the following world view results: the human animal is the source of all meaning, value and purpose and, as a result, the human animal has the "right" to do whatever it chooses to other entities in order to insure its own survival and security...Historically, anthropocentric-naturalistic humanism has helped to heighten modern humanity's new sense of self. This new self, already defined in important respects by Descartes, is the autonomous, intrinsically valuable, self-made "I", which is essentially different from merely "natural" entities...(p. 19)...On the one hand, we speak of ourselves as natural things in a meaningless universe; on the other hand, we speak of ourselves as intrinsically valuable persons in a universe that is ours for the taking (Ibid. p. 19).

A major falsity of declaring nature only valuable from a humanocentric lens emerges from the Cartesian worldview (Regan, 1983, 1998; Singer, 1990); namely, that nature is separate from humans and hence nature can be fragmented and utilised as resources for human desire. Regan (1983) cites the seventeenth-century French philosopher René Descartes as "…denying all thought, by which he means all consciousness, to animals. Animals, in his view, are *thoughtless brutes, automata,* machines" (p. 3). Unfortunately, Descartes had great influence over the scientific and medical communities of the time as he was considered one of the notable teachers and researchers of his era. Singer (1990) further reminds us of René Descartes' theory regarding non-human animals as machines; this mechanistic reasoning stemmed from so-called scientific experiments designed to advance medical science:

> They administered beatings to dogs with perfect indifference, and made fun of those who pitied the creatures as if they felt pain. They said the animals were clocks; that the cries they emitted when struck were only the noise of a little spring that had been touched, but that the whole body was without feeling. They nailed poor animals up on boards by their four paws to vivisect them and see the circulation of the blood which was a great subject of conversation (pp. 201-202).

This seventeenth century notion that animals are unlike humans in that the former are nothing more than machinery while the latter are thinking, breathing and feeling beings began to dissipate in the eighteenth century. Voltaire brought to light the realisation that humans and non-human animals shared many of the same capacities:

> There are barbarians who seize this dog, who so greatly surpasses man in fidelity and friendship, and nail him down to a table and dissect him alive, to show you the mesaraic veins! You discover in him *all the same organs of feelings as in yourself.* Answer me, mechanist, has Nature arranged all the springs of feeling in this animal *to the end that he might not feel?* (Ibid. p. 202).

Viewing non-human animals as highly dissimilar to us and incapable of experiencing feelings, physical pain or sensory perceptions thought to be solely the preserve of humans permitted Cartesians their need (or desire) to control the weaker and more helpless lives of non-human animals (Adams, 1998). If non-human animals can be thought of as lesser than humans, incapable of experiencing pain and suffering, then any moral consideration for the sake of non-human animals can be dismissed. Fortunately, today, we know better – we realise that non-human animals do experience physical, emotional, psychological and other sensory perceptions *not* unlike those of humans (Adams 1998; Rowlands, 2002).

> From an ethical perspective -- which is far from being a minor or trivial matter -- there is a range of considerations that related to animals that buttress an even stronger legal claim that may be made on their behalf. [...] They include their inability to give or withhold consent, inability to vocalise their own interests, their moral innocence or blamelessness, and their vulnerability and defencelessness. Perhaps the most relevant of these considerations here is the recognition that animals cannot represent their own interests. Individuals who cannot adequately represent themselves have to depend upon benign moral representation. This consideration marks animals, along with vulnerable human subjects, notably infants and young children, as a special case. There are, therefore, strong grounds for extending to these beings special consideration when it comes to legal decisions that may affect or harm their own interests (Linzey, 2009, p. 143).

The following philosophical argument substantiates the notion of humans embedded within nature and vice versa; hence, a *non-Cartesian* position upholds a non-anthropocentric paradigm.

> **Premise 1**: Both humans and non-human animals – nature – originate from the same entity of creationism. This can be explained by the Big Bang Theory whereby all living beings' origins stem from a common microcosm of creation. (Organised religion claims that a supreme being – God – created all life; not meaning to beg the question on creationism, my philosophy utilises non-religious explication of the origins of life).

Premise 2: Nature comprises all living entities on Earth and within the biosphere.

Premise 3: Therefore, given that humans and non-humans originated from the same microcosm, humans are an integral part of nature. We are embedded within nature, we are part of nature, and nature is within and a part of us.

Premise 4: Hence, given the premise that both humans and non-humans stem from the same origin of creation, if humans possess intrinsic value (and inherent value), then so too do non-human animals and nature.

Selby (2001) elaborates on this same notion of interconnectedness among all living entities of the universe: "Everything is dynamically connected and related to everything else…nothing can be completely understood save in relationship to everything else… [w]hat happens locally is also a global phenomenon (a part of the whole, itself acting to inform the whole)"… (Ibid. p. 3). Selby further quotes physicist David Bohm (1983, 1990): "everything is enfolded within everything else" (Selby, 2001, p. 4). Both Selby and Bohm explore a metaphysical subatomic world whereby all entities – micro-organismic and macro-organismic – are interrelated and interconnected stemming from a common origin of creationism and continuing as flowing and highly interactive life forms – forms that depend upon each other and intertwine one another.

Callicott (1985) expresses his concept of interrelatedness with nature through what he terms *the principle of axiological complementarity* (p. 275). He suggests that the destruction of nature, the demise of the environment, lends to his own degradation and devaluation of his own life.

> […] [A]s one contemplates the destruction of biomes and the
> consequent loss of perhaps hundreds of thousands of species
> that the palpable disvalue of the prospect is at once
> personal…I personally feel a very real loss of value to *myself*
> as I reflect upon the progressive destruction of the natural
> environment…[T]he injury *to me* of environmental
> destruction is primarily and directly to my extended self, to

the larger body and soul with which "I"…am continuous (Ibid. p. 275).

Callicott concludes that,

> [s]ince nature is the self fully extended and diffused, and the self, complementarily, is nature concentrated and [focussed] in one the intersection, the "knots," of the web of life or in the trajectory of one of the world lines in the four dimensional space-time continuum, nature is intrinsically valuable, to the extent that the self is intrinsically valuable (Ibid. p. 275).

Following from the preceding philosophical stance, if we believe that humans have or possess value, then it is a reasonable and logical assumption that non-human animals and the rest of nature also possess value (Ralston, 1998). To argue against this assertion condones false reasoning (i.e., deeming one life form as inherently valuable while denying another life that same value) and upholds the maintenance of a fragmented notion of humans separate from nature – such resistance upholds Cartesian justification in its purest sense.

The reason why we project feelings and emotions towards the other-than-human is due to the fact that we recognise the other-than-human as capable of cognisant awareness – we realise that they possess a conscious realisation of pain, suffering, pleasure, joy, relatedness to others. Only the fragmented, compartmentalised and speciesist Cartesians would dare scoff at emotional expressions of empathy, compassion, sympathy, sadness, helplessness and despair directed towards our non-human counterparts.

Embracing emotions as strong and solid argumentation and justification for encompassing non-human animals into our realm of moral consideration is significant (Donovan, 1996; Luke, 1996) – hence, our inclusion of those deemed to possess intrinsic value – is not only valid, but required from a standpoint of our embeddedness within nature (Callicott, 1985; Metzner, 1995; Selby, 2001) and the other-than-human. And, yes, the other-than-human does not merely possess value because they are valuable to us (humans), but because they are inherently valuable (Ralston, 1998):

[W]hen our awareness focuses on the individual lives of
plants and animals, each is seen to share with us the
characteristic of being a teleological [centre] of life striving
to [realise] its own good in its own good in its own unique
way (P. Taylor, 1998, p. 84).

Countering the theory of human egoist superiority in that humans
assign value to nature is a model stemming from quantum physics that
embraces all living entities as continuous waves of interactive energy
(Selby, 1999). This theorisation not only enables us to view ourselves
embedded within nature but permits a holistic perspective of all
entities of the universe as possessing "both...wave and particle
states..." (Ibid. p. 128); a living organism exists for its own sake;
hence, the particle state – an individual organism flourishing, thriving
and adhering to the remainder of the universe. Simultaneously, the
individual organism exists as an integral and integrating part of a
larger whole – it moves throughout and within the whole of the
universe; hence, the individual organism continues as a moving
element of life within a larger wave of continuous flux and
complementarity (Ibid.). The quantum view of living systems averts
dichotomous separations of *human/other-than-human* valuation.
Instead, this more holistic view celebrates all entities of the biosphere,
of the universe, as highly connected, inter-related and interdependent
flows of energy.

3.3 Transforming Our Relatedness towards Nature

When we think of human rights, *a sense of morality* is one of the
foundations for asserting human rights in the first place. We believe
that committing cruel acts towards fellow humans is immoral; at least,
those acts committed without provocation (i.e., the victims have done
nothing to initiate or instigate the acts of cruelty perpetrated upon
them). Then why do we not also feel the same way about committing
acts of cruelty towards non-human animals *who have done nothing to
initiate or instigate acts of cruelty against us*? Doesn't the cruelty we
commit against non-human animals and nature say something
profound about our species?

The fundamental principle of morality which we seek as a
necessity for thought is not, however, a matter only of

arranging and deepening current views of good and evil, but also of expanding and extending these. A man is really ethical only when he obeys the constraint laid on him to help all life which he is able to succour, and when he goes out of his way to avoid injuring anything living. He does not ask how far this or that life deserves sympathy as valuable in itself, nor how far it is capable of feeling. To him life as such is sacred. He shatters no ice crystal that sparkles in the sun, tears no leaf from its tree, breaks off no flower, and is careful not to crush any insect as he walks (Schweitzer, 1998, pp. 95-96).

Schweitzer's words meld with my own philosophical views of living my life as humanely as possible. Does this mean that I never harm any creature, whether an insect or the leaves on a tree? I do my best not to interfere with nature. I do not tear leaves from trees. I am careful to avoid stepping on snails and earthworms. I am not perfect; the human species is not perfect. However, living humanely is not about perfection. It is about living consciously so as to minimise any negative impact on the natural world.

The question is not *Can we live humanely*, but *Are we willing to live humanely*? This is not about degrees of abstinence from harming insects, trees or larvae. It is about our willingness and intentional actions and behaviours to refrain from bringing harm to non-human animals and to not leave a destructive footprint on the environment, on nature.

Perhaps, the realities of radical animal liberationist philosophy are too painful for most people to acknowledge and therefore, denial (Luke, 1996) overshadows the true horror of our inhumane relatedness to the other-than-human.

It is the sheer irrationality of conventional attitudes toward animals that strikes some of us as humanity's worst moral failing. It's bad enough to mistreat animals for blatantly selfish reasons, but to defend this mistreatment by means of transparently shoddy arguments is almost as objectionable. It is not just the welfare of animals that is at stake here. The integrity of human reason is also on the line. Where is our intellectual pride? (McGinn, 1996).

McGinn wholeheartedly expresses disgust and anguish at human apathy toward non-human animal suffering. Addressing McGinn's assertion, however, we need to be careful about accrediting the human race in a superior mode to non-human species due to intellectual capacity; such assertions may be construed or interpreted in ways that affirm anthropocentrism.

> It is true that a human being may be a better mathematician than a monkey, but the monkey may be a better tree climber than a human being. If we humans value mathematics more than tree climbing, that is because our conception of [civilised] life makes the development of mathematical ability more desirable than the ability to climb trees (Taylor, 1998, p. 80).

Possessing a greater intellectual ability does not make one possess greater moral worth (Luke, 1996); hence, moral consideration ought not be awarded, a priori, based on intellectualism (Singer, 1998) – a mechanistic rationalist ideology. This false superiority accredited through possession of intelligence carries dangerous assumptions for all living beings – within the human species as well as between humans and non-humans.

> It is an implication of this principle of equality that our concern for others ought not to depend on what they are like, or what abilities they possess – although precisely what this concern requires us to do may vary according to the characteristics of those affected by what we do. It is on this basis that the case against racism and the case against sexism must both ultimately rest; and it is in accordance with this principle that speciesism is also to be condemned. If possessing a higher degree of intelligence does not entitle one human to use another for his own ends, how can it entitle humans to exploit nonhumans? (Singer, 1998, p. 30).

Habitual speciesism may be a matter of a flaw in our failure to understand and fully comprehend our shared space and place in the biosphere – most people simply choose not to acknowledge or are unable to grasp notions of linking their highly anthropocentric behaviours with their corresponding end results of cruelty and suffering of non-human animals at massive and global proportions. Through cultural relativism (Shepard, 1995) – what human culture deems normal and acceptable behaviour – and historically (Ryder, 1989; Taylor, 1999), humans have exploited non-human animals, for the most part, without consciously contemplating or reflecting on the negative repercussions meted out to non-human animals. I interject the concept of cultural relativism with reference to anthropocentrism insofar as I believe that the two concepts intertwine autonomously; concretely, anthropocentric ways of living historically have impeded the freedoms and rights of non-human animals; likewise, the concept of cultural relativism explains that such historic hierarchical relatedness of human over non-human animal has engraved a normalised and socially accepted way of retaining humans as supposedly the top species and stewards of the remainder of the animal kingdom. The exploitation, oppression and massive apathy towards other species, for example, farm animals utilised for human dietary consumption (Adams, 1998; Barnard, 1995; Lyman, 1998; Marcus, 1998; Robbins, 1987), has endured from one generation to the next over thousands of years (Johnson, 1997); hence, anthropocentrism has incurred as habituation of the human species (Margulis, 1998).

> Australian anthropologist Derek Freeman observes that the doctrine of cultural relativism, which has dominated modern thought, may have blinded us to the deviate [behaviour] of whole societies by denying normative standards for mental health (Shepard, 1995, p. 24).

Affirming Freeman's assertion, one can begin to understand how cultural relativism has inculcated our cruelty towards non-human animals; namely, that from centuries of cruel and inhumane practises, we as a species have convinced ourselves that such cruelty is normal and acceptable. Certainly, from a radical animal liberationist view, the multiple ways in which we exploit, torture, and kill other species repudiates the inherent messages of humane education insofar as encouraging healthy states of mental, physical, and/or spiritual balance. For example, consider the slaughterhouse worker: this individual makes a living by contributing massive torment, anguish and untimely demise to millions of innocent animals. These innocent and unsuspecting living beings (e.g., cows, pigs, chickens, goats, sheep, turkeys, and others) as discussed earlier, are capable of feeling pain, emotional distress, alienation from family, agony at witnessing fellow family members and community members meet their bloody death (Robbins, 1987). Such horrific suffering evinces such evil, inhumane and morally reprehensible outcomes, that these experiences of the factory farm parallel the unspeakable atrocities meted out in Nazi concentration camps during World War II. How can the slaughterhouse worker maintain a healthy mental state? This person is responsible for murdering countless lives and causing immeasurable agony and torment for innumerable animals. The slaughterhouse worker is spiritually detached from her/his animal victims. Such an individual fails to make critical connections of spiritual and emotional relatedness between themselves and nature, between their own experiences and those of other species (Ryder, 1998), between their capacity for pain and suffering and the same capacity held by their non-human victims.

> There is…very good scientific evidence that other animals
> can suffer as we do. When hurt, they scream and writhe like
> we do; their nervous systems are similar and contain the same
> biochemicals that we know are associated with the experience
> of pain in ourselves (Ryder, 1998, p. 49).

Of course, let us not accuse this slaughterhouse worker of contributing autonomously to the torture and demise of these unsuspecting victims. It is the public demand for meat that creates these concentration camps for non-human animals (Adams, 1998). It is always easier to have someone else do our killing (Robbins, 1987); if people were forced to kill their own animals for consumption, we would in all likelihood witness a dramatic increase in the practise of vegetarianism (Ibid.).

> [During] the nineteenth century, abstinence from animal flesh
> gradually became established among a minority of the middle
> class. Slaughtering and slaughter houses began to be
> concealed from public view, and the animal origin of meat
> dishes obscured, as [recognisable] carcasses were less
> frequently served at table…(Ryder, 1989, p. 97).

Most slaughterhouses are located in rural areas away from the mass populous (Robbins, 1987). Urban facilities are usually giant warehouse type buildings without windows – this is to hide the hideous truths (Adams, 1996; Luke, 1996) behind the walls of these torture chambers. Psychologically, the 'out-of-sight, out-of-mind' mentality sustains people's continuance of the behaviour of devouring animal flesh; as long as they do not have to see the suffering, hear the cries, witness the agony of the tortured animals, they can justify their habitual behaviour through denial (Luke, 1996). In a sense, a psychic numbing (Roszak, 1995) on a societal level is necessary in order for such a massive degree of denial to sustain; the mystery and challenge of this societal failing is that such an inherently terrorising and tortuous institution – the institution of meat eating – can the pain and suffering of billions of non-human animals remain the normalised and systemic global acceptance (Caine, 2001) for human behaviour!

4

Embracing Bio-Centricity and a
Psychological Connection with Nature

4.1 Introduction: Understanding Bio-Centricity

Schweitzer (2001) expresses, once again, a humane and ethical as well as moral stance for which humans need to act insofar as invoking compassion and kindness:

> If [man] goes out into the street after a rainstorm and sees a worm which has strayed there, he reflects that it will certainly dry up in the sunshine, if it does not quickly regain the damp soil into which it can creep, and so he helps it back from the deadly paving stones into the lush grass. Should he pass by an insect which has fallen into a pool, he spares the time to reach it a leaf or stalk of which it may clamber and save itself (p. 96).

Bio-centricity recognises interconnections, interdependencies and inter-relatedness between and among all life forms (Selby, 1995). Adherence to a bio-centric outlook confirms the planet as a massive system comprising micro- and macro-systems – namely, life systems (Lovelock, 2000 [1979]). This paradigm is contingent upon initially viewing the big picture of the planet – macro-systems where life flourishes: oceans, forests, water tables, deserts, mountains, icecaps, and other natural geographies; additionally, included are the millions of species residing throughout these geographical arenas. As proffered by Margulis (1998), "Gaia is the series of interacting ecosystems that compose a single huge ecosystem at the Earth's surface" (p. 120). This of course does not connote that the individual beings are only in existence to comprise the systems for which they are part and parcel to; each living being also carries an inherent value unto her/himself: the other-than-human experiences many of the same transitions – physical, psychological, emotional – as do humans. We humans are part of Gaia; however, I doubt any human would concede to the notion that we are only here to fulfil a systemic need of the earth; hence, non-humans are also not merely fulfilling Gaian demands, but possess ends unto themselves as unique individuals.

Furthering bio-centricity to encompass micro-systems allows theoretical, philosophical and practical emphasis on living communities – humans, birds, fish, mammals, reptiles, insects, plants, micro-organisms, etc. Concretely, the bio-centric perspective acknowledges all these systems and living beings within systems as having an inherent place in the biosphere (P. Taylor, 2001) – they exist and therefore, deserve to exist (Rowlands, 2002). One who advocates bio-centricity does not question the existence of any species; s/he recognises all species as belonging to a great chain of living beings, systems and the whole of the universe.

> The bio-centric outlook on nature has four main components. (1) Humans are thought of as members of the Earth's community of life, holding that membership on the same terms as apply to all the nonhuman members. (2) The Earth's natural ecosystems as a totality are seen as a complex web of interconnected elements, with the sound biological functioning of each being dependent on the sound biological functioning of the others. [(3)] Each individual organism is conceived of as a teleological [centre] of life, pursuing its own good in its own way. (4) Whether we are concerned with standards of merit or with the concept of inherent worth, the claim that humans by their very nature are superior to other species is a groundless claim and, in the light of elements (1), (2), and (3) above, must be rejected as nothing

> more than an irrational bias in our own [favour] (P. Taylor, 1998, pp. 74-75).

In the most literal and rational sense, we have no proof whatsoever that humans possess moral superiority (Luke, 1996) over other species. There is no evidence that humans are more deserving than any other species insofar as entitlement of sheer existence (Rowlands, 2002). Our abilities to communicate in human languages, to engage in rational thinking (although this seems rare these days), and our so-called intellect do not connote humans as superior to non-humans; in fact, if we utilise abilities as measuring sticks for hierarchical placement of any species, humans fall short much of the time.

> [V]arious nonhuman species have capacities that humans lack. There is the speed of a cheetah, the vision of an eagle, the agility of a monkey. Why should not these be taken as signs of *their* superiority over humans? (P. Taylor, 2001, p. 79).

In the most profound sense, when humans claim superiority over non-human life forms, they are doing so from a human-centred perspective – obviously, the human ego takes precedence for placing humans at the top of a *false hierarchy* of species. Human-egoism, as it denies other species equitable moral consideration, operates from irrational and unfounded biases favouring humanocentric ideologies (Luke, 1996; Regan, 1983; Singer, 1990). A human-chauvinist does not consider the possibility that non-human animals possess abilities and strengths superior to human animals. Humans assume that they are superior beings to the non-human; humans use multiple rationalisations for sustaining this way of thinking.

> [The capacities of non-humans] are not as *valuable* as the human capacities that are claimed to make us superior. Such uniquely human characteristics as rational thought, aesthetic creativity, autonomy and self-determination, and moral freedom, it might be held, have a higher value than the capacities found in other species. Yet we must ask: valuable to whom, and on what grounds? (P. Taylor, 2001, p. 79).

Paul Taylor's inquiry is valid regarding questioning the values of any given abilities and to whom such value serves. However, his claim of *uniquely human characteristics* remain unfounded: we do not know for certain that non-human animals are not capable of rational thought, non-human animals are capable of exerting creative expression (i.e., the orang-utan who figures how to obtain food in 'out-of-reach' places or the chimp who, through trial and error, succeeds at opening a coconut by tempering it with a rock), and self-determination is evident in many species – how else could they have endured and survived the many challenges, obstacles and passing time of their historical existence?

Embedded within the conceptual framework of bio-centricity is the ethic of *reverence for life*. By adhering to bio-centric principles of valuing each life for its own sake – for its own inherent worth – we can claim that we respect and revere the existence of each living being. There is little room for compromise on this premise as indicated by Schweitzer (2001):

> The ethic of reverence for life [recognises] no such thing as a relative ethic. The maintenance and enhancement of life are the only things it counts as being good in themselves. All destruction of and injury to life, from whatever circumstances they may result, are reckoned by it as evil…Man does not make ethical progress by assimilating instruction with regard to accommodations between the ethical and the necessary, but only by hearing ever more clearly the voice of the ethical element, by being ever more under the control of his own yearning to maintain and to enhance life, and by becoming ever more obstinate in his opposition to the necessity of destroying and injuring life (pp. 98-99).

According to Devall and Sessions (2001), "The intuition of bio-centric equality is that all things in the biosphere have an equal right to live and blossom and to reach their own individual forms of unfolding and self-[realisation] within the larger Self-[realisation]. This basic intuition is that all organisms and entities in the ecosphere, as parts of the interrelated whole, are equal in intrinsic worth" (p. 158). The *self* refers to the individual living being, in this case a human; the *Self* refers to the individual as an embedded member of a larger whole: the whole of Gaia. This concept is elaborated in the following quote:

> Bio-centric equality is intimately related to the all-inclusive Self-realization in the sense that if we harm the rest of Nature then we are harming ourselves. There are no boundaries and everything is interrelated. But insofar as we perceive things as individual organisms or entities, the insight draws us to respect all human and nonhuman individuals in their own right as parts of the whole without feeling the need to set up hierarchies of species with humans at the top (Devall & Sessions, 2001, p. 159).

Terrance O'Connor (1995) delivers a psychological awakening of our connection with nature; hence, with all other life on Earth. Although he does not specifically use the term bio-centricity, we may infer a life-centred message from his proffering:

> If this is not my planet, whose is it? If this is not my family, whose is it? If not my responsibility, whose? I am both the victim and the [victimiser]. I am the cause and I am the cure. When I act out of this [realisation], I act not out of guilt but out of self-love, a love that includes my family, which includes my planet. When I look, I see. When I educate myself, I break through my denial and see that humankind is facing an absolutely unprecedented crisis. When I act from this knowledge, I act not out of obligation or idealism, but because I live in a straw house and I smell smoke. I realize the truth that, in Krishnamurti's words, "You are the world, and the world is on fire" (Ibid. p. 153).

4.2 Our Psychological Connection with Gaia

It seems almost impossible to engage humane and environmental education without understanding our psychological connection with nature. Whether we live in a city, a small town or a rural community, we are surrounded by nature: trees, plants, flowers, birds, chipmunks, snails, earthworms and a multitude of other living organisms remind us of the natural world in which we are embedded. This world also includes mountains, forests, rivers, lakes, oceans, deserts and other natural geographies – the very space and place where we reside – envelope us in the essence of nature. Does our natural environment affect us? Do we feel different when strolling along the beach, listening to the crashing waves, feeling the warmth of the sun on our face and the touch of the warm and golden sand on our feet as opposed to the way we feel when we are stuck in heavy traffic on the freeway at 5 p.m. on a Friday afternoon? Do the sounds of running water and chirping birds have any effect on our moods? Do waterfalls have any soothing effect on our psyches? Why do so many people enjoy watching fish swim whether in aquariums or during deep-sea diving expeditions? What is the attraction of bird watching? Does the environment affect us emotionally, psychologically and spiritually as well as physically?

> When we are *in* the natural environment, rather than reading about nature or hearing a lecture on nature, we are granted a unique experience, depending upon our able senses, to see, hear, smell, touch (hopefully in an unobtrusive manner), and become acquainted with the living systems, species, and individual species members (Caine, 2003, p. 50).

Experiencing nature through our able senses allows us to connect with nature in that we bring both our conscious and subconscious acknowledgement of our *self*. We are affected by weather conditions, for example; some people experience what has been termed *seasonal depression* during the winter months. Because the days are shorter and darker (and in some places, snow, rain and long periods of overcast skies can add to the winter feel), some people experience low ebbs in their mood. (I am the opposite of most in that I experience elated moods on overcast days and a deprivation of energy and a "less than happy" disposition on very hot sunny days). In other words, many people do experience mood altering states stemming from weather conditions – i.e., conditions of nature. Thus, we are affected psychologically/emotionally by these changes in the atmosphere. Another example is the endeavour to escape the noisy city, and seek solitude and relaxation at a sandy beach, a mountain resort or a lush and green golf course; many people report feeling (and even looking) more relaxed and at peace after having spent quality time in one of these "more natural" settings.

When we are able to pause in our busy lives and truly experience nature in all its glory and wonder, we are reminded of nature's magic; we need to be reminded frequently that we are nature and that spending all of our time sitting in cubicles, classrooms, offices, and concrete towers conflicts with our natural need to engage the rest of the bio-sphere. We need to see ourselves as in-rhythm with other life forms rather than assuming a superior valuation over other-than-human living beings. When we view the wolf, the elephant, the orang-utan, the fox, and the zebra as one of us – as fellow earthlings – only then will we undeniably understand and embrace the rest of nature as our family, our community, our shared planetary companions. "Once we relinquish our need for the control, exploitation, and the hierarchical analysis of other-than-human life forms, we start opening ourselves to the beauty, love, and creativity in all of nature surrounding us" (Caine, 2003, p. 49).

Humans are part of nature. We are highly integrated within and from nature. We do not exist in an isolated bubble exclusive only to humans. In a very literal sense, we are synthesised of water and dust. All animals are composed of these same elements. Whether one adheres to the Big Bang Theory or to a religious doctrine, we are all – human and non-human – connected to the *Universe*. Multiple interpretations for what constitutes the universe are evident throughout academic disciplines, religious institutions, and among individual mind-sets. From a bio-centric perspective, the universe is comprised of the biosphere – all living and non-living entities herein – animals, plants, rocks, water, air, Gaia herself, are embraced as an enormous system of multiple and diverse living systems (Lovelock, 2000 [1979]; Margulis, 1998).

David Suzuki warns us of the psychological and irreparable dangers in exploiting the natural environment and in fragmenting ourselves from the rest of nature:

> When we forget that we are embedded in the natural world, we also forget that what we do to our surroundings we are doing to ourselves. Recently a new discipline has been created that combines the study of the human mind with the study of natural communities. Eco-psychology is an attempt to reconnect us with our natural home and to remedy some of the harm caused by our exile in the modern city. Eco-

psychologists argue that the damage we do to ourselves and our surroundings is caused by our separation from nature. Instead of trying to adjust to the existing social order and accept the status quo, they argue that for true mental health we must challenge the norm and take into account the interrelatedness of people and all other life-forms…If we continue to think of ourselves as separate from our surroundings, we will not be sensitive to the consequences of what we are doing, so we can't see that our path is potentially suicidal (Suzuki, 2002, pp. 179-180).

Joanna Macy (1995) signifies our need to shift our current ways of relating to nature; she calls for a shift in environmental consciousness:

We can see that our planetary crises are impelling us toward a shift in consciousness. Confronting us with our mortality as a species, they reveal the suicidal tendency inherent in our conception of ourselves as separate from the competitive beings. Given the fragility and limited resources of our planet, given our needs for flexibility and sharing, we have to think together in an integrated, synergistic fashion, rather than in the old fragmented and competitive ways—and we are beginning to do that. Once we tune into our interconnectedness, responsibility toward self and other become indistinguishable, because each thought and act affects the doer as much as the one done to (p. 258).

One of the greatest challenges for human beings is bringing to consciousness the realisation that we are connected to the biosphere – cognitively, emotionally, psychologically, and for some of us, a sense of a spiritual connection with nature pervades (Caine, 2003) – we exist as extensions of the biosphere and as integrating players within the biosphere.

Psychology, so dedicated to awakening human consciousness, needs to wake itself up to one of the most ancient human truths: we cannot be studied or cured apart from the planet (Hillman, 1995, p. xxii).

Robert S.E. Caine

Abraham Maslow's (1954, 1968) theory for attaining *self-actualisation* begins with the human's attainment of psychological needs, followed by safety needs, belongingness and love needs, esteem needs, and finally, although very few actually reach the top of the self-actualising pyramid, self-actualisation needs (See **Figure 4-1**). Maslow's self-actualisation theory is an excellent model for excelling the person towards a greater sense of self-confidence, self-worth and self-empowerment. However, a component of relatedness to the outside world is not encompassed by Maslow's theory – such relatedness may be inherent in the attainment of self-actualisation and perhaps Maslow did not feel it necessary to spell out every entity that comprises the self-actualised individual. I certainly will not criticise Maslow – his contributions to the psychological community are immense and invaluable – at least, for the benefit for humankind.

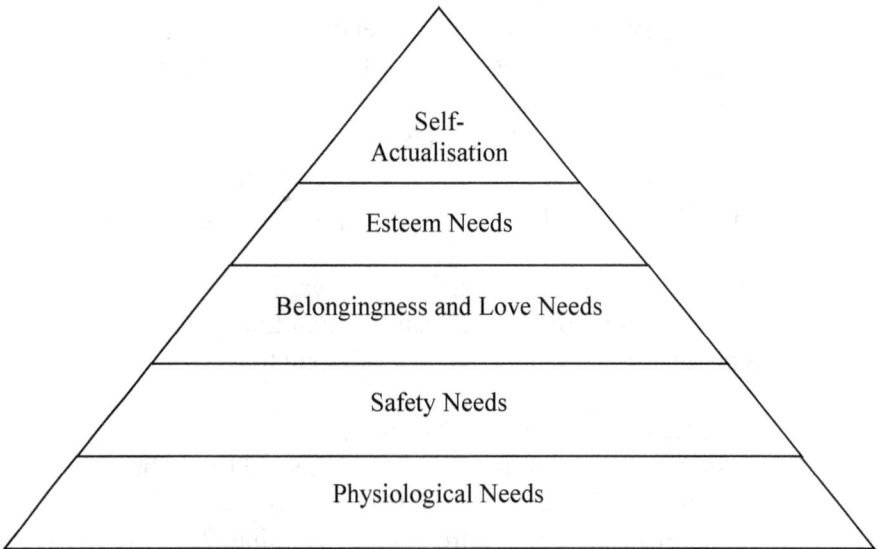

Figure 4-1: Abraham Maslow's Need Hierarchy (Adapted from McAdams, D.P., *The Person*. Orlando, Florida: Harcourt Brace Jovanovich, Publishers, 1990).

That said, humans need to work towards a greater goal than *self-actualisation* – they need to co-operatively work towards *Self–actualisation* or *bio-actualisation* – working towards the betterment of the planet: peace among humans, respect between humans and non-human species, nurturing of nature, and recognition of the planet as both a whole life system and innumerable micro-bio-systems of inherently valuable living beings.

If we, as a single species, work towards our own self-actualisation without acknowledging the whole of the biosphere, we remain incomplete – we never achieve a true sense of *Self* – the larger *Self* that is integrated with the whole of the biosphere, rather than merely as an individualistic and narcissistic self; we will have negated our true nature – literally, the fact that we are extensions of nature. I do not intend to emasculate Maslow's theory of attaining self-actualisation as it stands at present nor do I intend to diminish its import for the healthy existence of the human animal; quite the contrary, I affirm Maslow's theory as directing us towards an overall betterment of ourselves – that said, I further assert that within that realm of self-actualisation, of attaining an actualised self of normative functioning, relating and thriving, we must also include within that realm, our embeddedness in nature; hence, utmost respect and care for nature, for the other-than-human, cannot be diminished nor negated from the self-actualising process(es) – by evoking care for nature, for other species, for the planet, we simultaneously invoke care of the *Self*. "[We] cannot restore our own health, our sense of well-being, unless we restore the health of the planet" (Brown, 1995, p. xvi). Psychologically, emotionally, and cognitively, we are only as healthy as the state of the whole living system.

> By assuming a deep, abiding connection between psyche and Gaia, eco-psychology could produce a timely reappraisal of the environmental movement's political strategy. It might generate a new, legally actionable, environmentally based criterion of mental health that could take on prodigious legal and policy-making implications. To suggest with the full weight of professional psychological authority that people are bonded emotionally to the Earth reads a powerful new meaning into our understanding of 'sanity,' a meaning that might even achieve the same legal and policy-making force that now attaches to physical hazards like toxic waste (Roszak, 1995, p. 15).

Experiencing nature as a part of ourselves and as mandating survival of the planet is essential if we are to fully recognise and understand our place within the natural world – that is, not that we need to or ought to control or steward nature, but that we need to care, nurture and honour the natural world for what it is: an immense living system sustaining billions of living organisms comprising rich and diverse micro-communities. As expressed by Sarah Conn (1995), apathy towards the destruction of nature is a danger that we now face.

> The news about environmental degradation is hard to avoid. Anyone who walks, breathes, looks, or listens knows that the air, the water, and the soil are being contaminated and that nonhuman species are disappearing at alarming rates. Yet the great majority of us, in… [the U.S.] and in much of the Western world, seem to be living our lives as if this were not so. Because we experience the self as separate from the Earth, we feel either overwhelmed by or removed from what we learn about environmental deterioration; we become helpless or indifferent in the face of it, and unable to respond except with numbness and denial (Ibid. p. 161).

Mechanistic thinking, often devised through traditional science education and deriving from Cartesian psychopathology, encourages separation and fragmentation between humans and nature. It is precisely this type of education that sustains dangerous mindsets of viewing the world as a place solely for humanocentric exploitation and occupation. Theodore Roszak (1995) is well aware of the dangers of continuing to teach young people in this anthropocentric medium:

> The "procedure" we teach children for seeing the world this way is the permissible repression of cosmic empathy, a psychic numbing we have [labelled] "normal." Even schools of psychotherapy as divergent as humanistic psychology could only think of "self-[actualisation]" as a breakthrough to nothing more than heightened personal awareness (Ibid. p. 11).

Terrance O'Connor (1995) reminds us of the dangers of maintaining our status quo(s) lifestyles that wreak havoc with the environment and he draws our attention to our psychological denial of such degradation and desperate need for changing the status quo.

Let me say something about the status quo. The status quo is
that the hole in the ozone layer is as big as the United States.
The status quo is that some scientists are predicting that by
the middle of the next century global warming will result in
most of the coastal cities in the United States being below sea
level, and will make the grain belt a wasteland. The status
quo is that acid rain, besides destroying the lakes and forests,
is now considered to be the leading cause of lung cancer after
cigarette smoke. The status quo is that thirty-five thousand
people die of starvation every day. Also every day, two or
more species become extinct, not due to natural selection but
due to deforestation and pollution . . . [To] me [this] says that
the status quo is that the planet is dying! The planet is dying
because we are satisfied with our limited relationships in
which control, denial, and abuse are tolerated (Ibid. pp. 150-
151).

Sarah Conn (1995) suggests that we do in fact grieve the loss of Earth
and nature's wonders. She further indicates a psychological analogy
that parallels our experience of loss of space and place with nature's
experience of a progression towards death of species and demise of
the planet.

The Earth hurts; it needs heeling; it is speaking through us;
and it speaks the loudest through the most sensitive of us. I
believe that that pain wants to speak through a great many
more of us. When people are unable to grieve personal losses
openly and with others, they numb themselves, even
constricting their muscles in order not to let the grief show.
This can become chronic, leading them to see, hear, feel, and
breathe less. The same process of numbing and constriction
occurs with our loss of connection to a sense of place in a
viable, thriving ecosystem. Many of us have learned to walk,
breathe, look, and listen less, to numb our senses to both the
pain and the beauty of the natural world, living so-called
personal lives, suffering in what we feel are "merely
personal" ways, keeping our grief even from ourselves.
Feeling empty, we then project our feelings onto others, or
engage in compulsive, unsatisfactory activities that neither
nourish us nor contribute to the healing of the larger context.

> Perhaps the currently high incidence of depression is in part a signal of our bleeding at the roots, being cut off from the natural world, no longer as able to cry at its pain or to thrill at its beauty (Ibid. p. 171).

Like Conn, Macy (1995) also emphasises our integral connection with nature and evinces a parallel of the pain of the planet with experienced pain within us.

> We are not closed off from the world, but rather are integral components of it, like cells in a larger body. When part of that body is [traumatised]—in the sufferings of fellow beings, in the pillage of our planet, and even in the violation of future generations—we sense that trauma too. When the larger system sickens, as is happening in our present age of exploitation and nuclear technology, the disturbance we feel at a semiconscious level is acute. Like the impulses of pain in any ailing organism, they serve a positive purpose, these impulses of pain are warning signals (pp. 241-242).

Steven Harper (1995) urges us to practise conscious awareness and attentiveness to nature and the processes in which we impart from nature and contribute to the natural world.

> With practice and patience, sensory awareness can be cultivated to a more [focussed] awareness I call "attentiveness." In wilderness, we begin to develop a sustained continuum of mindfulness. We are not necessarily [focussed] on a single object, but rather on the stream of awareness itself. A journey through wilderness is in itself an awareness continuum. We are invited to observe with attentiveness what emerges around each bend of the trail, what unfolds before us over each hill. This does not mean that we have forgotten or lost the past...or that we do not creatively drift into the future...We are instead attentively aware of wherever our awareness flows: the past, present, or future. In a sense, the means becomes the end, and our journey becomes an unfolding process to which we become attentive (Ibid. pp. 189-190).

Harper's assertion is an integral part of what I believe environmental curricula needs to encompass. Through environmental education, we need to remind our students and ourselves of the import of attending to the natural flow and processes of nature – not controlling engagement that we impart upon nature, but rather the universe's plan(s) for the natural world. This level of attentiveness and conscious awareness reminds us that we should not and need not attempt to steward the Earth and nature's residents, but that we are mere observers and perhaps it is in our best interest (and the interest of nature) that we go with the flow so to speak[7]; such an assertion provides an interesting theory that we may in fact benefit from attending to nature's schedules, workings and transitions – this is utmost humility for the human species when we realise that we are but a minute and insignificant player of the biosphere.

Not all environmentalists and nature activists believe that we possess much power to alter the natural world. Lynn Margulis expounds our inability to destroy nature. She suggests that in spite of our (human) exploitation of the natural world, nature will, in the end, sustain itself beyond human infiltration.

> We people are just like our planetmates. We cannot put an end to nature; we can only pose a threat to ourselves. The notion that we can destroy all life, including bacteria, thriving in the water tanks of nuclear power plants or boiling hot vents, is ludicrous. I hear our nonhuman brethren snickering: 'Got along without you before I met you, gonna get along without you now,' they sing about us in harmony. Most of them, the microbes, the whales, the insects, the seed plants, and the birds, are still singing. The tropical forest trees are humming to themselves, waiting for us to finish our arrogant

---

[7] Of course, if we see an animal in danger, injured, or very ill, I do believe that we have a moral obligation to intervene to help and assist that animal. For example, I recently viewed a video whereby a baby elephant fell into a large hole, but could not climb out; other elephants of the herd were unable to assist the baby elephant out of the hole; the video showed how a few people intervened for good by tying ropes around the trapped elephant and pulling him to safety, allowing him to rejoin his herd. This is an example whereby people are intervening nature; however, such intervention is for the good of both the baby elephant and his family; not intervening would have resulted in horrific outcomes: namely, the eventual death of the baby and the traumatised elephant family due to the loss of one of their own.

logging so they can get back to their business of growth as usual. And they will continue their cacophonies and harmonies long after we are gone (Margulis, 1998, p. 128).

The stronghold sustainability of nature, portrayed by Margulis in the aforementioned passage, is a vision I admire for the sake of nature's resistance to human intervention; however, I do not believe that humans are incapable of destroying nature beyond repair. We have desecrated natural geographies to the extent of bringing thousands of species to extinction, barren deserts where forests once stood, and lakes and rivers so polluted with toxic chemicals, that no fish or other animal can thrive in these liquid death traps. In essence, humans are destroying the planet; we are succeeding at overpowering nature in tortuous and murderous ways.

Margulis emphasises the strength of nature in spite of human intervention; however, she fails to address the massive losses of countless lives due to humanocentric narcissism. Moreover, Margulis does not speak of the billions of individual animals who have suffered horrific agony and death at human hands. We could never reverse the atrocities committed against these animals; we could, given a miracle of social consciousness towards bio-centric ethics, cease all activities that subject nature to needless and merciless pain and suffering. (This monumental idealistic transformation is discussed in chapter six, specifically, within the philosophical and ideological moral stance of vegan ethics).

4.3 Altering Our Perspective(s) and Our Psyche Towards Humane Relatedness

[T]he bio-centric outlook recommends itself as an acceptable system of concepts and beliefs to anyone who is clear-minded, unbiased, and factually enlightened, and who has a developed capacity of reality awareness with regard to the lives of individual organisms (P. Taylor, 1998, p. 85).

Any social transformation requires major shifts in social consciousness. Society needs to engage a critical approach of current mainstream attitudes in order to alter our behaviours. If we think humanely, we are more likely to act humanely. This is a monumental challenge for most people as it calls into question their very fundamental attitudes, habits and lifestyle choices; for such a transformation to occur, people must be willing to critically reflect on their every decision: language usage (that may be anthropocentric such as comments or attempts at humour that degrade animals), dietary choices (adhering to a pure plant-based diet that does not infringe on the rights and integrity of animals' lives; seeing animals exploited in the agricultural industry not as food products, but as unique, individual living beings with feelings, thoughts, families, friends/companions, and a strong desire and instinct to thrive), clothing (refraining from wearing dead animal skins: i.e., leather, suede, fur), their treatment of family pets (truly viewing these companion animals as possessing needs and desires as well as understanding the fact that the human caretakers are literally the lifeline for these beings), and their attitudes towards all other non-human animals on farms, in laboratories, in entertainment industries (e.g., circuses, zoos), in shelters, and in the wild. To truly realise a humane ethic that embraces all living beings with moral consideration, people will need to shift their ways of thinking and believing away from the cultural relativism of speciesism and towards a non-speciesist foundation for contributing to a more convivial and humane society; further, they will need to rethink their daily decisions that directly/indirectly effect the lives of other beings.

> A liberation movement demands an expansion of our moral horizons and an extension or reinterpretation of the basic moral principle of equality. Practices that were previously regarded as natural and inevitable come to be seen as the result of an unjustifiable prejudice. Who can say with confidence that all his or her attitudes and practises are beyond criticism? If we wish to avoid being numbered amongst the oppressors, we must be prepared to rethink even our most fundamental attitudes (Singer, 1998, p. 26).

4.4 Humane Values as Effective Change Agency

Humane education offers a vision of a more compassionate world. As a form of anti-violence education, humane education presents opportunities for invoking more peaceful and less exploitative ways of living. A focus on interconnectivity among all species propels this slow shift from a mindset of individual narcissism, competition and us/them dichotomous analogies to intent for community inter-relatedness – both human and non-human community – co-operation, and *both/ands* inclusiveness. A humane discourse avoids hierarchical ordering, rationalisation for speciesism, and power structures that sustain oppressor/oppressed relationships. Instead, this field of compassion recognises all species as Earth residents – as members of the same biosphere, promotes egalitarian moral consideration (Rowlands, 2002; A. Taylor, 1999) – particularly, in cases of pain, suffering and protecting the sanctity of life, and encourages values of respect, empathy and kindness.

One of the greatest challenges, yet one of the most compelling motivations, of humane education is to convey the message of psychological, emotional and physical well-being of humans who choose to adopt a humane lifestyle. Obviously, non-human animals who are protected, nurtured and encompassed within a circle of compassion benefit immensely – literally, their lives can be saved. However, the majority of humans, I believe, need a more personally effecting motive for engaging such a massive overhaul of their lifestyles. Humane education endeavours to deliver benefits for all concerned – human and non-human – however, realistically, humans need as much convincing as possible before breaking themselves of habitual routine ways. John Lawrence Hill (1996) demonstrates this very need:

> Psychologically, we cannot expect the world to be any kinder to us than we are to it. Consequently, the way in which we interact with the world reverberates in our psyches and in our self-conceptions. We are psychologically, as well as physically, bound to the world. We cannot – and generally do not – expect healthy selves in an unhealthy world. Nor do we expect to find the healthy psyche engaged in acts of unmitigated selfishness or outright brutality. We cannot help but place ourselves…in the shoes of the Other whom we victimize or neglect. The doctrine of karma has potent psychological, if not cosmic, significance to our own continued well-being (p. 78).

If we can realise our connection with the other-than-human life forms as well as our cosmological integration within and of the universe, then we can begin to acknowledge our similarities with other species, our common needs for a healthy environment, and our shared interests as a body of diverse earthlings. As explicated by many humane and environmental theorists, we are physically, emotionally, psychologically and spiritually bound to other species, to the natural world, and to the whole of Gaia – only through such acknowledgement can we engage more humane ways of flourishing and thriving.

5

Recognising the Parallels of Oppression: An Eco-Feminist Perspective

5.1 Introduction: The Eco-Feminist Paradigm

I have included the eco-feminist paradigm (stemming from an animal liberationist perspective) within my framework for integrating humane values within the non-anthropocentric environmental education model. Upon delving deep into the research, I discovered several feminist theorists who adhere to values of compassion and empathy for the other-than-human. Carol Adams (1995, 1998, 2001), Deane Curtin (1991, 2001), Josephine Donovan (1990, 1996), Brian Luke (1992), and Valerie Plumwood (1998, 2000) are just a few of the prominent feminist philosophers who acknowledge parallel oppressions of both marginalised humans and non-human animals. They are eager to point out the ever-present patriarchy that maintains control over the less powerful of our society/our world. Adams, for example, is not shy to claim that non-human animals are now experiencing a form of oppression that is all too familiar to women and people of colour. This is a highly significant premise in terms of supporting the urgency for animal liberation; until human consciousness realises the parallel for pain and suffering among diverse living beings – human and non-human alike – we remain challenged to address the torment of millions of living beings in slaughterhouses, factory farms, scientific laboratories, universities, and research facilities.

It needs to be noted that not all feminists embrace animal liberationist ideology; however, the focus within this chapter hones in on the theorists who do acknowledge our non-human counterparts. Henceforth, the eco-feminist theorists discussed herein approach the need for environmental integrity and view nature as an *oppressed other* in need of protection and nurturing. The melding of eco-feminism and animal liberationism seems to conjoin in a natural and supportive marriage that foments the oppression of multiple groups rather than compartmentalising one group from another. If there is ever to be a case for "strength in numbers," this is it! It is my fervent hope that my readers will discover that there is truly no difference between causing a human to needlessly suffer or causing a non-human animal to needlessly suffer. If a man attacks a woman and physically overpowers her, causing her bodily injury, the woman is a victim of his oppressive nature/act. If a human attacks a non-human animal and physically overpowers her, causing her bodily injury, the animal is a victim of the human's oppressive nature/act. This premise and argument should become clear in the pages that follow.

5.2 Eco-Feminist Perspective for Humane Transformation

> Ecofeminism calls for an end to all oppressions, arguing that no attempt to liberate women (or any other oppressed group) will be successful without an equal attempt to liberate nature. Its theoretical base is a sense of self most commonly expressed by women and various other nondominant groups—a self that is interconnected with all life (Gaard, 1993, p. 1).

It is not surprising that many people who have experienced oppression and who have been viewed, treated and regarded as less than equal in society tend to advocate for liberation of others – women, people of colour, gays and lesbians, and yes, even non-human animals. The majority of animal liberationists, animal compassionists and even vegetarians tend to be women (Adams, 1998) – men are often inhibited to show any emotions or signs of caring towards animals for fear of being ridiculed by other men as not being "man enough" (Adams,

1996, 1998; Donovan, 1996; Luke, 1996). Several ecofeminist writers and philosophers draw a comparison between oppression against women and oppression against nature (Adams, 1993, 1996, 1998; Birkeland, 1993; Gruen, 1993; Donovan, 1993, 1996; Hessing, 1993; Kheel, 1996 [1985]; Plumwood, 1998).

> Ecofeminists have described a number of connections
> between the oppressions of women and of nature that are
> significant to understanding why the environment is a
> feminist issue, and, conversely, why feminist issues can be
> addressed in terms of environmental concerns. For example,
> the way in which women and nature have been
> [conceptualised] historically in the Western intellectual
> tradition has resulted in devaluing whatever is associated with
> women, emotion, animals, nature, and the body, while
> simultaneously elevating in value those things associated
> with men, reason, humans, culture, and the mind. One task of
> ecofeminists has been to expose these dualisms and the ways
> in which [feminising] nature and [naturalising] or
> [animalising] women has served as justification for the
> domination of women, animals, and the earth (Gaard, 1993,
> pp. 4-5).

Many ecofeminists see the animal liberation movement as one more fight against patriarchy. It comes down to power relations: men / women; white / black; human / non-human animal; us / them. Ecofeminist philosophy engages these dualities through consciousness of such power relations issues and brings them to the forefront of its genre. Janis Birkeland (1993) is one such contributor to this ongoing discourse:

> ...[the] very essence of ecofeminism is its challenge to the
> presumed necessity of power relationships. It is about
> changing from a morality based on "power over" to one
> based on reciprocity and responsibility ("power to").
> Ecofeminists believe that we cannot end the exploitation of
> nature without ending human oppression, and vice versa. To
> do both, they reason, we must expose the assumptions that
> support Patriarchy and disconnect our concept of masculinity

from that of "power over" others and the rejection and denigration of the "feminine" (p. 19).

Birkeland further suggests a direct link between patriarchy (male domination) and environmental degradation:

> Ecofeminism is a value system, a social movement, and a practise, but it also offers a *political analysis* that explores the links between androcentrism and environmental destruction (p. 18).

Lori Gruen (1993), also drawing from the feminist theory that patriarchy lends itself to systemic oppression of women, animals, and other *others*, expresses the need for educating for liberatory awareness and action against patriarchal society:

> The categories "woman" and "animal" serve the same symbolic function in patriarchal society. Their construction as dominated, submissive "other" in theoretical discourse (whether explicitly so stated or implied) has sustained human male dominance. The role of women and animals in postindustrial society is to serve/be served up; women and animals are the used (p. 61)…[ecofeminist] theory will [recognise] sympathy and compassion as a fundamental feature of any inclusive, liberatory theory. An inclusive ecofeminist theory suggests that compassion is crucial to undoing oppression in both theory and practise. "Others" are not only [marginalised] by contemporary cultural practises, but negated by the process of defining a powerful "self" (p. 80).

Ecofeminists see sexism and speciesism as interconnected – both women and non-human animals are controlled and manipulated by male dominated systems (Adams, 1996 [1995]). This comparative analysis is not only quite effective in persuading advocates of anti-oppression education to encompass the non-human communities within their realm of protectionism, but such an assertion delivers a wake-up call to *oppressed others* to not continue the cycles of oppression upon weaker and more helpless members of our society.

Carol Adams (1996 [1995]) provides just a few of the dualisms apparent throughout the ecofeminist/animal liberationist discourse:

> The best way to convey this analysis of the overlapping, interdependent relationship of sexual inequality and species inequality is by referring to our current racist patriarchy as instituting a *sex-species system*. An ecofeminist analysis of racist patriarchal dualisms identifies dyads that [organise] our world. These dyads include:

man	woman
human	animal
white	[coloured]
mind	body
reason	emotion

> (Ibid., p. 175).

As in any struggle against oppression and discrimination, there is strength in numbers. It not only makes sense from a perspective of greater numbers for women, people of colour, gays and lesbians, socioeconomically disadvantaged and other *others* of society to enjoin their efforts against patriarchy, but there are also legitimate claims for these aforementioned groups to bring their grievances to the fore of social consciousness. Gruen further elaborates on this very point:

> Ecofeminists must challenge such dualistic construction and, in so doing, attempt to establish a different system of values in which the normative category of "other" (animals, people of [colour], "Third World" people, the lower classes, etc.) is re-evaluated. By [recognising] that the exploitation that occurs as a result of establishing power over one group is unlikely to be confined to that group only, ecofeminists are committed to a reexamination and rejection of all forms of domination (Gruen, 1993, p. 80).

In other words, it is suggested by ecofeminists such as Gruen that when one group becomes victim to oppression, in all likelihood, another group will join the ranks of the oppressed – for example, a woman may be discriminated for being a woman, but also for being black or lesbian or disabled or of a lower socioeconomic status; hence, multiple oppressions converge upon the individual to an extent of overlapping persecution. This is the very argument asserted by Gruen: that both ecofeminists and animal liberationists need to work together towards a common goal of anti-oppression.

> Both feminists and animal liberationists would do well to reflect upon how their inclusion of certain "others" is often accomplished at the expense of other "others." [...] Feminists all too often fail to consider the various ways in which oppression operates, particularly as it affects nonhumans, because, they proclaim, "We are not animals!" While the work of both feminists and animal liberationists has raised awareness of the oppressive conditions under which most women and animals live, and has often led to important reforms to improve these lives, the roots of oppression remain intact (Gruen, 1993, pp. 83-84).

Marti Kheel (1993), like Gruen, is aware of the relationship of oppression for both women and non-human animals. She signifies the importance of feminists addressing the degradation, destruction and apathy towards nature. But Kheel also stresses a greater need for working towards social transformation; she indicates that some ecofeminists are stagnating at pointing out the problems without making the effort to take action in a positive direction of proactive behaviour. Kheel places greater emphasis on conscious awareness of patriarchy/oppressive systems and less emphasis on understanding any theoretical principles:

> ...ecofeminists have been deeply committed to social transformation. The method of transformation that ecofeminists have subscribed to, however, is premised on the insight that one cannot change what one does not understand. Understanding the inner workings of patriarchal society is [emphasised] precisely so that society might be transformed. The transformation that ecofeminists wish to bring about is, thus, often implicit in their critiques. If the images of women and nature under patriarchal society have facilitated the exploitation and abuse of both, then, clearly, new ways of

perceiving the world must be sought. The natural world will be "saved" not by the sword of ethical theory, but rather through a transformed consciousness toward all of life (Kheel, 1993, p. 244).

When one of us suffers inequality, then all of us suffer inequality; this suggested domino effect stems from the premise that all of us (human and non-human) are life entities of the same cosmos / planet / universe.

Whether we reference feminist animal compassionists or eco-feminists (environmentalists with a feminist view), we find the overall philosophy to favour emotional and caring ethics rather than purely rational argumentation. Some feminist theorists criticise rationalists for reasoning fundamentally from a cognitive realm of activism and for failing to seriously consider and respect emotional and non-rational support of animal liberation (Donovan, 1996 [1990]). Furthermore, the feminist school often criticises male dominated systems for lending to and exacerbating species and environmental exploitation, not to mention oppression against women:

> From the cultural feminist viewpoint, the domination of nature, rooted in postmedieval, Western, male psychology, is the underlying cause of the mistreatment of animals as well as of the exploitation of women and the environment (Ibid. p. 41)…Reason…belongs to man. The animal…knows only irrational terror. But the scientist feels no compassion for or empathy with his victims because [for] rational beings…to feel concern about an irrational creature is a futile occupation. Western [civilisation] has left this to women…[through] the division of [labour] imposed on her by man […] (p. 42).

Kheel (1996 [1985]) further challenges the notion of Western dualism regarding the oppression/control over the *other* whereby polarities of valuation are contrived:

> Western dualistic thought sees the world in terms of static polarities—"us and them," "subject and object," "superior and inferior," "mind and body," "animate and inanimate," "reason and emotion," "culture and nature." All such dualities have two characteristics in common: (1) the first half of the duality is always valued more than the other, and

(2) the more valued half is always seen a "male" and the less valued half as "female" (p. 18).

Deane Curtin (1996 [1991]) further elaborates on Western culture's influence over maintaining us/them dualities of male/female, male/nature, human/non-human animal submitting male domination as a fundamental foundation for social, political and planetary control. Curtin, attaining shared assumptions from Karen Warren, also emphasises the need to make the connection between Western domination over women and over nature:

> Ecofeminism is the position that "there are important connections—historical, experiential, symbolic, theoretical—between the domination of women and the domination of nature" (Warren, 1990, p. 126). It argues that the patriarchal conceptual framework that has maintained, perpetuated, and justified the oppression of women in Western culture has also, and in similar ways, maintained, perpetuated, and justified the oppression of nonhuman animals and the environment (Curtin, 1996 [1991], p. 60).

Curtin's point of realising that caring can enlighten one to consciously acknowledge her/his (direct or indirect) contributing to the oppression of others parallels a very similar articulation put forth by animal liberationist philosophy: it is not so much the blatantly obvious cruelty towards animals that is of sole concern – although such cruelty is consummate in endeavours and advocacy to end suffering of animals – but the inadvertent contributions that seemingly innocent, ignorant and naïve individuals make towards the propagation and sustainability of animal suffering. When one visits a local fast food restaurant and devours a hamburger, s/he is not consciously aware of devouring the flesh of a once living, breathing, thinking, feeling and loving being; this type of oppression stems from an *unknowing* contribution to suffering; namely, the individual is not consciously pondering from whence her/his food derived. In the case of parallel oppression of women, as hinted to by Curtin, when Western women purchase an article of clothing that was manufactured in an oppressive and patriarchal culture, they, in all likelihood, do not consciously ponder the notion that by purchasing this garment, they are contributing to ongoing sustainability of the oppression of women working in oppressed countries, earning poverty wages, and working under less than desirable conditions. Whether we are talking about oppression of women or of non-human animals or of nature, and whether we are suggesting direct oppression (root causes) or inadvertent oppression (unknowing contribution), the results are the same: sustained oppression and suffering.

Val Plumwood (1998) contributes her stance on the Western view for domination over non-male, non-rationalist and feminist perspectives:

> As ecofeminism points out, Western thought has given us a strong human/nature dualism that is part of the set of interrelated dualisms of mind/body, reason/nature, reason/emotion, masculine/feminine and has important interconnected features with these other dualisms. This dualism has been especially stressed in the rationalist tradition. In this dualism what is characteristically and authentically human is defined against or in opposition to what is taken to be natural, nature, or the physical or biological realm (p. 298).

Plumwood also directs our attention to the very notion that we humans are often thought of as separate from and apart from nature; that somehow, we are outside of the realm of nature; this division of the self – rationalist self/natural self – becomes problematic in making the connection that we are in fact an irremovable essence of nature.

Plumwood (1998) beautifully sums up the parallel oppression of women and of nature:

> And it is not only women but also the earth's wild living things that have been denied possession of a reason thus construed along masculine and oppositional lines and which contrasts not only with the "feminine" emotions but also with the physical and the animal. Much of the problem (both for women and nature) lies in rationalist or rationalist-derived conceptions of the self and of what is essential and valuable in the human makeup. It is in the name of such a reason that these other things—the feminine, the emotional, the merely bodily or the merely animal, and the natural world itself—

have most often been denied their virtue and been accorded an inferior and merely instrumental position (p. 293).

Approaching a non-anthropocentric vision, Plumwood (1998) offers the supposition that humans are inseparable from nature and that humans are incomplete *selves* without their realisation of their enmeshed relationship with nature.

> ...[in] order to provide an alternative to anthropocentrism or human self-interest, ...[we need to recognise] the distinctness of nature but also our relationship and continuity with it. On this relational account, respect for the other results neither from the containment of self nor from a transcendence of self, but is an *expression* of self in relationship, not egoitic self as merged with the other but self as embedded in a network of essential relationships with distinct others (pp. 307-308).

Plumwood reaches a conclusion that signifies a deeply rooted cultural problematique of rationalist assumptions:

> Anthropocentrism and androcentrism in particular are linked by the rationalist conception of the human self as masculine and by the account of authentically human characteristics as [centred] around rationality and the exclusion of its contrasts (especially characteristics regarded as feminine, animal, or natural) as less human (p. 309).

Melody Hessing (1993) discusses the various schools within ecofeminist perspectives: radical ecofeminism, liberal ecofeminism, socialist ecofeminism – nevertheless, she articulates common strivings for all proponents of these realms of thought: namely, end goals of empowering women and oppressed others to meet the challenges of patriarchy; Hessing (1993) summarises the necessary future objectives to be attained and embraced in order to acquiesce future understanding and inception of non-patriarchal equity and justice.

> Human social relations are [characterised] by a fundamental subordination of women by patriarchy (and, in socialist arguments, with capitalism); women share this experience of oppression with the natural environment; women's lives, and

the work that they do, reflect a respect for and compatibility with the natural environment; women's concepts of how we should live with one another should be considered as models for environmental harmony; women's actions have been successful in achieving some degree of environmental protection, and require continuing support to bring about social change; and significant changes to social institutions and the larger social and economic framework are necessary in order to achieve the goals of sustainability, economic well-being and social justice (p. 20-21).

Although these foregoing ecofeminists draw parallels between oppression against both women and nature, not all ecofeminists embrace animal liberationist ideologies as easily transposed throughout the struggle for women's fight against patriarchy. The resistance of some ecofeminists to include non-human animals – hence, to acknowledge the goal of humane education to encompass all living beings within the discourse of anti-oppression education – within *their* realm of anti-oppression education is suggested by Selby (2000):

Humane education's linking of non-human and human oppressions and its insistence that concern and compassion for all forms of life should coalesce also speaks to the need for a coalition with anti-racist and anti-sexist education. There appears, however, to be marked reluctance, even resistance, to exploring shared concerns (and airing likely tensions) save amongst some ecofeminist educators (p. 274).

Plumwood (2000) notably conjoins environmental ethics with a feminist ethic of care whereby she asserts that we need to draw from emotional and relational concepts rather than rational and hierarchical relationships with the other-than-human. She eloquently proffers an alternative method for instilling a discourse of eco-feminist ethics into a conjoined discourse of feminist and animal liberationist/naturist ethics:

Extensions of a feminist ethics of care to ecology have brought a new set of ethical concepts and issues to the fore, have stressed the importance of modest and [localised] ethical concepts drawn from the sphere of personal life, such as care, gratitude, friendship, trust, generosity, and attentiveness and openness to the other, seeing a potential for wide application to the practise of ecological concern and to respect for animals and nature, both wild and domestic. Advocates of a feminist ecological ethics of care have seen it as grounded in identity and the concept of the self as expressed in relationship to others (p. 222).

In acknowledgement of parallel oppression of the human/non-human *other*, Plumwood (2000) also offers a most interesting analogy of the coloniser/colonised duality of oppressor/oppressed as this duality applies to both human and non-human relationships. Plumwood speaks about the coloniser as one who sees himself as possessing higher value than the colonised; hence, the coloniser places himself as the centre of social, political and hierarchical importance over the colonised. Plumwood's poignant parallel between coloniser/colonised and us/them dichotomies aligns with the human/nature duality of humans acting in ways whereby people dominate nature for humanocentric narcissistic desires while nature (and non-human animals) are viewed as something/someone to be dominated and controlled.

> The kind of (re)consideration the dominant human technoculture must now give to nature acknowledges the need for a redistribution of value, space, and resources in favour of the other, for a negotiated relationship which acknowledges that the interests and needs of nonhuman nature present a limit to human ambitions, designs and demands. It must acknowledge the human continuity and interdependence with nature it has denied in its [dualised] conception of human identity: but it must also acknowledge the independence of nature it has denied in constituting itself as the [centre] and treating nature as no more than a set of replaceable and interchangeable units answering to its needs (pp. 218-219).

When Plumwood speaks about the coloniser/colonised duality, this relationship can be equally and adequately applied to both the man over woman and the human over non-human animal dualities. Hence, when we design and implement an environmental education model that emphasises non-anthropocentric equity, we need to maintain this assertion that more often than not, humans do act/serve/control as colonisers over the non-human animals/nature (the colonised). The next subsection provides a deeper analysis of dominating hegemonies. I request the reader to bear in mind, while reading this next subsection, the parallels that may exist/do exist with both oppressed other humans and other-than-humans. It is essential to imagine the experiences, the pain, and the suffering of these multiple others.

5.3 The Struggle against Dominating Hegemonies

Just as we have begun to recognise and acknowledge injustice within human interactions — sexism, racism, homophobia — we need to take our anti-oppression vehicle much further in the direction of anti-violence — namely, to address systematised and normalised speciesism that thwarts violence towards other living beings (Ryder, 1983; Singer, 1998; P. Taylor, 2001). We are aware of systematised oppression against women — i.e., sexism: in some cultures, women are deemed property of men; in Westernised countries, women earn less monetary compensation for comparable work performed by their male counterparts; and globally, men far outweigh women in positions of power (Adams, 1996). Racial tension continues to dominate newscasts as diverse racial groups clash over power struggles. Racism, regardless of the groups involved, especially continues to fragment and divide differing ethnic groups (West, 1990) in North America and globally. Homophobia does not adequately get addressed or challenged in educational, political or social issue forums (Wittig, 1990) — gays and lesbians have a long and challenging struggle against ignorant and heterosexist hegemony that condemns diversity of sexual orientation.

Just as heterosexual hegemony declares domination over homosexual individuals, the human species assumes domination over non-human individuals. I signify these isms – racism, sexism, heterosexism – as parallels to speciesism and to the struggle to eradicate oppression of one more *other*.

> Like racism and sexism…[speciesism] is a form of prejudice
> that shows a selfish disregard for the interests and sufferings
> of others (Ryder, 1983, p. 12).

People judge other people harshly and vehemently on account of differences of gender, race, sexual orientation, and multiple spectra of individual differences. This is perhaps why anti-violence education is crucial throughout schools (Smith & Carson, 1998), community programmes and community support organisations. Unfortunately, education does not fulfil its moral responsibility of engaging students in ways that foster utmost respect towards nature and the other-than-human – humanocentric idealism almost always takes precedence throughout university/post-secondary curricula as signified by David Orr (1994):

> Higher education has largely been shaped by the drive to
> extend human domination to its fullest. In this mission,
> human intelligence may have taken the wrong road (p. 9).

From a practical stance, within the educational systems that be, we need to commence and continue the discourse of anti-oppression education. This discourse needs to be inclusive and acknowledge as many groups as necessary to bring to social consciousness the us/them, male/female, oppressor/oppressed dualities that exist. The discussions have begun that address issues of racism and sexism; however, as already stated, heterosexism is more often than not ignored; certainly, speciesism is almost never mentioned! Although the task seems daunting at first glance, there remains one crucial premise that perhaps gives encouragement and motivation for engaging in this discourse: the need for compassion. I do not believe that it is far-fetched to acknowledge the torment of non-human animals at the hands of man; at least, this notion is no more radical than acknowledging the torment meted out to women or other oppressed humans – pain is pain, suffering is suffering, torture is torture, the innocent victims, regardless of species, still cry when tortured.

I have occasionally heard the protest, *How can we concern ourselves with cruelty towards animals when so many people continue to suffer?* As a moral activist struggling for animal liberation, I interpret the preceding question as an on-going attempt to minimise needs/considerations towards non-human species. The question itself begs a philosophical argument in its very nature of proffering an either/or dichotomy of moral concern; i.e., we must *either* advocate for human rights *or* deny human rights in favour of non-human animal rights. I vehemently disagree—we can engage in a liberationist mode that confirms and advocates for *both* humans *and* non-human animals (Regan, 1983; A. Taylor, 1999). Furthermore, such an inclusiveness discourse can be implemented throughout post-secondary curricula.

The time has long past for us to uncover and face our atrocious and relentless inhumane treatment of other species. Like sexism, racism, heterosexism, ableism, classism and other operative *isms* of oppression, speciesism connotes violence and injustice (Adams, 1998). At the commencement of the twenty-first century, we are actively addressing, deconstructing and attempting to alleviate racist and sexist conflicts throughout Western society — anti-oppression discourse is spread wide and notions of political correctness are assisting in the expansion of anti-sexist and anti-racist policy. Heterosexism is more difficult to combat — we live in a highly heterosexist world — due to irrational and fear-driven motives, homophobia exacerbates hatred and oppression towards gays, lesbians and bisexuals who are compelled to endure prejudice, discrimination and homophobia throughout daily encounters with a predominantly heterosexist society (Gever, 1990). Even within educational settings (i.e., schools), homophobia is still tolerated by schools' failure to address the issues of prejudice against sexual orientation (Sapp, 2001). As signified by Jeff Sapp, an openly gay educator, "...*interpersonal homophobia* happens when we say nothing after hearing an anti-gay remark. If we are silent about [homophobic behaviour], then we are contributing to the problem" (p. 22). On a wider societal base, this recognition of the danger of silence exacerbates any form of bigotry or prejudice – within this realm of justice we need to include speciesism. As long as we continue to remain silent about the unjust and inhumane atrocities suffered by our non-human neighbours, their pain and suffering will continue. Just as I protest oppression based on gender or sexual orientation, how can I ignore the oppression of billions of innocent animals who continue to experience relentless agony due to humanocentric ignorance, cruelty and apathy? I realise the danger of silence; hence, I cannot ignore such massive oppression – the overwhelming torment suffered by these fellow earthlings is all too pervasive to preclude from the realm of anti-oppression education throughout elementary, secondary, and post-secondary settings.

5.4 Including Non-Human Animals as the Oppressed 'Other'

We have practised and accomplished the art of compartmentalising each other, poised to focus on differences rather than similarities, and ready to judge an *other* based on our subjective values. An on-going discourse pervades on university campuses, in social service organisations and throughout communities concerned with multiple oppressions that seem to have formed a strong foundation of inter-relatedness among fellow human beings — we are beginning to confront social injustice.

Correspondingly, societal concern over speciesist oppression is narrowly limited to animal compassionists and animal liberationists, proponents of vegetarianism/veganism and animal protectionist groups and to a large extent, eco-feminists — but the highly systematised oppression towards non-human animals is perhaps the most pervasive and inherent foundation of oppression stemming from human society (Caine, 2001; Rowlands, 2002; A. Taylor, 1999).

Anthropocentric attitudes enable profound apathy towards these *others* — 'who cares if a mouse or rat suffers in a research facility as long as such experimentation might help find a cure for human disease?' Obviously, such sentiment, or lack thereof, stems from strictly anthropocentric foundation (Donovan, 1996; Luke, 1996) — humanocentric ideology that claims that humans are deemed the superior species of the universe; therefore, all other life forms rank inferior to humans. Whether such human-centred allocation galvanises within conscious discovery or an unconscious realm, the rendition of speciesism and speciesist oppression results. This is one of the central tenets of my assertion for bringing normalised and systematised oppression against non-human animals into social consciousness throughout environmental education — if we are going to pervade in exploiting and torturing other species, we need to at least act on a *conscious* level — of course, I do not condone *any* exploitation of non-human animals or of the natural environment, but propose that *were humans to bring such systemic oppression against non-human/natural others into consciousness, said oppression would diminish dramatically, if not completely.*

Specifically, for a human to look a non-human animal (e.g., cow, pig, rabbit, chicken) in the eye and actualise and comprehend the ability of the non-human *other* to experience pain, emotion, loss, fear, and a shared interest in purpose of life is central to sanctioning of anti-anthropocentric and pro-compassionate transformation (Robbins, 1987; Rowlands, 2002). Empathic inquisition as to the experience of the *other* — literally, empathising with how the *other* experiences emotions, perceives her/his surrounding environment, and suffers through unjust exploitations — specifically, challenging normalised anthropocentrism, signifies the most extensive and expansive acknowledgement of speciesist attitudes, behaviours and paradigms; such actualisation, I believe, will prove to be the most radical transformation (Caine, 2001) in the history of human existence. It requires relinquishing centuries old traditions, hegemonic discourse (hooks, 1990), cultural practises (P. Taylor, 1998), religious fallacies of human supremacy (Caine, 2003; Linzey, 1998; Randour, 2000), and numerous structural and routine schematics of institutionalised anthropocentrism. Andrew Linzey (1998) proposes a rationalist view for propelling a transformation towards a non-anthropocentric society:

> People will not be easily cajoled, intimidated, threatened, or bludgeoned beyond their moral senses into a new world; they need to be rationally persuaded. The only viable strategy is to lay before them the vision of living peaceably with animals, arguing for its rational foundations, and encouraging individuals to take one step after another along the road to a less exploitative world (p. 91).

Linzey's assertion notwithstanding, we need to also embrace non-rational argumentation for invoking non-anthropocentric relatedness – premises that stem from sympathy based theorists (Adams, 1996; Donovan, 1996), a caring ethic (Gilligan, 1982; Manning, 1996), and eco-spiritual and holistic perspectives (Caine, 2003; De Silva, 2001; Dwivedi, 2001; Fox, 1998; Macy, 2000) invoke and deliver powerful messages for bringing about a more humane transformative view of life and our relationship with the planet and other species.

The rational and the non-rational arguments need to conjoin in mutual support to extend a more solid and cohesive foundation for animal liberation and non-anthropocentric paradigms (Caine, 2001). Marti Kheel (1996) in her discussion of environmental theorists, proffers the reality of uniting the dualities of emotion and reason. More specifically, in her argumentation for vegetarianism, she asserts that "emotions and sympathies might be considered more relevant in an argument for moral vegetarianism than an appeal to reason" (p. 31). Brian Luke (1996) emphasises a non-rationalist "...caring perspective that expects a human-animal bond, and that challenges any hindrances to this natural, normal, and healthy bond, allows us to continue moving toward a society in which animals have been liberated from human tyranny" (p. 100). Kenneth Shapiro (1996 [1994]) maintains that *caring* serves as a central tenet of the animal liberationist movement: "The most accurate image of the animal rights advocate is that of a caring individual who persists in assertively and, when necessary, aggressively exposing animal suffering" (p. 144).

In the big picture of the universe, non-human animals experience an overwhelming pathos of marginalisation – perhaps some people who feel marginalised in their own lives can empathise with these animals. Josephine Donovan (1996) asserts that "marginali[s]ed people may have an alternative perspective or standpoint that is more valid than the dominant view because it sees realities—pain and need—that are elided by controlling ideologies, which are motivated to distort the truth to perpetuate the status quo" (p. 162).

5.5 Compassion: A Gift of Life

I prefer to argue from a position of compassion. Since so many eco-feminist/animal liberationist theorists also argue from a stance of compassion: Adams (1995), Curtin (1996), Donovan (1990, 1994), Gilligan (1982), Kheel (1996), Linzey (1998), Luke (1996), Newkirk (1992), Randour (2000), Robbins (1987), Rollin (1990), Rowlands (2002), and Weil (1991) – I include this subsection as a significant contribution to my writing and of course, in support of my overall philosophy. I utilise the term *compassion* as referring to having feelings and emotional attachment and commitment to another being. Additionally, compassion requires that one take pro-active measures to alleviate the pain and suffering of another and, contrarily, that one refrain from bringing about or causing the pain and suffering of another (except in cases, for example, when a medical doctor or veterinarian needs to administer a painful shot to a patient; in this case, the pain caused is for the purpose of tending to an ailing or sickly being). Additionally, I adhere to a position of compassion because it is a powerful amalgamation of experiences and feelings that I have personally known many times over. Compassion is a non-rationalist position; therefore, even the individual who may not be privy to rational thought may still be able to experience the feelings associated with compassion. If an individual knows pain and suffering and witnesses another individual experiencing pain and suffering, s/he is more likely to relate to the experience of the other.

Dictionary definitions of compassion tend to be too brief and simplistic; however, I found this one very brief definition that serves well as an introduction to the concept of compassion:

Compassion: Deep awareness of the suffering of another coupled with the wish to relieve it.

(ITP Canadian Dictionary (1998). Scarborough, Ontario, Canada: ITP Nelson, A division of Thomson Canada Limited).

Compassion is central to humane eco-feminist education. As expressed by Zoe Weil and Rae Sikora (1999) of The Centre for Compassionate Living, the terms 'humane' and 'compassion' go hand in hand:

The word humane means having what are considered the best qualities of being human. We each define for ourselves what those "best qualities" are, but among them many of us would include: love, kindness, compassion, mercy, justice, integrity, courage, honesty, and wisdom. Being a humane educator means fostering these qualities and helping to [instil] compassionate values in the next generation. In this way, humane education is like preventive medicine – preventing the ills of some of our cultural habits and beliefs by creating awareness of suffering and offering new choices (p. i).

David Selby (1995) prescribes this very notion for implementing a humane learning environment that respects living creatures and acknowledges the dignity and inherent value of other living beings.

> Humane education, concerned with fostering dynamic compassion for all life and respect and reverence for the planet, calls for an alternative epistemology, one that accords at least equal prominence to relational and affective modes of knowing (p. 45).

Many feminist writers invoke compassion for non-human animals through their comparative analyses of the oppression and exploitation of women and non-human animals (Adams, 1993, 1996 [1995], 1998, 2002; Curtin, 1996 [1991]; Donovan, 1993, 1996 [1994]; Gaard, 1993; Gruen, 1993; Heller, 1993; Luke, 1996 [1992]; Manning, 1996 [1992]). These writers expose patriarchal oppression against women – oppression that has crossed boundaries of social, political, economic and systemic proportions; such 'second class citizenry' allows sympathy for the oppressed, but also furthers sympathy and compassion *from* the oppressed to an even further oppressed group: non-human animals.

Beyond discourses stemming from humane and eco-feminist positions, compassion can also be argued for and aligned with religious and spiritual premises. Gary Kowalski (1991) refers to both humans and non-human animals as being "made of the image of God" (p. 109); therefore, all these beings share in their origin of creation and the possession of a soul.

> To be "made of the image of God" is to be *somebody* rather than *something*. A thing is merely the sum of its parts. Bricks and buildings are good examples of things. They can be reduced to molecules and atoms without losing much in the analysis. A *somebody*, on the other hand, is greater than the sum of its part – people, deer, bears, and horses are examples here – and when we try to dissect or reduce them to their underlying components, we miss their very essence…Can we open our hearts to the animals? Can we greet them as our soul mates, beings like ourselves who possess dignity and depth? To do so, we must learn to revere and respect the creatures who, like us, are a part of God's

> beloved creation, and to cherish the amazing planet that
> sustains our mutual existence…Animals, like us, are living
> souls. They are not things. They are not objects. Neither are
> they human. Yet they mourn. They love. They dance. They
> suffer. They know the peaks and chasms of being…With us,
> they share in the gifts of consciousness and life. In a
> wonderful and inexpressible way, therefore, God is present in
> all creatures (pp. 109-111).

Andrew Linzey (1998), from his perspective of Christianity, asserts God as a divine entity of love and compassion. He eloquently argues that we must embrace all of God's creatures with the same sense of compassion and love.

> What has not been seen [in churches] is that the love of God
> is inclusive not only of humans *but also all creatures*. It took
> Christians many years to [realise] that we cannot love God
> and also keep humans as slaves. It has taken even longer for
> Christians to [realise] that we cannot love God and also
> regard women as second-class humans. Now is the time for
> Christians to [realise] that we cannot love God and hate the
> Creator's nonhuman creatures (p. 21).

The concepts and ideals stemming from the need for compassion can be adopted from a variety of sources and perspectives: learning morality, understanding and empathising with oppressed others, religious referencing. That notwithstanding, it is essential that compassion assembles in the forefront of the classroom and throughout curricula. Humane eco-feminist education within an environmental education curriculum is the vehicle for fostering such a learning environment. The environmental educator must be willing to push the traditional boundaries out further to encompass relational modes of knowing that not only address left-brain thinking (breaking wholes into parts), but also right-brain thinking and relating (recognising wholes rather than parts) (Selby, 1995). Students need opportunity to visualise and acknowledge non-human others as *wholes*: whole living beings with lives that include family, community, sensory perception and meaning. While a traditional curriculum – say a biology lesson – might approach learning about another species by dissecting the once living animal to analyse its parts, a humane eco-feminist educator can emphasise the animal in its living form – this does not mean bringing a live animal into the classroom, but discussing, informing and researching the habits, environments and dynamics of various species (without having to attain dead animals for students to poke and prod needlessly).

5.6 The Universes' Gift to Me (A Personal Feminist Non-Rationalist Perspective)

Animals can teach us how to love, how to allow ourselves to trust, and how to care for another as well as being cared for by another. I learned these very lessons and compassion from my dearly departed *Anna Bunny*. Anna was a beautiful chocolate brown bunny who I adopted from the Toronto Humane Society. It is difficult to describe in words how Anna touched my heart, but she had a gift of conveying a pure essence of unconditional love. I used to spend hours holding Anna in my arms and cuddling with her on the chesterfield or on my bed. She allowed me to hug and kiss her, to nurture her, and she seemed to trust me completely. Bunnies are usually anxious and not too comfortable with being handled; Anna always remained with me and seemed very relaxed when I held her. She taught me how to appreciate love, how to relax in times of anxiety and stress, how to take a break from the world's expectations and share quality time with the ardour of creation: namely, the love and comfort of a non-human animal. Anna, although no longer with me physically, still fills my heart with overflowing love and appreciation for animals and for nature. For me, no love compares with the love attained from innocent animals like Anna; non-human animals love unconditionally, do not demand of us unreasonably, and do not judge us for our shortcomings. I have never experienced such a magical love and a sense of inner peace as I did with Anna Bunny – or as I have with all of my other companion animals: Woody, Sterling, Chester, Noah, Sonoma, Maya, Berkeley, Stella, Mr. Fish, Silky Fish, Fluffy, Pumpkin, Forest and Sir Maximillion.

Compassion is an experience that belongs to the individual; s/he either feels it or does not. For me, the idea of compassionate living includes a lifestyle whereby I act intentionally so as to minimise my negative footprints on the environment and abstain from harming animals and nature to an utmost degree. I feel deep compassion for animals. I truly love them. Such feelings are not always easy to convey through the written word – nor are they only valid through writing or academic inquiry. For anyone who has ever loved an *other* – human or otherwise – that person understands the power and strength of compassion and love.

5.7 Closing Remarks

We can choose a both/ands inclusiveness: rational, emotional, and *any* other justification for the end goals are welcome – all perspectives combined strengthen the resolve for attaining non-anthropocentric ideologies, realisations and transformations (Caine, 2001). This chapter has delved into the non-rationalist school of eco-feminism, particularly, a humane eco-feminist environmental education perspective. Oppression, as we know, comes in a wide and diverse array of forms. Whether we are referring to discrimination due to gender, race, sexual orientation, or species identification, the duality of oppressor/oppressed pervades in today's society. We have a unique opportunity in education to foster an environment not only of tolerance, but acceptance of differences. Further, to the end goal of this book, we need to remain conscious of the experiences of pain and suffering – we need to recognise and acknowledge that we humans are not exclusive to these experiences; our non-human counterparts share in this realm of reality. The next chapter carries this discussion even further into the animal liberationist discourse that provides practical solutions for alleviating the pain and suffering of non-human animals through the adaptation of a vegan lifestyle.

6

Vegan Ethics – The Animal Liberationist Movement: Educational Transformation towards Compassion

6.1 Introduction: Overview of Vegan Philosophy

Environmental Education has the potential to include a wide and varied array of topics depending upon the perspective, philosophy, and/or theorist advocating the curricula. There are environmentalists who adhere to "lighter green" thinking in that they advocate for actions such as recycling, composting, and cutting back on pollutants. There are "darker green" environmentalists who advocate more in-depth transformative changes such as refraining from using any chemicals that are harmful for the environment (e.g., pesticides, non-organic fertilizers) and/or purchasing only food products that are organic and grown with the absence of all chemical pesticides. Towards the more radical end of the spectrum of dark green environmentalism we find those who advocate and practise veganism[8].

---

[8] It needs to be noted that vegetarians may or may not ingest some animal derived products; for example, a lacto-vegetarian still consumes dairy products, but not animal flesh or eggs; an ovo-vegetarian consumes eggs, but not dairy or animal flesh; a lacto-ovo-vegetarian consumes both dairy and eggs, but not animal flesh. A vegan abstains from all animal derived products and is considered the most "radical" form of vegetarianism.

A vegan is one who refrains from eating any animal derived products (e.g., animal flesh, dairy, eggs, gelatine, honey) *and* who refrains from wearing any animal derived articles of clothing (e.g., wool, fur, suede, leather) *and* who refrains from purchasing any products from companies or manufacturers that are tested on animals or contain animal derived ingredients. Hence, one who adheres to vegan ethics follows the aforementioned lifestyle and choices of compassionate living.

The motivation behind choosing a vegan lifestyle may be as varied as the people who choose to be vegan. That said, I am proudly a vegan; most people that I know who are also vegan tend to focus on very similar motivations for why they choose to be vegan: compassion for animals, not wanting to bring harm, pain or suffering to animals, a desire to protect the environment, and a healthier way to maintain one's physical body. Some people say that they also feel healthier emotionally and psychologically by abstaining from eating animal flesh, and I have even heard testimony from individuals claiming an elevated sense of spirituality post-transformation to a vegan lifestyle.

Humane Education is perhaps one of the most challenging approaches to erudition with regards to successful delivery in that the field calls for individuals to question, re-evaluate, and evolve their ways of thinking and of living from habituation of exploitative beliefs and behaviours towards more peaceful and convivial ways of existing; consequently, veganism remains on the far periphery of scholastic and academic arenas.

Veganism stems from a position of *radical animal liberationism* (Rowlands, 2002); such language and perspectives counter the bulk of human behaviour. For example, it is estimated that less than 4% of the United States population practises vegetarianism (Hill, 1996). If Hill is correct in his statistical finding, then about 96% of the United States (and Canada) population consumes animal flesh as food products.[9] "[Meat] eating is permitted because the majority says it violates no moral standard, and because the culture as a whole permits and endorses it" (Ibid. p. 179). Hence, this component of Humane Education – veganism – remains a highly controversial discourse for mainstream erudition (Gredley, 1998).

Vegans almost always protest other exploitative uses of non-human animals: using animals in medical research, military experimentation, psychological research, hunting animals whether for sport or meat consumption, as well as any other uses of animals that serve humankind in highly anthropocentric terms and practises.

The overarching topic of vegan ethics is massive. One main component of veganism is obviously related to dietary choices and how one views food and nutrition. The main focus here, however, is a correlation of veganism as a form of anti-violence education, compassionate living, and a perspective to integrate into environmental education and environmental ethics.

Angus Taylor (1999) reiterates the need for a transformation towards a more compassionate world whereby non-humans are embraced within a realm of moral consideration:

> For society to recognize animals as members of the moral community would be to put an end to the prevailing idea that these creatures are essentially resources. This would have far-reaching implications for agriculture and industry, for scientific research, for many occupations, for land use, and for animal populations themselves. It would signal a profound reorientation in the basic attitude of human beings

---

[9] According to a Vegetarian Times Study (2008), exact percentages of vegetarians and/or vegans are ever-changing. This more recent study indicates that about 7.3 million Americans are vegetarian, which only accounts for about 3.2% of the nation's population. However, the same study shows that an additional 22.8 million people currently follow a vegetarian-inclined diet. "The 2008 study also indicated that over half (53%) of current vegetarians eat a vegetarian diet to improve their overall health. Environmental concerns were cited by 47%; 39% cited 'natural approaches to wellness'; 31% cited food-safety concerns; **54% cited animal welfare** [my emphasis]; 25% cited weight loss; and 24% weight maintenance (vegetariantimes.com, 2008). It is my hope that one day, 100% of the population will cite animal liberation and the desire to no longer contribute to the pain and suffering of animals will prevail as the primary motivation behind a pure (vegan) plant-based diet.

to the other sentient beings who live on this planet. A world in which animals had been liberated would be a world dramatically changed from the one we live in at present (pp. 17-18).

The human-centred bias is extraordinarily flawed in that it negates all non-human beings as inferior to human interests; hence, environment, non-human species, the planet itself are regarded as resources for human consumption. Anthropocentrism casts a hazardous direction for social and global order; these ways of knowing are handed down from one generation to the next. Whether in the home, the classroom, the community centre, the media, industry, government, private enterprise, or other outlets, children are taught human-centeredness from the human-egoist motivations that permeate all aspects of human society. If a child is taught that a cow is a natural resource for human use (i.e., milk, meat), s/he learns to relate to the cow as an object for human consumption – the child does not learn of the cow's family ties, emotional experiences, psychological and physical needs, or any individualised characteristics of any given cow. Ironically, children's books covertly hide the truth about what humans do to cows, how they treat cows, or the merciless torture and death cows endure in factory-farms. We only know what we are taught or what we choose to investigate – systemically, the majority of the human species does not possess awareness to investigate our (human) exploitative actions against gentle animals such as cows.

This chapter delves into veganism inviting theoretical stances of various writers, researchers, and philosophers. Further, a parallel is drawn between the motivation(s) for veganism and its influence on compassionate and non-violent ways of thinking, relating, and living. This chapter alone serves as a springboard to greater and more extensive discussion on our relationship with non-human animals as fellow earthlings rather than as food products. Furthermore, and central to this book, this chapter advocates for and affirms the need for integrating concepts of veganism throughout environmental education. As discussed previously, if we educators do not teach our students the truth about our exploitation of non-human animals, then such animals continue to suffer extraordinary pain for humankind and such pain remains silenced from the public forum.

Finally, as it is virtually impossible to discuss veganism without giving the reader some idea of what our non-human earthlings experience as a result of non-vegetarian diets, there is a section that permits the reader to capture a glimpse of the daily suffering and agony of so-called "food animals" – I strongly believe that this latter section is critical in order for the reader to truly understand the moral and ethical connections of veganism with anti-violence and pro-compassion perspectives.

This chapter, in my opinion, is perhaps the most critical and crucial segment of my book; if we are to transform our society towards one of compassion and kindness for non-human animals, then we need to engage the theories, the discussions, and the realities of our cruel and inhumane treatment of our non-human fellow earthlings. Such humane transformative erudition needs to commence in the elementary and secondary education arenas – this discourse must then continue throughout post-secondary institutions as a movement towards a less exploitative and a more humane society. Veganism is a powerful life-affirming movement and ideology that brings harm to no one, but permits freedom and liberation for billions of earthlings. Veganism will evolve, I hope, as the next significant transformative movement of anti-oppression and anti-discrimination discourse, and ultimately, prove to be the most monumental and pivotal transformation ever known to humankind.

6.2 Vegan Ethics

Vegan ethics is fundamental to the very foundation of humane education, environmental education, environmental ethics, and compassionate living. We need to introduce a humane perspective throughout elementary and postsecondary institutions with reasons, motivations and objectives for attaining what I believe to be crucial in this struggle towards humane living.

Veganism is a radical movement in that it addresses some of the very roots of our society (Marcus, 1998): food production and consumption, clothing manufacturing, medical research, along with many other practises that involve the use/abuse of animals. Veganism is founded upon absolute abstention to consume any animal derived product – whether food, clothing, medication derived from animal sources, or an abundance of other products either containing animal derived ingredients or products whereby animal testing has occurred in the production process. Vegan ethics propel influential teaching away from these exploitative and oppressive ways of relating and living and towards more humane and loving ways of thriving on Earth – ways that do not impede other species or the natural environment. Vegan ethics is not about *commanding* all humans to refrain from contributing to exploitation of non-human animals – although this is a very essence of the final results – rather, the vegan epistemology draws our attention to the realities of our less-than-humane treatment of other species; in turn, *veganism* offers us a chance to engage in critical thinking activities that force us to reflect upon our current ways of relating to the other-than-human and, possibly, invoke alternative ways of relating to the other-than-human. The teaching of vegan ethics, humane values and humane alternatives to humanocentrism is, I believe, central to a humane standpoint in its fullest objective, the advancement towards a truly humane world.

Tom Regan (1998) speaks from a *vegan perspective* in that he "calls for…the total abolition of the use of animals in science, the total dissolution of the commercial animal agriculture system, and the total elimination of commercial and sport hunting and trapping" (p. 46). He expresses his outrage and frustration in our treatment of non-human animals and the resistance of our recognition of such atrocious suffering.

> There are times, and these are not infrequent, when tears come to my eyes when I see, or read, or hear of the wretched plight of animals in the hands of humans. Their pain, their suffering, their loneliness, their innocence, their death. Anger. Rage. Pity. Sorrow. Disgust. The whole creation groans under the weight of the evil we humans visit upon these mute, powerless creatures. It *is* our heart, not just our head, that calls for an end, that demands of us that we overcome, for them, the habits and forces behind their systematic oppression. All great movements, it is written, go through three stages: ridicule, discussion, adoption. It is the [realisation] of this third stage – adoption – that demands both our passion and our discipline, our heart and our head (p. 51).

When I read Tom Regan's words, I empathise emotionally and psychologically with his message. I too have experienced debilitating emotional depression at my witnessing society's apathy towards the holocaust of non-human animals. I too am angry and outraged at people who thoughtlessly contribute to the torture and demise of innocent animals. And I am disgusted with people who jokingly ridicule my personal decision to live a vegan lifestyle – those who laugh at the pain and agonising exploitation of unsuspecting, family-oriented, loving animals – innocent and loving beings who have brought no harm to our species.

Reaffirming Regan's words, let us consider other anti-oppression movements that experienced the same journey of ridicule, followed by discussion, and eventually adopted into social consciousness. Women and people of colour have experienced such challenges first-hand. Today, gays and lesbians continue to struggle to attain social equality – given our extensive history (as a species) of oppression and discrimination, our struggles through rights of worship/rights to not worship, women's rights, and (American) civil rights, I remain irritated and discouraged that the main of society continuously resists and opposes positive change against any unjust and irrational form of prejudice and discrimination that brings harm, pain, and suffering to innocent victims. Mainstream society continues to target *any group* as a social scapegoat for the problems of humanity. Unfortunately, non-human animals will need to patiently await *their* liberation while humans continue to act blindly towards them. Nevertheless, this unfortunate history of inhumane relatedness further explicates the need for humane education in our schools; we need to change these patterns of oppression and replace them with models and ideas of tolerance and respect for all living beings.

Like Regan, I assert that the very act of raising animals for food production, the behaviour of eating animal flesh, and the notion that non-human animals ought to serve as means for human ends -- all these habitually anthropocentric suppositions are fundamentally wrong and immoral.

> The fundamental moral wrong here is not that animals are
> kept in stressful close confinement, or in isolation, or that
> they have their pain and suffering, their needs and
> preferences ignored or discounted. *All* these *are* wrong, of

course, but they are not the fundamental wrong. They are symptoms and effects of the deeper, systematic wrong that allows these animals to be viewed and treated as lacking independent value, as resources for us – as, indeed, a renewable resource. Giving farm animals more space, more natural environments, more companions does not right the fundamental wrong, any more than giving lab animals more anesthesia or bigger, cleaner cages would right the fundamental wrong in their case. Nothing less than the total dissolution of commercial animal agriculture will do this, just as, for similar reasons…[morality] requires nothing less than the total elimination of commercial and sport hunting and trapping. The rights view's implications…are clear – and are *uncompromising* [author's emphasis] (Regan, 1998, p. 51).

Mark Rowlands (2002), another proponent of vegan ethics, proffers what he terms an *impartial position*, which parallels John Rawls' *veil of ignorance*, discussed in chapter three. Regarding vegan ethics, Rowlands asks us to imagine that we are born into the world not knowing whether we will be a human animal or a non-human animal; to rationally decide whether we feel that it is acceptable to utilise non-human animals as food sources for human consumption, Rowlands renders the following dilemma:

The choice is between two worlds. World 1, where humans eat meat, but where this is produced by some idyllic free-range[10] system of animal husbandry followed by a quick and painless death for the animals. World 2, where humans are exclusively vegetarian. In the impartial position [where humans are not privy to whether they are going to live as a human or as a non-human animal], which world is rationally preferable? To work this out, we need to assess what you potentially gain and lose from each world. Suppose, first, you turn out to be human. Then, in World 1 you have, and in World 2 you lose, certain pleasures of the palate. If you turn out to be an animal eaten by humans, on the other hand, then

---

[10] The term "free-range" refers to a system of farming whereby animals are not housed in factory farms with small cages and extremely confined quarters, but are allowed to roam in fields and large fenced meadows.

in World 2 you have, and in World 1 you lose, your life...Being deprived of certain pleasures of the palate is one thing, but being deprived of your future, even in a weak sense, is being deprived of the possibility of having any pleasures, or having any of your preferences satisfied. Ever. (p. 117-118).

It is evident that an animal liberationist, if consistent in her/his thinking, reasoning, and actions, also adheres to vegan ethics. If an individual continues to engage in consuming animal derived products, then s/he cannot possibly be a true animal liberationist; hence, animal liberationist ethics and vegan ethics reside cooperatively, convivially, and as naturally supportive of one another philosophically, relationally, and systemically. As Regan (1998) firmly states, the animal liberationist (rights) view is *uncompromising* (p. 51) – as it should be. How can we give in to compromise when the lives of billions of innocent, gentle, loving animals are destroyed by human-centred greed and apathy? One animal in a laboratory is one animal too many; one animal in a slaughterhouse is one animal too many! *I do not and will not compromise the lives of these animals* – from a moral and ethical sense, compromising their lives for our desires and gain is nothing short of inhumane preludes to psychopathic relatedness – atrocities committed against non-human animals by humans who are either spiritually dead, unconscious in their behaviours, simply ignorant to the issues at hand, or a multitude of other reasons why our species denies, ignores or represses the unrelenting holocaust of our non-human fellow earthlings.

6.3 Historicity of Vegetarianism

Animal liberation, vegetarianism and compassion for the other-than-human are not new paradigms of the twentieth/twenty-first century. Many prominent theorists, intellectuals, educators, and philosophers advocate rights for non-human animals – many have practised vegetarianism as a confirmation of their non-anthropocentric ideologies. "...Leonardo da Vinci [was] a vegetarian [and] he [was known] to buy caged birds in order to release them – [he viewed] humankind as tyrannous" (Ryder, 1989, p. 46). Sir Thomas More (1478-1535) advocated mercy towards non-human animals (p. 46).

"Richard of Wyche (1197-1253), Bishop of Chichester, when he observed animals being killed for food, [pondered]: 'you, who are innocent, what have you done worthy of death?'" (p. 96).

The normalised and systematised ways of exploiting, torturing and killing other species has evolved as justified and globally accepted behaviours; these atrocities are sustained as *non-issues* to mainstream society's discourse and behavioural norms (Rowlands, 2002; Shepard, 1995). For example, the majority of humans eat animal flesh – vegans are in the minority of human society – hence, the proclaimed vegan endures continuous inquisition as to her/his nonconformist lifestyle (Adams, 2001; Hill, 1996; Robbins, 1987). Upon examining the environmental literature on 'sustainability', one would not retrieve any indication that veganism is on the agenda for positive social transformation; in fact, quite the opposite reverberates in an undercurrent of maintaining the current ways of living – sustaining the status quo of habituation of human-centredness.

One of my most *radical* assertions is that eating animal flesh contributes to systemic violence – I do not believe that we (humans) can cause such massive agony, pain, suffering and murder of literally billions of animals, devour their flesh, naming it *food*, and not have such atrocities affect us with some negative repercussions. Joseph Ritson, a writer and philosopher of the late eighteenth, early nineteenth centuries, denounced meat eating as an act of violence.

> Joseph Ritson, the antiquarian, was one of the first to devote a whole book in English to vegetarianism. His essay on *Abstinence from Animal Food as a Moral Duty* was published in London in 1802. In it, Ritson argued against meat-eating on the grounds that it is unnatural, unnecessary, unhealthy and immoral. He repeated the notion that meat 'is the cause of cruelty and ferocity' among those who devour it… (Ryder, 1989, p. 96).

George Bernard Shaw (1856-1950) "wrote passionately in defence of nonhumans, attacking hunting, vivisection and meat-eating – preaching sermons, he said, based upon the humane lifestyle of his friend Henry Salt" (Ryder, 1989, p. 144). Henry S. Salt was a nineteenth century academician in England whose book *Animals' Rights*, published in 1892, proffered moral argumentation against the act of devouring animal flesh and, in general, treating non-human animals as inferior objects to be exploited at human will (Singer, 1990). Salt's emotional realisation of his foul participation of devouring animal flesh permits us to experience his inner turmoil:

> ...and then I found myself [realising], with an amazement which time has not diminished, that the 'meat' which formed the staple of our diet, and which I was accustomed to regard like bread or fruit, or vegetables—as a mere commodity of the table—was in truth dead flesh and blood of oxen, sheep, and swine, and other animals that were slaughtered in vast numbers (Robbins, 1987, pp. 132-133).

Pythagoras has been referred to as the first animal rights philosopher. "[Pythagoras] advocated vegetarianism, and he and his followers rejected the use of animals in religious sacrifice" (Taylor, 1999, p. 26). Theophrastus also rejected the act of eating animal flesh, proclaiming non-human animals as similar to humans with regards to their capacity for sensory perceptions and emotional experience as well as their ability to cognitively reason (Taylor, 1999). Porphyry (c. 232 – c. 304) argued that humans owe justice to non-human animals because they too are rational beings; however, even more so, we owe respect and moral consideration towards non-human animals because they are conscious beings capable of experiencing pain and terror (Dombrowski, 1984; Sorabji, 1993).

Andrew Linzey (1998) discusses the innocence of non-human animals and strongly advocates for animal protection and liberation from an unusual perspective of religious ideology. His systematic condemnation of organised religion's failure to embrace non-human animals into the circle of compassion is admirable and empowering to both religious and non-religious communities.

> ...[The] Church has done too much condemning with too little actual understanding. [I] suggest that the failure of the Church to champion humaneness is a fundamental failure on its own part to understand its own Gospel...[it needs to be] about service to the sick, poor, disadvantaged, diseased, imprisoned, and all others who are regarded as the lowest of all, and not least to the whole world of suffering nonhuman creatures, too...[For] too long Christian churches have been

part of the problem rather than part of the solution. We cannot love God and be indifferent to suffering creatures (Ibid. p. 83).

Another religious leader, John Henry Newman, voices his opinion of human apathy towards innocent non-human animals:

[Animals] are morally innocent...[What should] move our hearts and sicken us [is] that [animals] have done no harm. Next that they have no power whatever of resisting; it is the cowardice and tyranny of which they are the victims which makes their suffering so especially touching...there is something so very dreadful, so satanic in tormenting those who have never harmed us and who cannot defend themselves, who are utterly in our power, who have weapons neither of offence nor defence that none but very hardened persons can endure the thought of it... (Newman, 1868, pp. 133-145).

6.4 Philosophy of Vegan Ethics as Central to Environmental Consciousness

Humane and environmental education can consolidate their pedagogical and theoretical intents insofar as bringing together the need for understanding the very real connection among all living beings and the planet itself (O'Sullivan, 2001; Suzuki, 2002). Those who rein power over education – elementary, secondary, and post-secondary – boards of education, university chancellors and deans, need to realise the significance and the global need for adopting environmental education into core curricula. We, as thinking academics, need to inquire as to the true import of a child knowing how to calculate a math problem, how to structure sentences, or how to spell vocabulary words *if that child still does not understand the concepts of respecting life and planet*. If a child masters algebra or geometry, but spends his weekends stepping on snails and earthworms, can we call him educated? If a student is able to master his understanding of the periodic table in chemistry class, but derives pleasure from poisoning pigeons and throwing rocks at squirrels, how may we evaluate this individual as a human being? As critical thinkers, we educators need to reassess what exactly education needs to achieve and we need to redirect our priorities throughout curricula. This does not translate to extinguishing already existing curricula; however, my assertion does allow for integrating environmental ethics and environmental education throughout current programmes that permits learners a broader view of the world in which they live. Obviously, there is a purpose for knowing algebra, for understanding the periodic table, and for gaining a talent for writing effective and proficient essays; nevertheless, current curricula remains incomplete for teaching young people how to thrive humanely; educational programmes need to extend beyond the four walls of the classroom to embrace the natural world and all who abide on Earth. A truly comprehensive education facilitates learning of skills and abilities, but also facilitates the individual in learning about the environment in which he lives and how to exist cooperatively and convivially with nature and with other living beings in that environment. Once this is achieved, we can proudly acknowledge that we have taught our students to evolve as environmentally conscious beings.

Additionally, vegan ethics comprise the ultimate and uncompromising model (Adams, 1998; Caine, 2003; Marcus, 1998; Robbins, 1987) for invoking peace and non-violence throughout society and holistically within the biosphere; hence, biotic / environmental consciousness can be achieved.

Within this subsection, I discuss the ethical and moral foundations for veganism. My ideological assertion for veganism delivers what I hope will encompass a comprehensive theory for engaging non-anthropocentric and humane ways of relating, of knowing, and of living – compassionate living. Concretely, I assert a strong and endemic link between veganism and animal liberationism; specifically, as stated earlier, if one is to adopt the political and moral stances for liberating non-human animals from exploitation at the hands of humankind, one needs to, *a priori*, adapt a vegan lifestyle – otherwise, s/he risks inconsistency and failure at achieving the end goal for alleviating the pain and suffering of our non-human counterparts. My critical question at this point is as follows:

Why does the main of human society continue to consume animal flesh/bi-products on a daily basis?

There is a failure in people to recognise their own direct/indirect contribution(s) to such horrific cruelty forced upon non-human animals via their purchasing/consumption habits/lifestyle choices. This is due largely, I assert, in the fact that we do not teach these facts of reality within traditional and mainstream educational institutions. Students at all levels are subjected to nutrition curriculum that is indoctrinated into schools and universities by the Meat and Dairy Councils (Robbins, 1987). Obviously, a significant bias impedes the truth about animal suffering from ever entering discussion around issues of nutrition and our ongoing oppression of the other-than-human.

When we use non-human animals as resources, food products, victims of medical and scientific research, enslaved entertainment (e.g., zoos, circuses, marine parks), and other forms of exploitation, are we not sending a message to children that other species ought to remain precluded from deserving to thrive, not to mention worthy of respect and compassion? The hypocrisies are endless – parents allow their children to have a *pet* – e.g., a dog or a cat. Hopefully, the parents have taught the children proper and humane care of the animal. The child may grow to become very attached to the animal – emotionally, physically and in a meaningful relationship. Simultaneously, however, the child is served cow flesh, animal organs or other slaughtered animal parts for dinner – naturally, the animal parts are disguised with covert labels: beef, liver, drumsticks, chicken wings, etc. Whether the child is conscious or not as to where her/his food originated, there is a powerful and inconsistent message conveyed to the child (and to the parents for that matter). Some animals are our friends, loved ones and companions – these animals are deserving of our care (e.g., dogs, cats, some birds, hamsters). However, other animals are not deserving of our respect or love (e.g., cows, pigs, turkeys, fish) – in fact, these other animals are subjected to torture, separation from their families and community, and agonising death. This inconsistency is highly problematic. When a child is served the flesh of a murdered animal, the child is (inadvertently) taught violence (Adams, 1998) – the act of cooking an animal or parts of an animal, the act of eating an animal or parts of an animal are acts of violence (Ibid.). Most people do not want to hear this – such a reality check challenges habitual, historical and cultural behaviours (Adams, 2001; Caine, 2001; Hill, 1996; Rowlands, 2002; A. Taylor, 1999).

We can stand in the classroom and teach children that it is inhumane and violent to beat up a classmate; hopefully, they learn that physical fighting is not a peaceful way to resolve conflicts. Then at lunch, in the school cafeteria, we serve children a hamburger or fish sticks – now, the message (whether children are consciously aware of the connection of violence between humans and humans *and* between humans and other life forms – I suggest that such a conscious connection is extremely rare among children *and* adults) is that it is acceptable to kill animals and devour their flesh – an act of *condoned* violence.

We cannot, as a *civilised* society, condone violent killing, but we do – at least killing of other species. The killing and eating of non-human animals has been instilled as a normal way of living (Adams, 2001) – the imprisoning, torturing, killing, and eating of animals rarely is challenged as a form of societal violence (Caine, 2001). Nevertheless, I assert that such behaviour mandates scrutiny, examination and critical consideration as to the messages conveyed by and for society – systematised, normalised and institutionalised violence. Nevertheless, we do know that instilling humane ethics, teaching the value of life, invoking morals – right from wrong, can dramatically effect one's relationship with the outside world (Johnson, 1997). If an individual can be taught to respect life, not to harm other living beings, to feel empathy for others, to treat others with compassion and kindness, a strong case for humane living (i.e., veganism) can be made (Linzey, 1998). Links between violence towards non-human animals and towards fellow humans are numerous and significant (American Humane Association, 1992; Gredley, 1999; Rigdon & Tapia, 1977; Robertson, 1983; Tapia, 1971; Wax & Haddox, 1974; Weil, 1999).

We humans have a moral obligation to abstain from inhumane treatment of non-human animals. As an eco-spiritualist and animal liberationist as well as a vegan, I clearly understand and acknowledge our connection with nature (Caine, 2003), with the other-than-human life forms, and with the whole of the biosphere. There is a need for a balance to exist within the cosmology of the universe (Margulis, 1998) – balance of social justice (Taylor, 2001), deservingness to live and thrive (Rowlands, 2002), and a real need for all species to have their desires and needs met as nature intended (Rollin, 1990). When we exploit and harm non-human animals, we invoke an inhumane milieu for all earthlings, as explicated by Sagoff (2001):

> [To] allow animals to be killed for food or to permit them to die of disease or starvation when it is within human power to prevent it, does not seem to balance fairly the interests of animals with those of human beings. To speak of the rights of animals, of treating them as equals, of liberating them, and at the same time to let nearly all of them perish unnecessarily in the most brutal and horrible ways is not to display humanity but hypocrisy in the extreme (p. 91).

The single act of eating animal flesh is one the most major contributors to planetary destruction (Lyman, 1998; Robbins, 1987; Schlosser, 2002; Suzuki, 2002) wreaking havoc with the whole ecosystem of Gaia and engendering systemic speciesism causing billions of animals to suffer for unnecessary human desire.

Assisting animals in meeting their needs is not parallel to interfering with nature. If we see an injured animal lying in the road, as I have found on occasion, we do have a moral obligation to assist that animal in seeking medical attention. Many of us, upon spotting a human lying on the road, would not hesitate to call for help; however, how many of us have driven past injured or killed animals on highways and city streets only to continue on our way? Clearly, in this latter example, many people distinguish between the validity and value of the life of a human versus the life of a non-human animal. There is a profound failure to make the connection of all earthlings – the need to revere and advocate for the sanctity and protection of all living beings. This is precisely what veganism propounds to accomplish.

Keith Tester (1991) calls our attention to Henry Salt's views whereby vegan ethics plays an integral role in deciphering our relatedness to the other-than-human life forms. Salt (1980) emphasises a lack of justification of humans treating non-human animals inhumanely:

> Yet no human being is justified in regarding any animal whatsoever as a meaningless automation, to be worked, or tortured, or eaten, as the case may be, for the mere object of

satisfying the wants or whims of mankind. Together with the destinies and duties that are laid on them and fulfilled by them, animals have also the right to be treated with gentleness and consideration, and the man who does not so treat them, however great his learning or influence may by, is, in that respect, an ignorant and foolish man, devoid of the highest and noblest culture of which the human mind is capable (pp. 16-17).

Tom Regan (1998) further emphasises our duty to act on behalf of animals who cannot speak for themselves and therefore, are unable to protest against exploitation and torment of their kin.

As in the comparable case involving harm to human beings, our duty is to act, to do all that we can to put an end to the harm animals are made to endure. The fact that the animals themselves cannot speak out on their own behalf, the fact that they cannot [organise], petition, march, exert political pressure, or raise our level of consciousness—all this does not weaken our obligation to act on their behalf. If anything, their impotence makes our obligation the greater (p. 54).

I intentionally draw parallels between anti-violence and humane perspectives in education and vegan ethics. In fact, I believe that these areas of study are so interconnected, that we really cannot discuss one without also engaging the other. As already established, the crux of a humane perspective is to instil values of non-violence, biospheric justice and a sense of shared oneness with nature. One may deem the simple act of becoming a vegetarian or vegan overly simplified in regards to promoting peace for others; however, nothing could be farther from the truth – becoming vegetarian or vegan is a strong statement of asserting a need for revering life.

John Lawrence Hill (1996) eloquently discusses vegetarianism as a philosophical stance against violence. I refer here to some of his assertions of great import:

…[b]ecoming a vegetarian is the most direct way of evincing one's commitment to the doctrine of nonviolence to animals and to one's own good health. With a reduction in the demand for meat goes the suffering and exploitation of animals (Ibid. pp. xii-xiii).

Hill, like myself, advocates for the need to normalise vegetarianism; that is, to invoke vegetarianism as a mainstream way of thinking and living:

> ...[not] only is all this suffering preventable by adoption of a vegetarian diet, but no human pleasure is lost in the long run by doing so. Much of the pleasure that is derived from meat eating is the result of enculturation. People grow up accustomed to the taste of meat...[but] if vegetarianism were to become widely accepted, the next generation would grow up under vastly different conditions...[when] one factors in the health benefits inherent in vegetarianism, it is clear that, from a utilitarian standpoint, the vegetarian diet is preferable *even from the standpoint of humans, ignoring for the moment the total prevention of animal suffering.* When one includes the suffering experienced by animals at the hands of modern agribusiness, however, the call for an end to meat eating becomes downright compelling (Hill, 1996, p. 41).

6.5 Some Accounts of Agribusiness

I could easily write hundreds of pages of graphic exploitation and torment occurring in factory farms and slaughterhouses; however, such explications have been achieved effectively by notable writers (Adams, 1998; Marcus, 1998; Robbins, 1987; A. Taylor, 1999). I do feel that it is pertinent for me to include some very brief accounts of these environments in order to permit my readers an opportunity to relate to a vegan and animal liberationist perspective from a position of care and compassion. I also feel that revealing some of the horrors of what occurs in the 'food industry' will allow my readers to further understand my position and why I am so passionate about liberating animals; also, I hope that my readers will agree that such knowledge ought to be integrated within scholastic and academic environments.

JoAnn Farb (2000) writes about raising children to become the next generation of a more compassionate society. She talks of how she is raising her own children as vegans; for Farb, veganism constitutes a strong component of compassionate living as it has been proven to be a healthier way of living – hence, she is looking out the well-being of her children's health – and by adhering to veganism, she is expressing compassion for animals by not contributing to their pain and demise. Veganism is seen as an act of compassion by many other contributors of the fields of humane education, environmental education and animal liberation education (Caine, 2001, 2003; Marcus, 1998; Robbins, 1987; Rowlands, 2002; A. Taylor, 1999). John Robbins (1987) exposes the atrocities of factory farms in great and agonising detail; by drawing a parallel of the pain and torment experienced by these innocent animals with the human capacity for experiencing comparable emotional and physical pain, he aptly shows how compassion is mandated for both the human and the other-than-human. Erik Marcus (1998) and Mark Rowlands (2002) accomplish the same objective in their brilliantly written books whereby they permit their readers to compare the pain and suffering of non-humans with their own pain and suffering.

John Robbins (1987) has contributed one of most powerful books for social transformation towards vegan ethics. He relates accounts of unbelievable and unspeakable pain and suffering experienced by billions of animals in factory farms and slaughterhouses. His descriptive passages are accurate and vivid; nevertheless, I do not think that most people are consciously aware of the holocaust of non-human animals; certainly, most people are not consciously contemplating the overwhelming torture meted out to these poor beings – for if such knowledge was in the forefront of social consciousness, I would hope that most of us would abstain from contributing to such agony and torment.

6.5.1 Chickens

Chickens are intelligent creatures, aware of their surroundings, their family and community members, and they are birds with very specific needs. They require plenty of space for moving about and spreading their wings. Chickens, like other bird species, reside within their communities through a pecking order – the more aggressive birds at the top, others towards the bottom of the order – this allows the flock to flourish with leaders and followers. Unfortunately, chicken farmers do not consider any of these needs; farmers fail to recognise and acknowledge the individuality of these unique living beings. The following account of factory farming relates the inhumane treatment of chickens for profit.

> ...[today's] chicken farms are not really "farms" anymore, but should more accurately be called "chicken factories"...[the] chickens live their whole lives inside buildings entirely devoid of natural light...[these] proud and sensitive creatures are treated strictly as merchandise, with utter contempt for their spirits, with not a trace of feeling or compassion for the fact that they are living, breathing animals...[the] chickens are systematically deprived of every conceivable expression of their natural urges...[Male] chicks...have little use in the manufacture of eggs...[they are separated from the females and tossed into large plastic garbage bags where they eventually suffocate or are crushed by hundreds of fellow chicks on top of them]...

Newborn male chicks are also placed on conveyor belts that lead them into grinding machines where they are ground alive -- put to an immediate excruciating and terrifying death for the crime of being born a male chick. The 'chicken farmers' do not have a need for male chicks, especially since they are primarily only interested in procuring chicken eggs. Of course, once the female chickens have been exhausted from egg production, they too are killed and sold as what is termed 'fryers' by the industry. This sustains my strong argument against the consumption of eggs; the whole industry wreaks of cruelty and horrific killing.

> [the newborn] babies peep constantly in frail litter voices for their missing mothers. But they will never know the sound of their mother's voice, nor the warmth of her body, nor the comfort of her protection...[Factory farms] consisting of windowless warehouses, with tiers of cages stacked on top of each other from floor to ceiling, like shipping crates, the environment has been systematically designed to maximize the profits of the agribusiness corporations...[Unable] to establish any kind of social identity for themselves, the cooped-up animals [5 to 6 birds in each 12 inch by 12 inch wire cage] fight constantly...[are] driven berserk by the lack of space and the complete frustration of their primal need for

a social order. In their frustration they peck viciously at each other's feathers, frequently try to kill one another and even try to eat each other alive...[chickens more often than not have their beaks cut off with blunt hot knives as a method of preventing them from biting each other, hence damaging the "meat"; this process is extremely painful as the beak is filled with nerve endings and no anesthesia is used]...(Robbins, 1987, pp. 53-57).

6.5.2 The Cow and Her Babies

By nature, cows are very gentle and intelligent animals. They are also very loving animals; when in natural environments, mothers groom and nurture their young. They are able to distinguish their own babies from babies of another cow (Robbins, 1987).

Unfortunately, the baby calves are separated from their mothers at birth; such a separation is extremely traumatic for both mother and baby – the trauma is physical, emotional, psychological, and I believe spiritual – imagine what a human mother and a human baby experiences in this same ordeal; I doubt that it is much different for cows.

> Veal producers...separate mother and child at birth...because the large udder of today's dairy cow can be damaged by suckling, and the cow will produce more milk if attached to a machine...[According] to Dr. Jack Albright, Professor of Animal Science at Purdue University,...it is important the calves do not bond with their mother, as they would if she nursed them. If the calves are taken away from their mothers after this bond develops, the cow will cause a great deal of trouble and even try to break down fences to be with her calves...The newborn calves are taken to veal sheds, and placed in what are euphemistically called "stalls." These stalls will be their homes until they are slaughtered at the age of four months, unless, of course, they die first. A high percentage are not able to survive even four months so horrid are the conditions...Every year, one million newborn calves are shut up in such stalls in the United States...These youngsters not only never have a chance to romp or play; they never even walk! Remember these are babies, only a

day or so old, cut off from their mothers and imprisoned in this way. The newborns are isolated in stalls all of 22 inches wide and 54 inches long—far less than the space that can be found in the trunk of the smallest cars…[The] calves must hunch into a position no cow ever normally assumes. They cannot stretch out into their natural sleeping posture. They cannot turn around. Chained around the neck, the baby calves cannot even twist their heads to lick and groom themselves with their tongues, though this is one of their most basic and innate desires. They can move only a few inches back and forth, and side to side…As the days pass, and the calves grow, they become even more cramped, so that any movement at all becomes nearly impossible (Robbins, 1987, pp. 114-115).

6.5.3 Pigs

Pigs are also gentle creatures. They have great intelligence and are said to possess the same cognitive capacity as dogs (Robbins, 1987; Rowlands, 2002).

Instead of pig farms, today we have more and more pig factories…these robust creatures are placed in stalls so cramped that they can hardly move. If you were to peek inside one of the buildings in which these stalls are kept, you'd see row upon row…of pigs, each standing alone in his narrow steel stall, each facing in exactly the same direction, like cars in a parking lot…Pigs' feet and legs were designed to scratch for food, to kick or claw if needed for defense, and to stand and move on different kinds of natural terrain. But in today's pig factories, the floors are either metal slats or concrete…[Also], producers rave about the prospect of being able to force sows to give birth to over seven times the number of children nature designed them for…[P]iglets are taken away from their mothers much earlier than would ever occur in any natural situation. Without her babies to suck the milk from her breast, the sow will soon stop lactating, and then, with the help of hormone injections, she can be made fertile much sooner. Thus, more piglets can be extracted from her each year…[Upon the removal of her babies], the sow calls and cries for them, though her distressed sounds always go unheeded. Not having gotten the hang of modern factory life, she only knows that her whole being is filled with an inexorable instinct to find her lost babies and care for them…It is difficult for us to fathom the suffering of today's pigs. They are crammed for a lifetime into cages in which they can hardly move, and forced against their natures to stand in their own waste. Their sensitive noses are continuously assaulted by the stench from the excrement of thousands of other pigs. Their skeletons are deformed and their legs buckle under the unnatural weight for which they have been bred (Robbins, 1987, pp. 80-88).

The demise of a factory farm pig is frightening, cruel and reminiscent of the holocaust of World War II.

Before they reach their end, the pigs get a shower, a real one. Water sprays from every angle to wash the farm off them. Then they begin to feel crowded. The pen narrows like a funnel; the drivers behind urge the pigs forward, until one at a time they climb unto a moving ramp…Now they scream, never having been on such a ramp, smelling the smells they smell…[It] was a frightening experience, seeing their fear, seeing so many of them go by. It had to remind me of things no one wants to be reminded of anymore, all mobs, all death marches, all mass murders and extinctions…(Rhodes, R., "Watching the Animals," *Harper's*, March 1970; In Robbins (1987), *Diet for a New America*, p. 95).

6.5.3.1 Witnessing the Holocaust of Pigs

For years, I have participated in vigils and protests on behalf of the billions of pigs murdered every year in slaughterhouses and factory farms. As an active member of Toronto Pig Save, an animal liberationist advocacy group, I have stood by roadways, holding large protest signs, watching huge slaughterhouse trucks pass by, containing hundreds of pigs on their way to slaughter. Standing with my fellow animal compassionists, when a truck is stopped at a red light, we are able to see into the trucks, witness the fear and terror on the faces of innocent and intelligent animals. We hear their screams and cries, as many of us helplessly station ourselves as close to the truck as possible, often offering them pieces of fruit on hot days or misting them with cool water, desperately offering our support of their lives with kind words and prayers. Nevertheless, we are helpless to stop the truck. We watch as one truck pulls away at an intersection, only to be followed by another truck a few minutes later. They seem to come non-stop. Sometimes, over a period of three hours, we may see as many as a dozen trucks loaded with pigs, as many as 200 to 250 pigs per truck, on their way to the slaughterhouse. It is reminiscent of the holocaust of World War II, when millions of people were loaded onto trains and transported to Nazi death camps. For me, and for many fellow animal compassionists, this current holocaust of animals is no different from the atrocities of World War II. The fact that the victims are non-human does not and should not negate the fact that these are innocent beings who have done no harm to anyone, being imprisoned, tormented, and transported, often for hours at a time, during the freezing cold winter or sweltering hot summer, to their final destination: death camps.

As we stand on the centre island of the boulevard, desperately attempting to catch a glimpse of the faces of our doomed friends, we can see them clutching to each other; they are confused by the movement of the truck; this is not a natural event for pigs or cows -- they do not understand the whole concept of the moving vehicle, the unstable confinement whereby animals are often thrown into each other when the truck makes wide turns or comes to sudden stops.

Unfortunately, no matter how much we pray or tell our (non-human) friends that we love them, we cannot alter their destiny; we are helpless to liberate these animals from the death truck, from the horrific hell that awaits them at their final stopping place, or from the inhumane, downright cruel and horrid abuse they will endure within the psychopathic torture chamber also known as a slaughterhouse. Are the people who work in these death camps devoid of any compassion, empathy or sympathy for their victims? Do they view the pigs (or cows or chickens or turkeys or any other animal victims) as nothing more than the means to their paycheques? Obviously, the animal food industry views the animals as commodities, as products, as machines -- their feelings, their sense of being, their attachments to their children, their parents, their friends and their loved ones are never considered; they are not respected as living beings, as the unique and loving beings that they truly are, that many of us have experienced when spending quality time with them at animal sanctuaries.

I cannot help but view the actions and attitudes of slaughterhouse workers in the same way I would view the Nazis of World War II. Such monumental torturing and murdering of innocent beings is not natural; it cannot be deemed natural; for the billions of animal victims of these death camps, this is hell-on-earth. The feelings that well up in me from witnessing my friends being taken to slaughter are life altering and traumatic: anger, deep sadness, resentment of my fellow humans, disgust at the human species. Nevertheless, the trauma I experience from my knowledge of the suffering of my non-human friends is minimal compared to what these animals are actually experiencing. They have no chance of escape; no one is coming to liberate them from the slaughterhouse; their impending death is irreversible. The animals already in custody of these monumentally psychopathic chambers are doomed to an untimely and horrific death; however, those of us involved in the animal liberationist movement know that we must continue to speak out on behalf of our animal friends. We hope that in the not too distant future, people will wake up and realise that killing and eating animals is barbaric, cruel, unjustified, unnecessary, and completely psychopathic and sociopathic. All we can do at this time in history is continue to deliver our messages of compassion and with persistence, one person at a time, assist people in evolving towards a more compassionate lifestyle, an existence that upholds humane and kind regard for our fellow earthlings, a philosophy that denounces tormenting and murdering innocent animals for no rational discourse other than humanocentric narcissism.

During our protests and vigils, we occasionally receive support in the form of honking horns; however, we often hear ignorant and cruel people calling out to us such horrific phrases such as "eat bacon" or "I love bacon." I have even been standing on Lakeshore Boulevard when a car zipped by and an actual strip of bacon was thrown in our direction and landed on the road. What causes people to be so cruel and apathetic to such monumental suffering? Our congregated group is obviously there in support of animal liberation; our signs are very clear, particularly a large sign that shows a dog standing next to a pig and reads, "why love one and eat the other?" How can people pass by, see these signs, witness the trucks filled with pigs on their way to be murdered, and yet, feel nothing for the horrific pain, terror, and agony forced onto these innocent animals, all in the name of human taste for meat? Perhaps the cruelty thwarted our way (and towards the pigs) is a form of denial; maybe some people find the notion of slaughtering animals so horrific and so unbearable, that they choose to minimise the actuality of what these animals are experiencing; such lack of compassion or profound apathy may be nothing more than a defense mechanism, possibly for conscious (or subconscious) feelings of guilt for consuming a meat-based diet, and in turn, contributing to the unrelenting horrific abuse, torture, and killing of so many innocent beings. Regardless of the motivations or justifications for such apathy, I find it monumentally disturbing that the torment, imprisonment, and murder of so many of our fellow earthlings is met with so much ignorance, denial, and blatant indifference. This says something psychopathic (and sociopathic) about our society -- the human society. This is the primary reason why I am dedicating my life to speaking out on behalf of my non-human friends.

My fellow compassionists and I often query whether people would show such tolerance (in North America) if these trucks contained hundreds of dogs instead of pigs. Dogs and pigs are often compared in terms of similar intelligence, awareness of their surroundings and those around them, and a very conscious realisation of their friends, their family, and all those who play a role in their lives, including those who harm them and those who love them. These are not stupid animals; they are not machines emitting noises like the springs of a clock, as declared by Descartes. Rather, they are individual beings with unique personalities and abilities to form bonds with others: with members of their own species and other species, including humans. Many times, I have visited rescued animals from the meat and dairy industries at farm animal sanctuaries where these very few fortunate lives are lucky to find a forever loving home to live out their lives as nature intended. I have become acquainted with pigs, cows, chickens, turkeys, goats, sheep, even a llama; they are each of them, unique beings with very individualised personalities. There is no place where I experience a greater sense of peace and love than at one of the many animal sanctuaries. If only all the meat eaters and those ignoring the holocaust of countless animals could visit such safe havens, perhaps such a visit would prove to serve as the greatest and most profound educational event of their lives, a vital lesson in empathy and compassion.

6.6 The Connection of Humane Eating and Humane Environmental Ethics

To initiate a discussion regarding our connection with nature and with the whole of the environment, we need to establish just what is meant by "environment." When I speak of the environment, I am including the whole of the biosphere: physical geographical features, human and non-human animals, and all that exists that constitutes our universe. Therefore, according to my philosophical assertions for a humane perspective of environmental integrity, when I discuss the protection, sustainability, and thriving of the natural environment, I am embracing all of life within the biosphere as well as the lands, waters, and "non-breathing" entities that comprise Earth. If we are to engage humane erudition for teaching and learning about and for environmental integrity, then we need to account for the entirety of our footprint upon the planet; our actions have impact on the Earth itself, but also upon other species. Quite literally, and as a concrete example to make my point, if we dig up tons of soil for constructing communities for human use, we are not only removing the soil, but we are interrupting the flow of life within the soil: the earthworms and insects that live in the soil, the plants that anchor to the soil, the visiting species (birds, squirrels, chipmunks, deer, etc.) that graze and roam the soil. We are not merely removing dirt, but all the living beings that call that "dirt" their home and *their* community.

We are extremely disconnected from nature. The danger of such a disconnection is grave and carries potential and probability for catastrophic ends. For example, if we teach children that hamburgers grow in "hamburger patches", we are setting a precedent for desensitisation of violence and oppression (Robbins, 1987). I have experienced a few fellow educators give me their opinion that young children *may be traumatised* by the reality from whence their food derived. I respond with "what about the trauma of the animals made to suffer?" Are we in the business of teaching denial of reality or do we owe the truth to our students? I maintain that anyone who is going to participate in the torturing and killing of other living beings, directly or indirectly (through eating animal flesh) needs to know the facts about the tortuous, inhumane and brutal conditions and treatment under which these animals are forced to endure.

I find it intolerable that we hide the truth of factory farming from children. They need to be informed of what humans are doing to animals in the name of human-centric desires — only then can young people be given the opportunity to make their own choices as to whether they wish to contribute to such deplorable exploitation. For example, traditional nutrition curriculum does not discuss the housing conditions of farm animals. The fact that piglets are separated from their mothers only a few weeks after birth (Robbins, 1987) is not discussed. The fact that pigs, calves, cattle and chickens live in extremely crowded and confined cages and stalls, sometimes so confined, that the animal is unable to turn his body or even to sit on the ground (Marcus, 1998; Robbins, 1987) is an atrocity we choose to hide from children.

The choices in the school cafeteria, the dinner served at six o'clock, the endless fast food restaurants, the media advertising for hamburgers, and countless other examples of the normalisation and socialisation of meat-eating (Adams, 2001) are continuously bombarding children. Where are they supposed to learn of alternative models? How will the incessant suffering of living beings ever end if schools continue to teach the practise of eating animal flesh as an acceptable and normal way of human life? What are the chances for young people to learn compassion, respect for life, kindness and empathy if they are indoctrinated into eating the misery of once living beings?

In terms of teaching for humane environmental ethics, how we relate to other species is directly related to what type of environment we create or can potentially create. Whether or not we are conscious of our food choices is not the thrust for creating a humane environment; it is the very fact that we continue to utilise other animal species as food products that is central to the task for creating a humane environment.

When we discuss environmental issues, and we introduce the concept of a *humane environment*, we need to realise that the "environment" does not only include the physical geographies of Earth (e.g., water, mountains, forests, deserts, prairies), but also the millions of species of living beings that comprise "the environment." Therefore, it is essential that we consider the environment from a truly holistic perspective: respect for other living beings, protection of the natural lands, conviviality between and among all species – at least, insofar as we are able to control our tendencies to exploit and destroy the environment.

Educators teach children concepts such as conflict resolution skills, peaceful negotiation, respectful behaviour and tolerance for diversity, and foundations for what constitutes a good and upstanding citizen. However, simultaneously we encourage (overtly or covertly) a lifestyle of oppression, devastation, and apathy to the killing of millions of living beings daily (across the U.S. and Canada, not to mention other parts of the globe). In essence, we are committing the worst form of contradiction. How do we explain to students that other animals (e.g., cows) have the ability to feel pain, to suffer, to experience pleasure, to live as a member of their community, etc., but that it is acceptable to murder them and eat their flesh? I intentionally structured the foregoing hypothetical question with the purpose of bringing the harsh reality into consciousness. Too many people shut down (psychologically and emotionally) (Metzner, 1995; Shepard, 1995) when asked to ponder the ethical boundaries of inhumane treatment towards non-human animals. It is time to face the torment that we have forced upon other living beings — these animals cannot escape the nightmare of the slaughterhouse — why should we hide such monumental suffering from society, including children? Naturally, I expect criticism for my views — I am not abiding by the normalisation (Shepard, 1995) of animal suffering. I dare to say that we do *not* have the right to impede upon the lives of non-human animals in such a destructive and anthropocentric discourse.

Having a cow witness the killing of her friends, family and community, and finally leading her to her untimely and often excruciating death is the normalisation for the treatment of non-human animals according to mainstream society – a meat eating society. If the majority of society were opposed to such ill-treatment, vegetarianism would be the norm and the cruel and inhumane treatment of animals would cease (or at least be significantly diminished). Nevertheless, as expressed by Paul Shepard (1995), humanity's violence and hostility towards nature and the other than human pervades:

> "The modern West selectively perpetuates these psychopathic elements [against nature and non-human animals]. In the

> captivity and enslavement of …animals and the
> [humanisation] of the landscape itself is the diminishment of
> the [other], against which people must define themselves, a
> diminishment revealing schizoid confusion [and unhealthy
> and irrational separation from nature]" (p. 37).

Summarising Shepard's intent, humans forget that we are part of nature; it is not in our interest or in the interest of other living beings to destroy, torture or exploit *any living other*.

6.7 Concluding Remarks

If ethical argumentation for compassion and reverence for all living beings resulted in a universal ideology or a universal truth that it is morally wrong to torture, exploit and kill other species for human ends, at least the majority of humans would adopt a humane lifestyle; hence, veganism. Furthermore, if everyone adhered to a bio-centric ethic, veganism would gradually evolve as the "normal" dietary lifestyle — simultaneously, meat-eating would be viewed for what it is: barbaric (Adams, 1998) and inhumane.

Realistically, I do not expect the world to become vegan in my lifetime; however, I would be thrilled to see the "milk and meat model" eradicated permanently from curricula. With regard to teaching health, physical education and nutrition, the *system* (scholastic, academic and medical communities) needs to engage in responsible and holistic health care education pertaining to soundness of mind, body and spirit (Caine, 2003) — the vegan paradigm is an excellent approach to health and fitness promotion. Veganism and the concepts of vegan ethics are central and essential to promoting a truly humane environmental education programme.

As educators, we are often under pressure to restrain our personal biases. By including the vegan (or vegetarian) curriculum, we are not indoctrinating a parameter of behaviour or philosophy — we are encouraging students to engage in critical analysis of their choices and to interpret any consequences, benefits and/or advantages to such decision-making. Education should never be under scrutiny and rule of corporate conglomerates or big industry (in this case, the meat and dairy industries). Education is supposed to provide an arena for creative, free thinking and an environment where people can expand their perspectives, philosophies, and make meaning of their lives through discovery and exploration of newly acquired knowledge and experience. Holistic growth and humane relatedness are parameters for progressive, emancipatory and effectual learning.

7

Altering Science Education through Non-Violent Methods

7.1 Introduction: Promoting Non-Violence and Environmental Ethics in the Science Classroom

Environmental ethics promote respect and reverence for nature, for the other-than-human, and for the planet. This translates to the embracing of all living beings and refraining from inculcating harm and suffering upon these other beings. Traditional science education has often engaged students in dissection and exploration (exploitation) of animals – these "specimens" are usually obtained through companies that sell deceased animals to schools, universities, and other research facilities (Weil, 1991). Within such science curricula, students, regardless of whether they plan to enter the field of medicine, are required to participate in probing these bodies. Unfortunately, the message sent, directly or indirectly, is that we ought to be able to use non-human animals instrumentally for humanocentric gain; hence, non-human animals are utilised to find cures and treatments for human disease. In these same classrooms, are the science instructors also teaching about the lives of these now deceased animals? Do issues of compassion, respect, or empathy ever prompt the lesson plans? To truly engage in a humane environmental ethic, we need to acknowledge the lives of other species just as we expect to recognise the sanctity of human life; there is no difference between the pain and suffering of a human and the pain and suffering of a so-called laboratory animal.

Science education often utilises animals in lesson plans. Dissection, although on the decline in schools (Weil, 1991), involves cutting open animals in order to study internal organs and biological systems. Advocates of animal dissection in science education are usually, as expected, biology teachers, scientists, and individuals who fail to make the connection between human and non-human animal suffering – the proven fact that non-humans are capable of suffering in similar ways as humans. Some proponents of animal dissection accuse animal liberationists as having false sentiment (Mayer & Hinton, 1990; McInerney, 1993; Morrison, 1992) built into their argumentation against using animals in the classrooms. Upon delving into the on-going debate of animal dissection, the inquirer need be aware of some of the justifications asserted by pro-dissection advocates. Adrian R. Morrison (1992) justifies using non-human animals as means to human ends with the flimsy argument that *everybody else does it*. His claim is that science education is not invoking any more cruelty than the food industries or animal shelters.

> This obsession [of attacking biomedical research] with
> medical research is out of proportion with the ways
> Americans actually consume animals. In the United States,
> we use the vast majority of animals – more than six billion
> annually – for food. Animal shelters and pounds wastefully
> kill 27 million more. Medical research consumes only 20
> million animals annually – and nine out of ten of them are
> rodents, not higher mammals (Morrison, 1992, p. 20).

Obviously, anti-violence advocates (Bowd & Shapiro, 1993) are able to easily decipher this cop-out attitude and weak stance for invoking and sustaining further pain and suffering *since animals are already experiencing pain and suffering anyway*. Morrison chooses an argument that is self-disintegrating. He asserts that because the food industry and animal shelters commit detrimental and death causing acts, it is justified for the medical research sector to follow suit. In other words, because other individuals, industries, organisations and institutions commit acts of exploitation, torture and murder, it is not problematic that one more industry joins in the lynching. Such a position is arguing in favour of cruelty and inhumane atrocities. Additionally, and perhaps an even more offensive pronouncement by Morrison, the fact that *nine out of ten laboratory animals are rodents, not higher mammals* (Ibid, p. 20), should not rattle anyone's moral or ethical stance. Is this researcher stating that rodents do not feel any physical, emotional or psychological pain? Has this 'scientist' forgotten that rodents have pain sensors, central nervous systems, not to mention the ability to form bonds with family members, community members, and even humans? The fact that Morrison denies rodents as having any interests in not being harmed places his argument within the categorisation of speciesism (Singer, 1990).

Joseph D. McInerney is another researcher who fails to understand the basic concepts of pain and suffering and views the biosphere as fragmentary – humans and non-human species as separate and hierarchical, not interconnected. McInerney (1993) accuses the animal rights community of being overly emotional and irrational to the interests of science. The realities of biology, in McInerney's interpretation are in the primary and predominant interests of human beings. Furthermore, his article title is in and of itself a false dichotomy of *who is the prisoner*: 'Animals in Education: Are We Prisoners of False Sentiment?' A priori, McInerney attests to the notion that the animal rights community is holding the science community prisoner in an attempt to cease all research using animals. It is true that animal liberationists, although individual differences exist within the community, acquiesce that non-human animals should not be used in medical, scientific and educational research as means to human ends. However, the science community is not being held prisoner — just the opposite, the laboratory animals are the prisoners — the animals are the ones being held in captivity against their will, being tortured without relief, being subjected to unscrupulous, unnecessary and unethical procedures without any compassion for their feelings, emotional distress, pain and suffering. McInerney fails to, or refuses to, recognise the fact that people like him are the jailers, the oppressors, and the perpetrators of pain, suffering and biotic injustice — the victims are the helpless animals trapped in his prison camps he calls laboratories.

A final note on McInerney — and quite disturbing with regards to respect for the sanctity of life — is his protest against students wishing to opt out of biology dissection activities. He compares the refusal of dissecting an animal to the refusal of a student not wishing to participate in "...[gym] class, learning mathematics, studying the theory of evolution...for that matter attending school at all" (Ibid. p. 279) for religious reasons or other personal beliefs that would conflict with their lifestyle. I find it unacceptable that McInerney compares legitimate educational discourses on a parallel scope to the imprisonment, torturing and killing of innocent living beings. I personally have never encountered a student opting out of algebra for religious reasons; however, that notwithstanding, algebra does not indoctrinate students to practise acts of cruelty, disrespect, apathy, and violence. Dissection is an act of violence especially when conducted indiscriminately among junior and senior high school students upon animals whose suffering and exploitation are not taken into account during the so-called lesson. It does not matter whether the animal is killed prior to reaching the classroom or upon entering the classroom; the research subject is obtained in inhumane modes of operation, refused moral consideration for the sanctity of her/his life, invaded, examined, discarded and treated with complete lack of compassion, empathy, sympathy and as an individual having rights, purpose and inherent value.

Diminishing sentiment, emotions, and natural caring and compassion as valid arguments *for* causing pain and suffering to other species serves as an atrocity to humane ethics and the philosophical foundation of reverence for all living beings – the notion of sentiment as a recourse against animal exploitation is shared by many theorists and researchers (Adams, 1995; Curtin, 1991; Donovan, 1990, 1994; Luke, 1992; Manning, 1992; Rowlands, 2002; A. Taylor, 1999). By teaching animal rights philosophy and protestation against harming animals as *false sentiment*, as McInerney puts it, a covert message of pro-violence is conveyed; hence, students, particularly boys (due to stereotypical behaviour patterns of sentiment or emotional reasoning being considered inappropriate for boys, *real men*, or traits deemed acceptable to the macho dictum) (Adams, 1998), are taught that sentiment is not a valid, justifiable, or appropriate mode of operating in the world (Ibid.). Sentiment becomes devalued in the learning process; hence, a clear message that tenderness, kindness and compassion are not congruent with science is the dangerous and alienating directive transmitted to science students.

> Whenever people say 'we mustn't be sentimental,' you can take it they are about to do something cruel. And if they add, 'we must be realistic,' they mean they are going to make money out of it (Brigid Brophy, quoted in Robbins, 1987, p. 73).

Victor J. Mayer and Nadine K. Hinton (1990) advocate dissection as a learning tool in the science classroom, but claim that students need to learn how humans and non-human animals coexist in the grand design of nature – also the notion of caring for animals is emphasised. Red flag! How can exploiting animals for scientific research show any level of caring for those animals? And as far as addressing the *grand design*, are these scientists not negating the right to thrive (Rowlands, 2002) for all living beings? Non-human animals are just as much a part of the biosphere as human animals – the *objective* of learning how other species fit into the grand design of the biosphere and the *desecration* of other species seems obviously hypocritical, self-serving (human-egoistic) and deceitful in pretending that we are regarding other species in a respectful, empathic and caring way by killing them and cutting them into little pieces. Mayer and Hinton note that there are students who "[exhibit] an attitude against cutting up *things* [my emphasis]" (Ibid. p. 28). Nevertheless, these dissection advocates believe that "[it] is important that our students have hands-on experience with animals. They need to learn to care for them, appreciate them, and understand how they fit into the grand design of nature" (Ibid. p. 30).[11] Their message and assertion seems highly incongruent (and hypocritical) in itself. Encouraging students to view non-human animals as learning tools accommodates and exacerbates the problematic of species hierarchicalisation; hence, the propagation of humanocentric supremacy that functions to sustain anthropocentric violence.

Biology, physiology and anatomy instructors use a variety of animals for dissection: worms, frogs, cats, mice, rats, fish and even

---

[11] Most students who are required to participate in science dissection activities do not in fact enter medical school to learn veterinary medicine. Even for individuals wishing to practise as veterinarians, alternative methods and models are available for study. Also, students who actually attend veterinary courses are able to apprentice under supervision of fully qualified veterinary doctors who do not rely upon using laboratory animals for practise.

minks are commonly found in school science refrigerators. Dissection, from a moral and ethical stance, is highly problematic in multiple ways. The origin of the cadavers is often unknown or not stipulated; cats and rabbits may be sold from animal shelters unable to adopt these animals out to good homes — in turn, the shelters sell animals to biology supply companies who then sells them to schools, universities and research laboratories (Weil, 1991).

> When preserved animals are used, neither students nor teachers know for certain how the animals were raised or killed. One commonly dissected animal, the mink, comes from a fur farm where the animals are raised in intensive confinement, in crowded metal mesh cages. They are killed by suffocation, electrocution or by having their necks broken … [other] animals used for dissection, such as cats, may also suffer abuse during rearing, caging, transporting and killing. Biological supply companies, which supply most of the animals used in dissection, normally utilize the least expensive techniques for housing and killing the animals. These are rarely the most humane procedures (Weil, 1991, p. 51).

Weil (1991) further points out the prospects of desensitising students to the sanctity of life:

> When the dissection involves animals usually thought of as pets, such as cats, the procedure can be particularly distressing and psychologically harmful. Those opposed to dissection also point out the irony posed by dissection, arguing that one need not kill in order to learn about life (p. 52).

I assert another argument from a moral standpoint against species exploitation: in terms of scientific and medical research, humans have the option of volunteering for such procedures – they can participate in experiments either to explore possibilities of curing their ailments or they can choose to donate their bodies to science upon their demise. Non-human animals used in scientific and medical research do not volunteer, consent or choose to participate in experiments (Singer, 1990); they are forced to endure painful, stressful and often agonising procedures; the animals, because of their inability to vocally protest, suffer in the hands of apathetic and callous humans – their cries for help and pleas for mercy are never heard.

Many of the findings of animal experimentation are inapplicable to human ailments and disease (Barnard & Kaufman, 1997). Not only are human and non-human pathologies varied and many plausible treatments incompatible from species to species, but the highly structured environments in which animal research occurs aggregates superfluous factors – the stress of being handled, confinement and isolation can literally alter the physiological components of the animal (Ibid.).

> The only animal model for human disease is man himself.
> Vivisection is a disease in itself that no amount of animal
> research and suffering and killing will ever cure.
> Metaphysically, this dis-eased condition is in part a reflection
> of the state of mind and social consensus that condones
> terrorism and war (the killing of human beings) on the one
> hand and vivisection (the infliction of suffering and killing of
> animals) on the other (Fox, 1990, p. 93).

The fact of the matter is that much of the data and findings using non-human animals does not apply to the effects and benefits claimed in the cases of human illness (Singer, 1985). What about the ethical grounds for using animals in research? Do we have a right to subject other species to tortuous, painful and life threatening experimentation?

> An animal experimenter will almost inevitably deny that
> animals suffer in the same way humans do. Otherwise he
> would implicitly admit to cruelty (Masson & McCarthy,
> 1995, p. 227).

Andrew Trotter (1992) discusses dissection in biology classrooms as a form of teaching violence.

> The objections are many and varied: that dissection places
> knowledge above life, that it violates the rights of students
> who object out of conscience, that it creates a market for a
> supply industry that subjects animals to terrible conditions
> and painful deaths, that the specimen trade threatens species

(notably frogs) with extinction, that it teaches violence and lessens respect for life, that it is irrelevant to the needs of future scientists, that it is expensive and wasteful compared to alternatives (p. 22).

David Cantor (1992), an educational specialist at People for the Ethical Treatment of Animals (PETA) reflects upon a critical question of ethical concern: "Shouldn't teachers lead discussions of the ethical issues rather than dictate by their actions that the position most detrimental to animals is correct?" (p. 40). It is not only ethical, but also a given and accepted responsibility of educators to present diverse, well-rounded perspectives that may vary from their own.[12] Most biology instructors do not present the pro-animal liberationist discourse (Ibid.) — these teachers simply engage the students in their own agenda without regard to or consideration of those who may protest such violence.

> A wealth of educational tools and activities do not involve animals; teachers need only to decide to spare animals' lives in order to stop dissecting. The only real obstacles are inertia and lack of concern. An educator should maintain a presumption that where animals are being made to suffer and that they don't deserve to die merely to stimulate students' interest in science. (In fact, many students are turned off by science when given the false impression that to study it they must harm animals) (Cantor, 1992, p. 40).

Whenever the discourse of using animals in the classroom particularly in dissection and vivisection procedures approaches the roundtable of debate, the issue of *rights* surfaces as an argument both for and against animal experimentation (Richmond, Engelmann, & Krupka, 1990). The very basic rights of animals not to endure such horrific pain and

---

[12] My critics may suggest that I am guilty of not providing a perspective that varies from my own – namely animal liberationist – however, I assert that an effective educator can provide a wide array of perspectives and alternative ways of knowing without causing harm and suffering to other living beings. The fact that I condemn the use of animals in science education does not parallel a failure to provide a well-balanced science curriculum of multiple perspectives; it does translate to my resistance to contribute to what I believe to be needless suffering of innocent animals.

suffering must take precedence over any other premise of reasoning and rationalisation in the name of *science*. Moral rights, the right to not be harmed for example, need not necessarily be exclusively directed at human interests, nor should it be. Non-human animals have interests as well including interests of safety, freedom from harm by humans, and individualised intrinsic value.

> In order for individuals to qualify as the subjects of moral rights, they must be capable of suffering — mentally or physically — if those rights are not observed. In other words, they must have interests — an interest, for example, in not being caused pain. While other animals may differ quite radically from humans in various capacities (they are unable to speak our language or vote in elections), when it comes to feeling pain, distress, and frustration we know that the animals used in laboratories are very like us indeed (Langley, 1991, p. 274).

In invoking anti-violence education, it is obviously essential that educators and the system they serve function in a coherent and consistent manner that promotes humane regard towards all living beings. It makes no sense to lecture on peaceful living and the sanctity of life in the morning, only to engage students in dissection of animal victims in the afternoon.

7.2 An Alternative to Animal Torture

> "[T]he essence of the vivisectionist [animal experimenter] position is that, in the final analysis, the human right to health takes precedence over any consideration of animal rights or welfare" (Selby, 1995, p. 252).

Selby contrasts the anti-vivisectionist position, the position I uphold:

> "[t]he essence of the anti-vivisectionist case is that it is wrong to kill animals or cause them pain or suffering even in the name of human progress" (Ibid. p. 252).

The procedures these so-called scientists force upon innocent animals include, but are not limited to, pouring toxic chemicals into eyes (usually rabbits), shocking various animals with intense electric shock, force feeding chemicals (such as the infamous LD50 test whereby chemicals are force-fed into animals; the test requires that half the subjects are killed by the chemicals – this is also known as a lethal dose 50%. Unfortunately, some of these animals can suffer for days with agonising pain – both physical and psychological – before succumbing to their death). What makes this testing not only immoral but completely unnecessary (Bowd & Shapiro, 1993) is the fact that the same tests are performed for years; hundreds or even thousands of animals are needlessly tortured and killed so that these mad scientists can collect a pay-cheque. Is it really necessary to continue the research whereby bleach and other toxic chemicals are poured into rabbits' eyes to see if such substances cause detriment?

Animal testing is unreliable (Selby, 1995; Singer, 1990) for treating human ailments.

> Aspirin, which is beneficial for humans, kills cats and causes birth defects in rats, mice and dogs. Penicillin, a lifesaver for humans, is a deadly poison for guinea pigs and hamsters. Chloroform, an anaesthetic for humans, kills dogs, whilst morphine, a sedative for humans, sends cats into a frenzy. Such differences make results from animal tests difficult, and sometimes dangerous, to extrapolate to humans and there is the ever-present danger that animal experimentation will lead to some valuable product being rejected, or a dangerous one accepted, for human use (Selby, 1995, p. 253).

Peter Singer (1990) poignantly argues that animal experimentation, particularly in the field of psychology (where some of the most painful and inhumane experiments take place), are inherently hypocritical and unjustified for helping humans. He further suggests that many of these experimental psychologists are fully aware of their weak and invalid claim that animal experimentation is useful to anyone.

> [M]any of the experiments that are performed on rats can only be explained by assuming that the experimenters really are interested in the [behaviour] of the rat for its own sake, without any thought of learning anything about humans. In that case, though, what possible justification can there be for

the infliction of so much suffering? It is certainly not for the benefit of the rat.

So the researcher's central dilemma exists in an especially acute form in psychology: either the animal is not like us, in which case there is no reason for performing the experiment; or else the animal is like us, in which case we ought not to perform on the animal an experiment that would be considered outrageous if performed on one of us (Singer, 1990, p. 52).

Alternative forms of experimentation do exist and prove much more accurate and applicable to the human condition. *In vitro* testing utilises human tissue for testing toxicity of various chemical compounds. Computer models have been developed that simulate dissection practises; these programmes assist in biochemical, physiological, and epidemiological research.

Computer simulations of physiological and pharmacological processes can be used to replace much of the use of animals for educational purposes. Computer-aided drug design can also help design drugs according to required specifications. Computer-aided design is becoming increasingly common in cancer research (Rowlands, 2002, p. 140).

Mark Rowlands (2002) discusses several alternatives to animal testing including tissue culture testing, physico-chemical methods, computer simulations, and mechanical models. He argues against the use of non-human animals in any form of medical/scientific experimentation for reasons of equality of moral consideration and utilises the golden rule of *treating others as you would have them treat you.*

Tom Regan (1983) elaborates on the moral equality of all mammalian animals; specifically, he argues that just as farm animals cannot be regarded as "mere receptacals or renewable resources" (p. 364) for humankind, so too must we pay equitable consideration to mammalian laboratory animals (Ibid.). I would include all animals – not just mammals – and Regan does allow for the moral rights of all animals as conscious beings and/or potentially capable of experiencing pain:

> ...it may not be possible to say, with anything approaching
> certitude, whether a given individual is or is not conscious or
> does or does not experience pain, despite the fact that there
> are clear cases where individuals are conscious and sentient
> (p. 366)...

Regan continues his argument, although he persuades from a human-extentionist position – i.e., arguing in favour of the rights of other living beings due to their similarities to humans (e.g., monkeys and apes). Nevertheless, even this somewhat human-centred argumentation can lend to a higher propensity of animal liberation coming to fruition; in other words, if we need to argue in favour of the advocacy of animal rights by comparing other species to our own, hence surfacing empathy and sympathy and a sense of commonality among species, then we are wise to travel down this path of rationalisation (as opposed to rejecting it which may alienate animal rights advocates from mainstream population altogether).

> Though nonmammalian animals differ from us anatomically
> and physiologically in some respects, they resemble us in
> others, and it may be that the resemblances in some cases are
> more important than the differences. We simply do not know
> enough to justify dismissing, *out of hand*, the idea that a frog,
> say, may be the subject-of-a-life, replete with desires, goals,
> beliefs, intentions, and the like. When our ignorance is so
> great, and the possible moral price so large, it is not
> unreasonable to give these animals the benefit of the doubt,
> treating them as *if* they are subjects, due our respectful
> treatment, especially when doing so causes no harm to us
> (Ibid. p. 367).

Interestingly, Regan draws our attention to the scientific community and animal experimenters as referring to animal rights advocates as anti-scientific and anti-humanity. He responds with a valid and powerful counter-argument against such defiance and places the responsibility of truly humane scientific research, particularly with the drug research industries – who are largely responsible for the use of countless animals in research laboratories – and Regan rightfully and justifiably lays the responsibility at the door of the oppressor: the research experimenters:

One can...anticipate charges that the ... [animal liberationist advocates']...view is antiscientific and antihumanity. This is rhetoric. The [animal] rights view is not antihuman. We, as humans, have an equal prima facie right not to be harmed, a right that the rights view seeks to illuminate and defend; but we do not have any right coercively to harm others, or to put them at risk of harm, so that we might [minimise] the risks we run as a result of our own voluntary decisions. That violates their rights, and that is one thing no one has a right to do. Nor is the rights view antiscientific. It places the scientific challenge before pharmacologists and related scientists: find scientifically valid ways that serve the public interest without violating individual [animal] rights. The overarching goal of pharmacology should be to reduce the risks of those who use drugs without harming those who don't. Those who claim that this cannot be done, in advance of making a concerted effort to do it, are the ones who are truly antiscientific (Regan, 1983, pp. 380-381).

Peter Singer (1990) questions how fellow human beings can be so tolerant and accepting of the atrocities meted out to animals by so-called scientists and researchers; his inquiry invokes both an emotional and personal soul searching for both the scientists and the general public.

How can these things happen? How can people who are not sadists spend their working days driving monkeys into lifelong depression, heating dogs to death, or turning cats into drug addicts? How can they remove their white coats, wash their hands, and go home to dinner with their families? How can taxpayers allow their money to be used to support these experiments? How did students carry on protests against injustice, discrimination, and oppression of all kinds, no matter how far from home, while ignoring the cruelties that were – are still are – being carried out on their own campuses?

The answer to these questions lies in the unquestioned acceptance of speciesism (p. 69).

The last line of the above quote, "The answer to these questions lies in the unquestioned acceptance of speciesism" sets the foundation for my entire book, for my motivation to focus my studies and teaching on the liberation of non-human animals, and for my inner passion for advocating for respect, for peace, for compassion, and for love of our fellow earthlings. Concretely, humane alternatives do exist for teaching for and about the world in which we live. Ideally, no animal should ever suffer as a means for human learning; we know, a priori, that non-human animals carry the capacity for suffering: they feel physical pain, emotional distress, and psychological torment. How then can we continue to torture those who have done no harm to us?

7.2.1 Integrating Compassion throughout Curricula

Enlightening our students to the plight of other species is a good starting point for engaging a more humane discourse of curricula. **Table 7-1** presents just a few examples of general core subjects taught in elementary, secondary, and post-secondary institutions; some alternatives are provided demonstrating more humane curricula. Awareness of animal abuse and neglect can come to fruition in the classroom in multiple ways and throughout all subjects: in mathematics, we can create word problems about the numbers of homeless animals residing in shelters, the numbers of domestic animals abandoned each year, the species found in slaughterhouses and the percentage of each species killed each year for human consumption; in creative writing and writing composition courses, students may be offered topics of animal suffering, the gifts and abilities of various animal species, and even their feelings towards specific species provide rich backdrops for practising writing and comprehension skills; physical education classes can demonstrate similarities and differences regarding anatomical and physiological characteristics between humans and non-human animals. There are no limits to integrating non-speciesist curricula throughout elementary, secondary, and post-secondary learning. Such ideas and challenges also provide educators opportunities for creating and implementing an abundance of learning activities and valuable lessons for increasing global awareness of planet Earth.

In reviewing current traditional core curricula, one can decipher human-centred messages and mediums, integrate non-anthropocentric perspectives, and strive towards a humane bio-centric framework.

Core Subject	Alternative Humane Curricula	Humane Pedagogical Process
Biology	• Implementing alternative models to dissection. • Teaching about aspects of other species: physical, but also psychological, habitual, communal, familial and historical.	• Discussing moral and ethical concerns of animal experimentation. • Recognising parallels between human and non-human species: e.g., ability to experience pain and suffering.
Physiology	• Identifying similarities and differences within and between species; • Indicating similar physiological abilities between humans and non-human species.	• Acknowledging sensory perception as present in both humans and non-human animals.
Anatomy	• Identifying critical life systems, organs and physical attributes within humans and non-human animals.	• Recognising shared ability between humans and non-humans to experience pleasure and pain • Acknowledging similarities of anatomical characteristics between humans and non-humans. • Realising the moral implications of conducting experiments upon other species as parallel to conducting same experiments upon humans.

Table 7-1. Integrating humane curricula and humane pedagogy within core curricula.

7.3 Closing Remarks

Once students are able to relate to other species as fellow earthlings, the sciences, for example, will be approached from a more humane position – such a perspective may also translate to students' behaviour evolving as more humane towards other species throughout the community. The lessons invoked through such an alternative view can be potentially far-reaching in allowing individuals to develop a greater sense of notable values such as empathy and compassion.

We have arrived at a technological age of history whereby there is literally no excuse, no reason to utilise animals in medical/scientific research. The time has come for us to eliminate our narcissistic, humanocentric attitudes regarding our domination over other species. The benefits of science and sound medical research must begin and end without causing pain and suffering to innocent, defenceless animals. From an ethical standpoint, given egalitarian universal justice, there is absolutely no justification for the continuance of such oppressive and speciesist operational systems.

8

Nutrition Education: Humane and Healthy Eating for a Compassionate World

*Nothing will benefit human health and increase
chances for survival on Earth as much as the evolution to a
vegetarian diet* –Albert Einstein.

*If man aspires towards a righteous life, his first act of
abstinence is injury to animals* –Leo Tolstoy.

*Veganism is not passive self-denial. On the contrary,
it instils active and vibrant responsibility for initiating
social change by presenting a constant challenge to
consistently seek out the highest ideal* –Joanne Stepaniak.

8.1 Introduction: Teaching Unhealthy Eating Habits

Health and nutrition education carry the potential for influencing
one's daily lifestyle choices regarding fitness and diet. This chapter
serves three-fold: (1) it discloses the current nutrition curricula that
primarily permeates schools by special interest groups—namely the
meat and dairy industries, (2) it provides evidence for a more humane

dietary lifestyle (i.e., vegetarianism/veganism) based on medical research, comparative nutritional analyses between animal-based diets and plant-based diets, and ethical foundations for adapting a plant-based diet, and (3) it unveils the New Four Food Groups as prescribed by Physicians Committee for Responsible Medicine.

There exists a profound bias within nutrition education curricula throughout schools, universities, and even medical school programmes.[13] Present-day models follow the traditional recommendations set forth by special interest groups: the meat, pork, poultry and dairy industries; hence, enforcing *their* bias of what ought to constitute nutrition education. Most people do not realise that the nutritional information found in classrooms across Canada and the United States (as well as Europe) has been conveniently provided by these special interest groups at no cost to the schools or the boards of education. For elementary schools, animal-based food industries supply schools with colourful and attractive posters, puzzles and games that encourage the "normalisation"[14] of consumption of their products; throughout colleges and universities, these same industries influence health and fitness programmes by instigating administrations and faculties to integrate their materials -- representatives from the meat and dairy industries even approach schools and colleges for the purpose of offering free presentations to students regarding the so-called nutritional aspects of their products. No one, including teachers and university professors, ever questions these materials or programmes. Why should they? The educators (and administrators) themselves were inundated by the same influential propaganda when they were young; hence, most instructors, even those specialising in nutrition education, are not aware of the existence of alternative models for more humane and healthier lifestyles.

---

[13] Sadly, about 86% of medical schools throughout the United States and Canada offer no more than three hours of nutrition education to prospective medical doctors. Nutrition is not emphasised at all in these programmes; hence, doctors do not learn about the profound connection between diet and overall health maintenance (Anderson, 2007).

[14] The term *normalisation* refers to interpreting the provision of and intake of dairy and meat products as a normal activity throughout society. Additionally, such activity is without consideration of the inhumane and oppressive nature of such industries. Most people throughout society do not consider eating meat abnormal; they do *not* think of the origins of their food. Hence, the oppression and cruelty of the so-called normalised food products remain hidden from social consciousness.

8.2 Traditional Nutrition Education

Many of us grew up with the USDA's old Basic Four food groups, first introduced in 1956 (Marcus, 1998). Canada's food guide to healthy eating (stemming from the American archetype) is shown in **Table 8-1**. Under each prescribed food group is indicated a recommended number of servings based on age, level of physical activity, body type, gender (and prescribed intake if pregnancy or breast-feeding is an issue).[15]

Traditional Four Food Groups (USDA and Health Canada)			
Grain Products	Vegetables & Fruits	Milk Products	Meat & Alternatives
5-12 servings/day	5-10 servings/day	Children 2-3 years: 4-9 servings/day Youth 10-16 years: 3-4 servings/day Adults: 2-4 servings/day Pregnant and Breast-feeding Women: 3-4 servings/day	2-3 servings/day
Includes bread, cereal, rice and pasta	Includes all vegetables, fruits, fruit juices and salads	Includes milk, cheese, yogurt, and butter	Includes beef, poultry, fish, eggs, beans, tofu, and nuts

Table 8-1: Traditional dietary food guide (USDA and Health Canada).
The Ontario Curriculum, Grades 1-8: Health and Physical Education, 1998.

---

[15] The full model that includes level of physical activity, body type, and gender is found in the curricular model provided by the school boards and colleges; for example, the Province of Ontario offers a booklet to educators that contains more comprehensive information referred to above.

8.2.1 Critiquing Traditional Nutrition Curricula

I critique the *four-food-groups* model on two grounds: (1) medical research that indicates falsity of thinking behind the perpetuation of this on-going model and, (2) ethical/moral analysis of the perceptions and implications of including animal-based products within the food guide. The former critique will site medical evidence as to the detrimental and negative affectations of consuming animal flesh, animal derived products and by-products; the latter critique will support humane ideology that encompasses an appreciation of bio-centricity and values of compassion, respect, kindness and empathy for all living beings; hence, a vegan[16] ethic (Marcus, 1998) as well as a biophilic ethic (Selby, 1995).

8.2.1.1 Reliability of Curriculum for Healthy Living

Unless a teacher has taken a vested interest in healthy alternative lifestyles, s/he is unlikely to include "humane dietary alternatives" as choices for health education and lifestyle management. The Ontario curriculum does not ever mention the words *vegetarian* or *vegan* (Ontario Ministry of Education, 1998). I doubt that other curricula across Canada or the United States include these healthy alternatives as components of nutrition education.

Furthermore, schools have systematised and normalised meat-eating and dairy product consumption simply by the provisions of their cafeterias (for those schools that have such facilities). I challenge anyone to find a school cafeteria that is exclusively vegan, let alone vegetarian friendly. If schools advocate mission statements of assuring and providing learning environments of enlightenment, good judgement and mental and physical well-being, that message ought to be enjoined from the administration right down to the cafeteria. It is contradictory to offer nutrition education—namely, addressing issues of reducing fat intake, lowering blood pressure and maintaining a healthy body — while simultaneously serving meat, milk and other animal derived "food" items that are high in fat, high in chemical composition and low in good nutritional value (PCRM, 1998).

Am I advocating that the scholastic system adapts a vegan philosophy? In order to maintain consistency and avoid hypocrisy for

---

[16] A vegan diet is purely vegetarian. Vegans do not eat any animal flesh, dairy or eggs, or any product derived from animals.

teaching healthy living, a resounding YES! Educational institutions need to provide alternative models that do not serve the special interests of dairy and meat industries. Nutrition curriculum, as it presently stands, is contributing to on-going ignorance of healthier dietary choices by *not* including the vegan option. It is up to the individual teacher to provide knowledge and awareness of these eating alternatives — this is simply inadequate and unreliable since most teachers are not aware of alternatives nor do most teachers (or most of the population) even think about veganism as an option (Robbins, 2001); also, many educators simply do not have interest in altering traditionally accepted nutrition guidelines. Such negation is blatantly irresponsible of school boards to disregard this crucial area of health education.

8.2.1.2 Teaching Vegetarianism and Veganism as Part of Health Curriculum

In May 1998, the seventh edition of Dr. Spock's *Baby and Child Care* was published; Dr. Spock recommends a vegan diet for children (Spock, 2000). Professional nutritionists further note that vegetarian children grow up to be slimmer, healthier, and live longer than their meat-eating friends (Barnard, 1995; PCRM, Dec. 1998). Research indicates that many health problems such as some forms of cancer (Phillips, 1975), high blood pressure, diabetes, and others are significantly prompted by poor dietary habits (PCRM, May 2000). For example, vegetarians typically have lower blood pressure than do non-vegetarians (Rouse & Beilin, 1984; Lindahl, et al., 1984). According to the American Dietetic Association (ADA), vegetarian diets are healthful, nutritionally adequate, and provide health benefits in the prevention and treatment of certain diseases (Messina & Burke, 1997). It has also been noted that "[v]egetarians tend to have a lower incidence of hypertension than [do] non-vegetarians" (Beilin, 1994). Cardiovascular disease is a result of ingesting significant amounts of cholesterol and fat. However, switching to a vegetarian diet can actually prevent and even reverse heart disease (Ornish, et al., 1990). Furthermore, "[n]umerous epidemiological and clinical studies have shown that vegetarians are nearly 50 percent less likely to die from cancer than non-vegetarians (Phillips, 1975). "Vegetarians avoid the animal fat linked to cancer and get abundant fiber and vitamins that help to prevent cancer. In addition, blood analysis of vegetarians reveals a higher level of Natural Killer Cells, [specialised] white blood cells that attack cancer cells" (Malter, et al., 1989). The National Cancer Institute asserts that as much as 35 to 50 percent of cancers are due to foods.

Even with an abundance of evidence from the medical community and nutritional research, schools continue to teach poor dietary habits that increase risk of disease, potentially shorten life span, and contribute to innumerable ailments and illnesses. A more progressive, informed and rational nutrition curriculum is in order. In spite of special interest groups such as the dairy and meat industries, educators need to own a responsibility of influencing and encouraging healthy lifestyle components — this most definitely includes healthy eating programmes.

8.2.1.2.1 What Could Be Healthier Than Milk?

In spite of what we have heard about milk *doing a body good,* cow's milk is highly toxic and a major contributing factor to many illnesses and ailments (Barnard, 1995; Lyman, 1998; PCRM, Feb. 2000; Robbins, 1987). The dairy industry has successfully manipulated society into believing that everyone, especially young children and women, require cow's milk for a well-balanced dietary programme (Robbins, 1987). According to the Physicians Committee for Responsible Medicine (PCRM), "[t]here is no need for infants to be raised on cow's milk formulas. Aside from the colic-inducing proteins that bother many children on cow's milk formulas, cow's milk is a common cause of allergies" (PCRM, Dec. 1998). The American Academy of Paediatrics recommends that infants below one year of age not be given whole cow's milk, as iron deficiency is more likely on a dairy-rich diet (Ibid., Feb. 2000). Iron is another strong argument against the consumption of cow's milk. Growing children require a generous intake of iron—"[c]ow's milk is very low in iron and can induce a mild chronic blood loss from the digestive tract" (Ibid. p. 1).

The dairy industry pushes milk as a foundational ingredient for daily nutrition. However, medical and nutritional research contradicts the portrayed value of milk. "Dairy products [c]ontribute significant amounts of cholesterol and fat to the diet" (Pennington, 1998). However, beyond the obvious detriments caused and/or attributed to cow's milk ingestion lies a deception put forth by dairy interest groups. Namely, the dairy industry has people believing that cow's milk is a preventative cure for osteoporosis — nothing could be further from the medical truth. The Harvard Nurses' Health Study (Feskanich, et al., 1997) showed no evidence to back the claims made that milk strengthens bones. In fact, the opposite outcome was revealed by this study; "increased intake of calcium from dairy products was associated with a higher fracture risk" (PCRM, Feb. 2000). Other studies (Huang, Himes & McGovern, 1996; Cummings, Nevitt, Browner, et al., 1995) have also concluded that dairy derived calcium has no protective value on bones.

When teachers show the provided nutrition curriculum which includes dairy (as mentioned earlier, the dairy industry is contented to supply these materials at no cost to schools), it is highly doubtful that these educators make mention of *lactose intolerance* (lactose intolerance is an allergic reaction to dairy derived products). Some people do not possess the necessary enzyme to digest milk sugar lactose; hence, they may suffer symptoms such as gastrointestinal distress, diarrhoea, and flatulence (PCRM, Feb. 2000) upon consumption of dairy products. Lactose intolerance is very common among and across diverse cultures: approximately 95 percent of Asian Americans, 74 percent of Native Americans, 70 percent of Mexican Americans and 15 percent of Caucasians are affected (Bertron, Barnard & Mills, 1999).

Additionally, dairy cows are fed synthetic hormones in order to increase milk production (Lyman, 1998; Outwater, Nicholson & Barnard, 1997). Pesticides and other drugs are also frequent contaminants of dairy products (Lyman, 1998; PCRM, Feb. 2000). Bovine spongiform encephalopathy (BSE) is a fatal nervous system disease emanating from tainted meat. Scientists attribute BSE to the practise of feeding cattle the remains of sheep infected with *scrapie*, a disease with many similarities to BSE (Walker, Hueston, Hurd & Wilesmith, 1991; Marsh, 1993; Prusiner, 1995), and also, regular injections of antibiotics (Lyman, 1998) given to cows contributes to further bacterial and carcinogenic substances.

It is irresponsible for schools to teach the nutrition curriculum prescribed by the meat and dairy industries without offering evidence of negative and detrimental consequences of adhering to such a plan *and* without offering alternative dietary choices that are beneficial with regard to health maintenance. Such negligence places students at risk for a multitude of health problems.

8.2.1.2.2 Protein Scare Tactics

Parents are concerned that their children get enough protein for normal growth and good health. The meat and dairy industries are well aware of this concern and take full advantage of brainwashing people into believing that they must eat meat (i.e., beef, chicken, fish or other animal flesh) in order to assure ample consumption of necessary protein (Barnard, 1995; Marcus, 1998; Robbins, 1987). What is frightening is that most school boards and educators believe the "protein myth" (PCRM, July 1999). What is even more astounding is the vast number of licensed nutritionists who also believe the story told by these special interest groups. Moreover, to make matters worse, most medical doctors have little or no knowledge of data supported by nutrition research that indicates veganism as a significantly healthier eating alternative. In fact, most medical doctors remain profoundly ignorant about diet since about 85% of medical schools in North America offer no more than three hours of nutrition education as an optional component of the medical school programmes (Anderson, 2007) -- we are not talking about three credit hours, but three actual hours out of a five to seven year programme!

"With the traditional Western diet, the average American consumes about double the protein her or his body needs (PCRM, July 1999). The Recommended Dietary Allowance (RDA) for protein for the average, sedentary adult is only 0.8 grams per kilogram of body weight" (Munoz de Chavez & Chavez, 1998; Mangels, 2014). To advise a realistic and nutritionally sound guideline for dietary curricula, schools ought to provide the standard formula for figuring one's daily need for protein (see **Figure 8-1**).

Body weight (in pounds) X 0.36 = recommended protein intake in grams

Even this value has a significant margin of accuracy and in most cases, the actual and true need is even lower than indicated by the formulation.

Figure 8-1: Mathematical formula for deciphering protein need.

The indoctrination of *Health Canada's Food Guide To Healthy Eating* (Ontario Ministry of Supply and Services Canada, 1992) renders false information that is highly problematic for the process of teaching healthy lifestyles to students. According to the Physicians Committee for Responsible Medicine (July 1999), "[a]s long as the diet contains a variety of grains, legumes, and vegetables, protein needs are easily met" (p. 1). Plant proteins provide all the essential amino acids, and are much easier on bones and kidneys (Barnard, 2000).

Still, whenever I tell someone that I am vegan, the first question is inevitably, "where do you get your protein?" **Table 8-2** indicates just a few excellent sources of protein. Charts such as this one belong in classrooms throughout elementary and secondary schools as well as throughout colleges and universities that offer medical and nutritional programmes of study in order to convey a more balanced and trustworthy perspective for dietary protein intake needs.

Percentage of Calories from Protein	
Spinach	49%
Kale	45%
Tofu	43%
Cauliflower	40%
Lentils	29%
Tomatoes	18%
Potatoes	11%

Table 8-2: Protein needs are easily satisfied by a plant-based diet. The average person requires no more than 9 percent of total caloric intake from protein sources (Derived from Robbins, 1987. *Diet for a New America*, p. 177).

8.3 Why Is It Necessary to Quote Medical/Nutritional Research?

The average person in society is not well-informed about the truthful facts of healthy eating, let alone a healthy lifestyle. Think about the continuous generation-to-generation messages conveyed in schools. Parents today find themselves in a panic upon the news that their child wishes to become a vegetarian. Fears surface — my child will not get enough protein; my child will not grow to be big and strong; my child will become deficient in nutrients, etc.— but these fears are not only unfounded, they are clearly irrational. However, the fears are understandably very real to parents — they too were taught the same traditional dietary rhetoric (Adams, 2001).

The New Four Food Groups (PCRM, 1991) can assist teachers, parents, students and community members (including medical and nutrition professionals) in demystifying the myths of vegetarianism. **Figure 8-2** reveals some of the principles offered through the New Four Food Groups.

Getting the Facts Right on Nutrition.

◆ Calcium in most cooked leafy green vegetables is more readily absorbed by the human body than that from cow's milk.

◆ Plant foods contain all the protein you need. There is no need to combine foods in any special way.

◆ Vitamin C enhances the body's ability to absorb iron—Vitamin C is found mostly in fruits and vegetables.

◆ The optimal amount of cholesterol in the diet is zero. Cholesterol is found only in animal foods.

◆ The best source of fiber is found naturally in whole grains, legumes, vegetables and fruits. Animal products do not contain any fiber.

Figure 8-2: Demystifying myths of vegetarian and/or vegan dietary programmes (PCRM, 1991).

8.4 Grounds for Ethical and Moral Deconstruction of Nutrition Curricula

Obviously, there is an abundance of medical/scientific evidence supporting veganism as a healthy and sustainable diet. There is another premise (perhaps many others) for integrating and penetrating current curricula with a humane alternative dietary model: veganism. I refer to the focus of an animal liberationist paradigm. Admittedly, I am tempted to assert that the moral and ethical motivations for veganism ought to take precedence over all other grounds of argumentation; however, the liberationist perspective evolves as an empowered set of premises along with and in collaboration with medical/scientific assertions insofar as attaining end goals of a healthy diet and lifestyle.

The person who desires to practise, advocate and sustain compassion, proposes that we develop reverence for all life, encourages empathy towards all living beings, and adheres to the philosophy of bio-centricity (Selby, 1995) is called *radical*. Humans are apprehensive about attributing emotions, feelings, thoughts, desires or even the ability to form relationships to non-human animals for fear of being labelled *radical*. This is the ultimate irony — it has become socially acceptable, via desensitisation (Macy, 1995), to cause suffering to other living beings, but it is often interpreted as radical to express compassion and love of other living beings. I strongly believe that this radicalisation of animal liberationist ideology stems from a socialised systemic guilt of the ill-treatment meted out to our non-human fellow earthlings for humanocentric desires such as meat-eating and other anthropocentric exploitations of our non-human counterparts.

8.5 Begging the Question of Choice for Students

The Ontario Health and Physical Education curriculum (Ontario Ministry of Education and Training, 1998) prescribes specific expectations for learning acquisition. Under the subheading *Healthy Eating*, grade one students are expected to "identify the food groups and give examples of foods in each group" (Ibid. p. 12). The curriculum automatically assumes only one correct model for dietary planning: the traditional model that includes dairy and meat. This early indoctrination of the traditional "meat and milk" diet sets a precedent that carries a message intended to last a lifetime. I could speculate that the introduction to the traditional four food groups is introduced at a very early stage in education (grade one) in order to "brainwash" children to believe there is no alternative — only the one model is presented to children at a young and impressionable age to insure the special interests agenda. Henceforth, grade two students are expected to "create menus for healthy meals" (Ibid. p. 13). Here, two assumptions of *truth* are rendered: (1) grade two students can only plan menus based on the information given to them in grade one and, (2) the food choices provided in the traditional model comprise a diverse array of so-called healthy foods. Theoretically and philosophically, students are not enlightened of alternative dietary perspectives nor are they informed of the truly inhumane and oppressive nature from which animal-based foods derive.

Grade three curriculum follows the same agenda as grade two, but additionally confirms a greater *correctness* or *truth* to the traditional model. Grade three curriculum expects students to identify and describe the benefits of healthy food choices; however, a powerful assumption and implication pervades whereby the food choices provided by the curriculum are, in fact, healthy. Grade four *Healthy Eating* curricula potentially allows for alternative dietary perspectives; however, it would be at the discretion of the teacher —most teachers are not well-versed with veganism. The fourth grade expectation of "determining whether or not one's food choices are healthy" (Ibid. p. 15) is laughable and not without special interest bias. These young children have no clue as to the toxicity and carcinogenic capacity of their food choices. It is safe to assume that the average fourth grade child has no idea that cow's milk contains enzymes of a highly carcinogenic nature (Campbell, 2006). Furthermore, and beyond the medical/scientific evidence against promoting the traditional model, these impressionable students are not privy to the happenings and practises in slaughterhouses and factory farms. To further this last point, most young children are not capable of making the connection between food production and the massive suffering and killing of innocent animals. One famous fast food chain even went to the trouble of creating a fantasy place called a *hamburger patch* — children learn that hamburgers grow much in the same way as carrots, potatoes or corn (Robbins, 1987).

Higher grade levels (five through eight) follow the same pattern as grade four. Once the foundation of "meat and milk" is permeated in grade one, it becomes unnecessary to reinforce the aforementioned narrow premise of nutrition.

Insofar as higher education (college and university programmes) is concerned, a comprehensive programme in vegan/plant-based nutrition can easily and appropriately integrate multiple subject areas: philosophy, ethics, sociology, psychology, even academic and persuasive writing. Bringing the overarching topic of veganism into classrooms and lecture halls helps to motivate critical thinking skills and carries unlimited opportunity for evolving one's perspectives on how one fits into society and how one thrives as an Earth citizen -- optimally thriving without invoking harm or suffering to fellow earthlings.

Two points need to be re-emphasised at this juncture: (1) the nutrition curriculum described in the preceding paragraphs has been supplied free of charge to schools by special interest groups (i.e. meat and dairy industries) (Robbins, 1987), and (2) no alternative to this model has been included anywhere within the grade 1 through 8 curriculum (Ontario Ministry of Education and Training, 1998). The words *vegetarianism* and *veganism* never appear in the guidelines for Ontario's Health and Physical Education curricula (Ibid.). It is somewhat surprising that no one has made the effort to accommodate alternative perspectives within nutrition curriculum. Perhaps this laxity is due to ignorance of non-traditional dietary choices and/or a feeling of safety and security in knowing that the provided nutrition curricula has become a mainstay in the teaching/learning structure.

8.6 The New Four Food Groups

Promoting a healthy lifestyle is, in and of itself, an excellent reason for adapting a vegan nutrition programme throughout curricula within scholastic and higher academic environments. Physical education endures as a stable and necessary part of the curricula. Taking an active role in one's health and fitness is vital for a well-rounded and balanced programme of health maintenance (Ornish, et al., 1990). Additionally, one's diet significantly affects other aspects of lifestyle (Barnard, 1995). If a diet is high in saturated fats, there is an increased likelihood that the individual will carry extra body fat (Barnard, 1995; Robbins, 1987); this in turn will limit physical activity somewhat, not to mention other detriments to overall health procured from lack of healthy whole foods.

Aside from the health benefits obtained from a vegan diet, there is a benefit of healthy consciousness. Specifically, one who refrains from eating animal flesh and other animal by-products chooses not to eat the misery and suffering (Adams, 1998, 2001) endured by the animals who died for the dinner plate. From a holistic and bio-centric position, it is hard to believe that people who devour animals that experience such extensive torture and butchery are not effected in some negative way (Ibid.) — whether the outcome is failing health, emotional turmoil or psychological distress. Yet the majority of society eats the flesh of animals without giving a single thought to the fact that their so-called dinner was once a living, breathing life form (Adams, 1998; Robbins, 1987), a member of a family and of a community, and eventually an innocent victim of human-centric desires. This is why it is so crucial that everyone is educated about from where and from whom food originates. The state of denial that we are eating once living, loving beings needs to end. The truth of monumental suffering needs to be brought to the forefront of social consciousness (Caine, 2001) — otherwise, the torture, cruelty and inhumane treatment of non-human animals will continue.

The **New Four Food Groups** promotes a plant-based diet. The dual primary objectives of motivation behind this alternative dietary plan are for the betterment of health for humans *and* for the liberation and salvation of non-human animals. The four groups are (1) whole grains, (2) vegetables, (3) legumes, and (4) fruit (See **Table 8-3**). Nutritionally, these foods combine to provide a diet high in carbohydrates and fiber, low in fat, and without cholesterol (PCRM, 1991).

The Physicians Committee for Responsible Medicine (PCRM) considers animal-source foods such as beef, pork, chicken, fish, eggs and dairy as *optional* foods. PCRM suggests that these sources be consumed in very modest amounts. Obviously, the views expressed by PCRM are not founded on a liberationist paradigm of animal rights philosophy.

The New Four Food Groups			
Whole Grains	**Vegetables**	**Legumes**	**Fruit**
5 or more servings daily	3 or more servings daily	2 or 3 servings daily are adequate	3 or more servings daily are optimal
This group includes bread, rice, pasta, hot or cold cereal, corn, millet, barley, bulgur, buckwheat groats and tortillas. Build each of your meals around a hearty grain dish – grains are rich in fiber and other complex carbohydrates, as well as protein, B vitamins and zinc.	Vegetables are packed with nutrients; they provide vitamin C, beta-carotene, riboflavin and other vitamins, iron, calcium and fiber. Dark green, leafy vegetables such as broccoli, collards, kale, mustard and turnip greens, chicory or bok choy are especially good sources of these important nutrients. Dark yellow and orange vegetables such as carrots, winter squash, sweet potatoes and pumpkin provide extra beta-carotene. Include generous portions of a variety of vegetables in your diet.	Legumes, which is another name for beans, peas and lentils, are all good sources of fiber, protein, iron, calcium, zinc and B vitamins. This group also includes chickpeas, baked and refried beans, soy milk, tofu, tempeh and texturized vegetable protein.	Fruits are rich in fiber, vitamin C and beta-carotene. Be sure to include at least one serving each day of fruits that are high in vitamin C -- citrus fruits, melons and strawberries are all good choices. Choose whole fruit over fruit juices, which don't contain as much healthy fiber.

Table 8-3: PCRM, 1991.

However, given the scientists and researchers involved in the ongoing education provided by PCRM, I believe that the liberation of animals from factory farms and slaughterhouses also prevails as a primary motivation of this optimal dietary model.[17] PCRM is primarily concerned with promoting human health. I am primarily concerned with saving animals from suffering and exploitation. However, they are providing a service to humans *and* to non-human animals in encouraging a healthier, primarily vegetarian way of eating. The fact of the matter is that the New Four Food Groups is a healthier way of eating for everyone. This food programme needs to be integrated into current nutrition curricula, as well as food service facilities at schools, colleges, and universities.

8.7 Closing Remarks

From the obvious medical/scientific evidence, and in support of a healthier dietary programme, veganism is a sane and rational choice for teaching life-promoting and humane dietary erudition. For ethical reasons, the choice is even more enticing and convincing. Unfortunately, not everyone agrees -- were ethical argumentation for compassion and reverence for all living beings to evolve as a universal truth and globally accepted philosophy for the main of society, at least the majority of humans would adopt a humane lifestyle; hence, veganism.

---

[17] I believe that the researchers behind the New Four Food Groups, led by Dr. Neil Barnard, are highly motivated to discourage society from the continuation of viewing animals as food products. Perhaps, PCRM has decided to focus primarily on the benefits to human health rather than saving animals' lives; many people would not respond to the call for animal liberation; however, when people hear that their own health and their own lives can be improved and that they can be alleviated from disease by changing their diet, then perhaps the motivation to adopt a plant-based diet is stronger.

9

Coalescing Non-Anthropocentric Ideologies within Environmental Education and Environmental Ethics

9.1 Introduction: Integrating Curricula

Any subject area of scholastic or academic study can benefit from a humane perspective of relating and knowing. Humane education bridges constructed learning and comprehension with values for a more compassionate society, a more humane world. Although humane education currently resides on the periphery of curricula (Selby, 1995), this leading-edge perspective conveys powerful and positive messages for influencing and encouraging more peaceful and humane ways of being. The goals and objectives of formal education is to deliver knowledge for enabling the individual to survive and thrive in life – unfortunately, the equation is incomplete without teaching life affirming values that encourage co-operation, sense of community, and interconnectivity to all other entities of the biosphere. Such an assertion seems overwhelming at first glance; however, it is not unreasonable to teach our students how to relate to others in peaceful, negotiable ways that invoke collective advancement for all of society as opposed to current fragmented and compartmentalised objectives and activities.

The preceding chapters discuss bio-centricity, eco-feminism, and vegan ethics as these areas pertain and apply to environmental education and ethics. This chapter further enhances these theories and applications insofar as linking them together as a comprehensive and cohesive model for delivering environmental education within a non-anthropocentric perspective. Additionally, and extensively, this chapter demonstrates how the *non-anthropocentric perspectives* of bio-centricity, eco-feminism, and veganism serve to strengthen the following academic areas in environmental education: (1) anti-violence education, (2) futures education, and (3) eco-spiritual environmentalism. Following is a brief discussion of what constitutes humane pedagogy: methodology essential in the delivery of and for learning compassion for the environment.

9.2 Humane Pedagogy: Compassionate Methods for Learning

> We need to adjust our learning programmes and learning approaches so that students become aware of the commonalities that mark out all forms of oppression and are sensitised to the needs of other human beings and animals (Selby, 1995, p. 21).

According to David Selby, we need to engage and sustain pedagogical methods that encourage highly interactive and experiential learning environments (Ibid.). The humane classroom needs to evolve as a safe space of warmth, acceptance, non-judgement, equitable treatment of all class members, and a place where a truly democratic spirit can be experienced and celebrated.

> [The] humane classroom necessitates a harmonisation of 'message' and 'medium'. If some of the principle 'messages' of humane education concern compassion, kindness, harmony, justice, equity and peacefulness, then these need to be reflected in the climate, ethos and quality of relationships evident in the classroom. In practise this means a range of concrete things such as emphasis on dialogue between the students themselves and between students and teacher, a valuing of the contribution all can make to the learning process, co-operative learning, a decentralisation of sources of power, decision-making and initiative-taking within the

learning community, and sustained commitment to esteem-building and group-bonding processes within learning programmes (Selby, 1995, p. 35).

A humane classroom is a place of affirmation (Ibid.) where each individual can emerge as a self-confident, self-assured person of high self-esteem. Differences among individuals are celebrated; diversity is seen as the make-up of a rich tapestry. Humane pedagogy recognises the unique talents, gifts and abilities of every learner; to that end, both students *and* teachers are viewed as *both* teachers and learners. In other words, the classroom is not structured as a top-down operation in that the teacher is all-knowing and the students have nothing themselves to teach. Quite the contrary: all are respected as potential messengers and receivers of knowledge, process, and active participants in the teaching/learning process.

Graham Pike and David Selby (1999) identify four primary dimensions conducive and integral to a humane learning environment: spatial, issues, temporal, and inner dimensions (**Figure 9-1**).

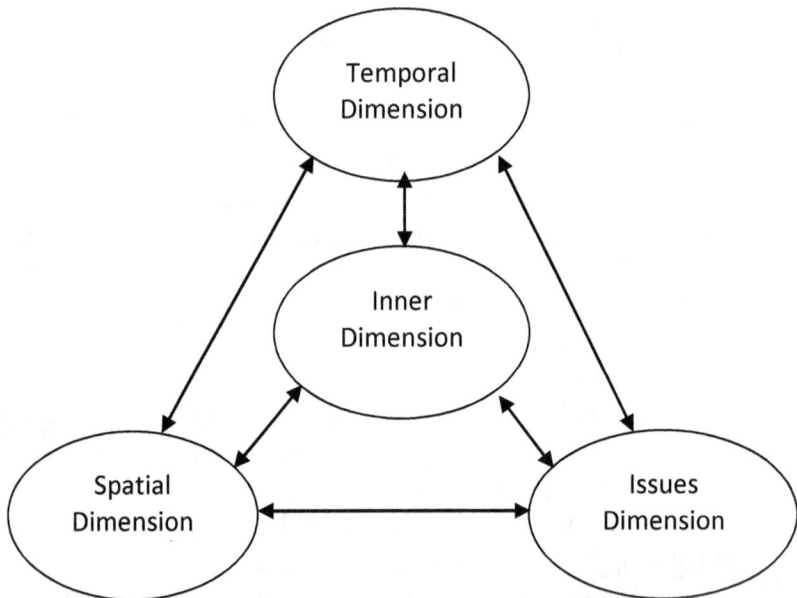

Figure 9-1: Pike & Selby (1999), p. 12.

Each of these dimensions is characterised by core traits inherent in their pedagogical philosophy and implementation. The *spatial dimension* draws our attention to the realm of interdependence. For purposes of humane education, the philosophy both of the field and within the classroom adheres to a global awareness of one's neighbours – both human and non-human. Existentially, every living being is interdependent upon every other living being. From a foundation of ecology, we – human and non-human – are interdependent upon environmental sources: air, water, soil, the sun's energy. "At a personal level, this dimension focuses on the interconnectedness of an individual's mental, physical and spiritual make-up" (Ibid. p. 12).

The *issues dimension* encompasses all relevant concerns of the students' lives (Ibid.). We need to extend our thinking, however, to include not just the local, but the global issues that do in fact affect all of us in our locale. For example, if we destroy rainforests in Brazil, as a result of the diminished oxygen we depend upon from rainforests' natural *oxygen factory*, we here in Canada or in England are affected by the environmental depletion in Brazil. This is also an example of the overlapping tendencies of these dimensions: globally, we are interdependent upon sources from around the world, not just locally; therefore, we clearly see how an *issue* of environmental degradation also brings about detriment to our need of *interdependency*. According to Pike and Selby (1999), the issues dimension also includes "...economic and political development, the environment, gender and race equity, health, peace and conflict resolution, rights and responsibilities" (p. 13). Furthermore, within this dimension, we need to examine with our students the concepts of interconnectedness: i.e., "An environmental issue, such as deforestation or water pollution, is likely to contain within it aspects that relate to development, health, equity, conflict and rights" (Ibid. p. 13). Additionally, it is important that students acknowledge and recognise perspectives other than their own. "Consideration of diverse perspectives, from a variety of cultural, social and ideological vantage points, will provide a broad platform of ideas from which individuals can form far-sighted and fair-minded judgments" (Ibid. p. 13).

The *temporal dimension* invokes an interesting and thought provoking discourse. Essentially, this dimension views time as fluid; hence, the past, the present, and the future are not deemed discrete time periods, but rather, all time is thought of as one essence of existence. "Our present thoughts and actions are shaped not only by our experience and understanding of the past but also by our future visions and aspirations" (Ibid. pp. 13-14). Humane pedagogy reveres time not as fragmented frames of events, but as a valuable reminder of our roles in the world as teachers and learners. More concretely, we cannot negate the happenings of the past – i.e., if we forget the wrongdoings of past evils, we are doomed to repeat them; also, we need to remain cognitive about our future – i.e., we need to realise that actions we invoke today may carry negative consequences for tomorrow.

The *inner dimension* embarks us on an exciting new way of viewing ourselves as active participants in the world. "While the journey outwards leads students to discover the world in which they live, the journey inwards heightens their understanding of themselves and of their potential" (Pike & Selby, 1999, p 14). These journeys – outwards and inwards – are not opposing, but rather complementary and essentially interdependent upon one another. The individual needs to understand the world around her/him in order to make sense of numerous events, cultures and individuals, the natural environment, and how s/he may see her/himself in that world. Simultaneously, the individual who is actively engaged in learning and self-exploration continues to evolve as a world member *and* as an individual of potential accomplishment and benefaction. Concretely, if the individual sees her/himself as a valuable member of society, perceives her/himself as self-confident, able, generous, compassionate and empathic to the suffering of others, then s/he can contribute positively to both self and others. The inner dimension of the learner – experiencing outward and inward growth – is psychologically, emotionally, and spiritually integrative with the self, with others, with nature, with the universe.

Humane education is about content; humane pedagogy is about process. Both content and process are essential in the teaching/learning environment. David Selby (2000) brilliantly expresses the developmental and substantive characteristics of humane pedagogy:

> The debate on the nature of a humane pedagogy has now
> begun as proponents consider how the core "messages" of

humane education – such as compassion, empathy, kindness, respect, responsibility, intrinsic value and equal consideration – should be reflected in the climate, ethos and quality of the relationships in the classroom (p. 275)…The humane teacher's ability to [recognise] and then respond to the "subtle indicators of energy and compassion" in young people by providing them with real-life opportunities to become involved in social action is also being [recognised] as a hallmark of the humane classroom (p. 276).

The messages inherent in humane pedagogy translates to "…[encourage] students to work for personal and social change (including change of a transformative nature)" (Ibid. p. 276). Students learn to think for themselves which behaviours are acceptable for the fomenting of a humane world; contrarily, they learn to critically reflect upon and scrutinise any behaviour that does not coalesce with humane values and objectives. Eventually, from ample and ongoing practise of critical thinking, reflection, and learning to evaluate one's own attitudes, behaviours, and ways of relating in the world, students can potentially adopt and adhere to humane ways of living and view themselves as positive contributors to a more compassionate world.

9.3 Linking Bio-Centricity, Eco-Feminism, and Vegan Ethics to Humane Non-Anthropocentric Environmental Education

Bio-centricity, eco-feminism, and vegan ethics (veganism) are natural mergers for the compilation of a framework for humane non-anthropocentric environmental education. Bio-centricity advocates for reverence and respect for all species and all individual organisms; this conceptual framework parallels the end goals of humane non-anthropocentric environmental education. In particular, the focus on a non-anthropocentric viewpoint echoes bio-centrism.

Eco-feminism (although variations exist within the field) extends the notions of oppression onto the natural environment; hence, just as women have historically experienced varying forms and degrees of oppression at the hands of a patriarchal society, so too now is planet Earth experiencing exploitation and degradation at the hands of humankind. Plumwood (1998) draws a parallel between nature and gender; she alleges a pattern of dichotomies that demonstrate the feminist need to defend the environment: man/woman, human/non-human-animal, economy/ecology – Plumwood further upholds the ideal that both women and nature have suffered due to patriarchy of historical proportions. Eco-feminism is a powerful and supportive adjunct to humane non-anthropocentric environmental education in that it invites those who feel slighted by patriarchy – women, people of colour, LGBTQ individuals – to draw comparisons between their own experiences of discrimination and exploitation and those experiences of other species and of Earth. For some, this may be a challenging stretch – many people are not comfortable with comparing themselves with non-human animals; however, upon discovering the similarities of pain and suffering between and among both humans and the other-than-human, and as one possible task of humane education, one may begin to develop a sense of empathy and compassion that denotes common experiences rather than focussing on difference of species.

Veganism is about abstaining from participating in any activities or behaviours that bring harm to non-human animals. Furthermore, veganism advocates for environmental integrity; hence, vegans tend to be environmentally conscious: they most likely partake in recycling, water conservation, minimise fossil fuel consumption, and of course, refrain from ingesting animals or animal by-products. Since factory farms and slaughterhouses contribute massive amounts of environmental desecration, the vegan, by abstaining from animal product consumption, practises a profound form of radical environmentalism. Referring to the basic economic concept of supply and demand, for every individual who chooses a vegan lifestyle, the demand for animal products decreases and so too does the need for supply. It only stands to reason from an environmental standpoint that fewer factory farms translate to a lessening of environmental pollutants into our atmosphere.

Humane environmental education melds ideals and philosophies from humane education and environmental education to form a more comprehensive outlook for living humanely in an environment shared by many species. Introducing non-anthropocentric assertions into this melding produces a very unique field that integrates animal liberationism with both humane education and environmental education foundations. Together, these three broad fields amalgamate with a potential for teaching and learning about the environment –

where we all live, and for the environment – providing a safe and healthy environment inclusive of all Earth residents. Concretely, humane non-anthropocentric environmental education encourages environmental protection, conservation, and integrity while reminding us that other species also reside on this planet and that we carry a massive responsibility to not only care for Earth for our own survival, but also for other species to survive and thrive on this planet they call home.

9.4 Integrating Humane Non-Anthropocentric Environmental Education Curricula with the Principles and Philosophies of Bio-Centricity, Eco-Feminism, and Vegan Ethics

Creating a framework of humane non-anthropocentric environmental education that embraces bio-centricity, eco-feminism, and vegan ethics begins with recognising and acknowledging the intricate and multi-dynamic relationships among the various components for this holistic erudition. **Table 9-1** exhibits the multiple possibilities for linking environmental curricula of anti-violence environmental education, futures education, and eco-spiritual environmental education with the principles and philosophies of bio-centricity, eco-feminism, and vegan ethics.

9.4.1 Anti-Violence Education through the Acknowledgment of Bio-Centricity

Anti-violence education and the positive influences stemming from non-violent means of conflict resolution, co-operative attainment, and peaceful ways of knowing and living needs greater attention both within scholastic and academic environmental education curricula. In pursuing non-violent means of alleviating global tensions and sustaining a world whereby pain and suffering is curtailed to an utmost degree, the assertions and ideological perspective of bio-centricity, radical humane transformation, and the multiple humane values proffered through humane environmental education deserve attention at centre stage in the classroom.

Humane education serves as a complementary paradigm for anti-violence education (Caine, 2002). Integrating humane pedagogy and humane theory and practise within and throughout environmental education curricula lays foundation for ethical groundwork mandated by transformative teaching and learning processes. With violence so prevalent throughout our society — locally, nationally, internationally and globally — the time to recognise the multiple interconnections of influence and causation of societal violence has come to pass. Moving towards more progressive and pro-active initiatives in transforming our species into a more compassionate existence is paramount and central to forging a bio-centric and humane world. The so-called traditional 'business as usual' lifestyles are not working — wars continue, poverty flourishes, violence pervades, and needless suffering persists and without relief.

Humane Non-Anthropocentric Environmental Education (Partial Framework)			
Humane Environmental Education Curriculum			
Philosophies and Principles		**Anti-Violence Education**	**Futures Education**	**Eco-Spiritual Env.- Education**
	Bio-Centricity	Bio-Centricity/ Anti-Violence Education (9.4.1)	Bio-Centricity/ Futures Education (9.4.4)	Bio-Centricity/ Eco-Spiritual Environmental Education (9.4.7)
	Eco-Feminism	Eco-Feminism/ Anti-Violence Education (9.4.2)	Eco-Feminism/ Futures Education (9.4.5)	Eco-Feminism/ Eco-Spiritual Environmental Education (9.4.8)
	Veganism	Vegan Ethics/ Anti-Violence Education (9.4.3)	Vegan Ethics/ Futures Education (9.4.6)	Vegan Ethics/ Eco-Spiritual Environmental Education (9.4.9)

Table 9-1: Framework for Integrating Humane Environmental Education Curriculum with the Philosophies and Principles of Bio-Centricity, Eco-Feminism, and Vegan Ethics.

Consequentially, all earthlings suffer and are victims of the systematic and normalised brutality and suffrage of current anthropocentric and androcentric (Warren, 2001) activities. My focus herein embraces anti-violence education asserted through humane education as paradigmatic ideology for teaching compassion (Vockell & Hodal, 1977). Specifically, a subjective assertion of bio-centric peace — egalitarian justice across all species, between humans and non-humans — is the predominant focus of my theorisation that encompasses emancipatory moral regard for all living beings.

We also need to be consistent in how we approach resolution of social violence. There pervades a danger of delivering mixed messages to children regarding acceptable and unacceptable forms of violence. We, as a society, actually condone some forms of violence while we struggle to alleviate other forms of violence. The principles of bio-centric ethics clarify this discord in no uncertain terms as explicated in the following subsection.

9.4.1.1 Societal Hypocrisy of Diagnosing Children with Conduct Disorder

There are numerous reasons why a child might display and project violent and cruel behaviour towards an animal. Some of the excuses and explanations are the need to control, to retaliate, to satisfy a prejudice (against a particular species), to express aggression, to enhance one's own aggressiveness, to shock people for attention and amusement, displacement of hostility, or a variety of other egocentric desires (Arkow, 1997). The American Psychiatric Association categorises cruelty towards animals as symptomatic criterion for *conduct disorder* (American Psychiatric Association, 1994). "Individuals displaying inherent traits of conduct disorder usually have little empathy regarding feelings or the well-being of others" (Ibid.).

Numerous studies have indicated strong connections between childhood cruelty to non-human animals and later antisocial and psychopathological behaviours (Arkow, 1997; Ascione, 1993; Gredley, 1999; Kellert, 1996). Cruelty is learned behaviour. A highly dysfunctional family where abuse – physical, emotional, psychological and/or sexual – is the norm is a classic environment for teaching cruelty, neglect and abusive engagement (Friel & Friel, 1990;

Gannon, 1989; Woititz & Garner, 1990). Children who are raised *without* values of compassion, empathy and kindness endure the additional challenge of coping within society, but profoundly lacking in humane ethics and skills of comprehension for interconnectivity and inter-relatedness with others.

The obvious hypocrisy with the label and diagnosis of conduct disorder stems from adult society serving as models for acceptable behaviour. If parents, or other adult figures, display behaviours of cruelty, the child learns cruelty. Contrarily, if these models invoke values of peace, caring and respect, the child will most likely ascribe to more humane ethics in relating to their world. A priori, conduct disorder renders a highly inconsistent expulsion of selected living beings as not worthy of humane consideration. A mixed message pervades that it is acceptable to harm, to torture and to kill some beings, but not acceptable to do the same to other living beings is eminently incongruent with humane ethics. We need to query as to why a child is potentially labelled with conduct disorder when s/he kills the neighbourhood cat, but rewarded when s/he accompanies her/his father on a hunting trip and kills a deer. Does the diagnosis of conduct disorder condone selected forms of violence, but reprimand other forms of violence?

The messages we teach our children (the next generation) are discrepant with regards to the environment, coexisting with other species, and relating to fellow humans. By indoctrinating some forms of violence as normalised ways of living, a carry-over effect of projected violence is inevitable. When an individual learns that an act of violence is socially acceptable, s/he may transfer that permitted violence onto other situations. In invoking anti-violence education as a medium for compassionate living – i.e. humane ethics – we need to send messages of congruity, connectivity and consistency. It does not make sense to permit and condone violence in some situations (i.e., killing a deer), but to denounce the same decree of violence in other situations (i.e., killing the neighbourhood cat).

More fundamentally, if we are going to label children with behavioural problems — in this case, violent behaviour of torturing and killing animals — as diagnosed with conduct disorder, are we not then obligated to do the same for adults committing the same acts? What about slaughterhouse workers, butchers, vivisectors, and researchers who impel pain and suffering upon innocent defenceless animals? Is not the slaughterhouse worker who clubs the pig to death or slits the throat of a cow also committing an act of violence? Technically, if we are going to be consistent with the American Psychological Association's diagnostic criterion for conduct disorder, we need to label the slaughterhouse worker as violent, as suffering from conduct disorder, and even psychopathic — my own asserted inquiry, *How can anyone intentionally cause so much suffering, violent abuse and agonising torture towards innocent and defenceless animals and not be deemed psychopathic — particularly, when the individual perpetrating such atrocities feels no empathy or compassion for her/his victims?* I stand by my uncompromising position: Invoking massive cruelty, torture, suffering, horrific treatment towards families and communities of animals without any remorse or sense of wrongdoing is psychopathic! As judgmental as that may sound, I cannot surrender to the cultural relativism sustained in agribusiness or within a meat-eating society.

9.4.2 Eco-Feminism Supporting Anti-Violence Education

As discussed in chapter five, many eco-feminists view violence against nature and non-human animals as parallel to violence against women (Adams, 1993, 1996 [1995]; Curtin, 1996 [1991]; Donovan, 1993, 1996 [1994]; Gaard, 1993; Gruen, 1993; Heller, 1993; Luke, 1996 [1992]; Manning, 1996 [1992]). Feminist erudition focuses deeply upon oppression against marginalised groups in society. Nature and the other-than-human qualify as being the 'oppressed other.' Degradation and destruction against nature and non-human animals may be positioned as acts of violence against these entities. Since the feminist mindset struggles to liberate oppressed others from prejudice, discrimination, and acts of violence, it is not implausible to include the other-than-human within this realm of protectionism. Environmental demise may also be viewed as raping the Earth (Adams, 1998) – quite literally, exploiting Earth's natural resources and destroying natural geographies translates to altering nature to a state that may never fully recover. A parallel, yet controversial illustration may be drawn representing the violation against a woman who is raped and the violation against nature (Adams, 1998) through ongoing excavation and degradation. Both the woman and nature may

Robert S.E. Caine

endure for years in a struggle to recover; either may never fully recover from the suffered brutality and/or devastation.

9.4.3 Addressing Systemic Violence through Vegan Ethics

One of the primary objectives of humane education as an effective change agent is to permit multiple and diverse perspectives throughout curricula. If we (educators) are going to transmit messages of meat eating, sport hunting, using animals for biomedical research and other systems that sustain violence and oppression, we also have a moral and ethical obligation to present alternative paradigms that invoke more humane ways of knowing and relating, values of compassion and empathy, and an opportunity to engage in critical inquiry of systematised violence throughout the community, society and on a global scale. For example, if we are expected to teach the traditional four food groups that include animal flesh and animal derived products, we need to present an alternative health and nutrition curriculum that abstains from harming other species, the environment and the biosphere. Presenting opposing perspectives, pro/con, humane / inhumane, bio-centric / anthropocentric, co-operative / competitive, species inclusiveness / human-centeredness, is a compromise for many animal liberationists, myself included, in that I know of no animal liberationists who would condone ongoing detriment, exploitation and torment of the other-than-human Earth members; however, in providing multiple perspectives, we avail students of alternative humane ways of knowing (Vockell & Hodal, 1977, 1978); thus, we permit entry and expansion of humane ethics not currently offered in scholastic environments – concretely, bringing humane values into curricula allows students opportunity to critically ponder and reflect upon their own values and the multiple ways they wish to believe, act and live in accordance with nature.

Vegan ethics propounds to accomplish the bringing of alternative and more humane ways of thriving, ways that do not cause the suffering of our fellow earthlings. Veganism rejects using non-human animals as human food products, as scientific research tools, as objects for our entertainment, and as means to human ends – vegan ethics affirms the other-than-human as fellow beings in need of our care and compassion rather than our cruelty and exploitation. Ideally, I advocate humane erudition as mandated discourse for preparing the next generation in their role of social construction, participatory citizenship and anti-speciesist foundations. Synthesising bio-centricity, eco-feminism, and vegan ethics as a composite for delivering anti-violence education proffers a new perspective for viewing violence on a larger scale; however, the principles and philosophies of these fields resonate strong messages for getting along more peacefully on local, national, and global proportions.

9.4.4 Futures Education Curricula from a Perspective of Bio-Centricity and Social/All-Species Harmony

One may choose any evening news programme at random, and the reality of violence, despair, and a world filled with anger and sadness is prominent. Young people need an alternative scenario of how the world *could be* (Rubenstein, 1999). They need to be made aware that there are humane alternatives, less violent means of obtaining goals, and more positive perspectives for forming philosophical ideals and beliefs of why we are here and how we can effect a more humane and desirable world (Shostak, 2000).

Futures education discourse engages in probable, possible and preferable scenarios about and for the future (Caine, 2002; Selby, 1995; Smith & Carson, 1998). Of course, one needs to critically examine epistemological and ontological orientations of *the future* among the multiple definitions that pervade the field. Is the future one hundred years from now, twenty years from now, tomorrow, or does futures discourse encompass a continuous and cyclical series of *futures* – ongoing presents that comprise a futures perspective? We consciously plan, discuss and envision future events in our lives – habitually, we also act on unconscious levels in our daily activities – i.e., we engage in behaviours without consciously and critically examining our motivations, intents or objectives for such behaviours. It is precisely this latter point that I wish to focus my assertions and intentions of humane ideologies for a humane future.

Envisioning a future whereby we live in harmony with all species is an ultimate goal of true bio-centricity; animal liberationist ideology along with bio-centric environmental ethics furthers this notion by acknowledging and recognising inherent value and moral consideration for each and every species *member*. Reverence for all living beings remains critical of a preferable futures discourse that can be interjected into environmental education curriculum (Holbrook, 1998).

9.4.4.1 Neglecting Our Relationship with Earth and the Dangers of Ignoring a Bio-Centric Outlook

To begin, futures education is an area of academe that gets buried under more mainstream subjects – much in the same way as humane education. Not enough time, research and attention are accorded to futures education. Futures education endeavours to make connections between present actions/behaviours/ways of thinking *and* future consequences/outcomes/successes and failures. The futures field implores us to contemplate a future world based on our present actions. For example, our present-day actions will have a direct bearing on future conditions. If we continue to pollute the environment, weather patterns may alter in dramatic and threatening ways. If we continue to contribute to the extinction of thousands of species, we will be responsible for destroying and erasing whole communities of fellow earthlings; we will also decree irreversible damage to ecosystems. If we continue to uphold the monetary system as the reigning power over society, we will ultimately destroy ourselves.[18]

> Since formal conventional educational institutions are tailored to the needs of the consumer industrial society, it should not be surprising that our society's present direction aligns itself with programmes and procedures that ignore and inhibit human-earth relationships (O'Sullivan, 2001, p. 43).

Edmund O'Sullivan recognises our need to plan for a future whereby our planning, our actions, and our objectives consider the whole earth community – such a transformative way of living not only reveres nature and the natural world, but also brings sane and humane relatedness among ourselves and between ourselves and nature.

> A different kind of prosperity and progress needs to be envisioned which embraces the whole life community. All our human institutions, professions, all our programmes and

---

[18] According to Milbrath's (1996) extensive list of needed changes for a more sustainable future, he permits the need to "[d]iminish rewards for power, competitiveness, and domination over others…[a] sustainable society emphasizes partnership rather than domination, cooperation more than competition, justice more than power" (p. 197).

activities, need to function now in this wider life community context (Ibid. p. 46).

O'Sullivan (2001) further criticises the educational systems for failing to prepare young students as responsible and respectful global citizens – citizens who show positive regard and love for the biosphere.

> There are no questions asked on the planetary sustainability of this direction. This position accepts uncritically the demands of the global market on competition and consumption. The attitude towards the natural world is fundamentally *exploitative* (p. 52).

In fact, this is one of the major downfalls of the educational system: students are sent strong messages about making a living, competing locally and globally, and striving to progress in some chosen career; however, they are not provided with a foundation for developing an honouring and revering of the biosphere. They are not warned of potential catastrophic repercussions often perpetuated by big business and industries that profit from exploitative actions upon the environment.

David Hicks and Catherine Holden (1995) also discriminate between two subtle, yet distinct, conceptions regarding futures education: (1) teaching *about* the future, and (2) teaching *for* the future. The former merely indicates what may occur in the coming years; the latter "...requires exploration of [students'] ...hopes and fears for the future and the action required to create a more just and ecologically sustainable future" (p. 10).

From a bio-centric perspective, "[e]verything is connected to everything else; we must learn to anticipate second-, third-, and fourth-order consequences for any contemplated major societal action" (Milbrath, 1996, p. 194).

> Economic growth is a means and not an end, it cannot be our top priority, whereas a viable ecosystem must be society's top priority. Current rates of economic growth are impossible to sustain ... [our] current misplaced emphasis on growth must give way to a recognition that there are limits to human population growth, and to economic growth, otherwise

society will lose more highly treasured values such as the
continued good functioning of global biogeochemical
systems, the viability of ecosystems, the continued
availability of vital resources, and the health of all creatures
(Milbrath, 1996, p. 191).

Futures education is also about encouraging ongoing discourse of
values, ethics and morals. With regard to influencing children towards
a more humane way of life, we need to take a serious look at the
violence conveyed via the media (McEwan, 1993). According to
Burle Summers, president of the Ontario Moral/Values Education
Association, the upcoming generation of children differ significantly
from past generations in their "me first" (Ibid. p. 115) attitudes, and a
general lacking of proper etiquette and manners – qualities such as
"honesty, respect, courtesy, generosity, responsibility and self-
discipline" (Ibid. p. 115). One proposal for futures education is
founded on a fear of losing these values permanently if our present
course of action continues without intervention.

"Life in a viable ecosystem must be the core value of a
sustainable society. Viable ecosystems nurture all life, not just human
life" (Milbrath, 1996, p. 190). Of course, such recognition would
require major changes throughout society. It is obvious that our
current unsustainable society does not work and will not afford
continued life on Earth indefinitely.

Animal liberation advocates and humane educators alike need to
passionately strive to convey the message(s) of moral consideration
for non-human species; hence, animal liberationism. In order to
transform our current negatively consequential repercussions of
planetary destruction, we need to repel the overwhelming
anthropocentric attitudes, behaviours and societal status quo that
permeate society into thinking that our current course of action is on
target. The very existence of bio-diversity and the contextual intent of
bio-centricity are central to demonstrating the parallel needs and
desires for humans and non-human animals.

One part of the ecological crisis where we have particular
responsibility has to do with an ideology that equates
personal identity and success with consumerism, and with
possessing the symbols of power and social status. This drive

to consume…further strengthens the ecologically destructive
practises within our form of economy where the demand for
growth in profits leads to creating new markets for a
continual stream of technological innovations. The *insanity*
[my emphasis] of living in a state of ecological imbalance has
been…correctly identified in some quarters for what it is:
namely, a crisis in the direction our spiritual development has
taken over the course of the last four to five hundred years
(Hicks & Holden, 1995, pp. 146-147).

Hicks and Holden, in the above quotation, reference the formation of
identity – associating oneself with monetary, material and physical
possessions. This is unfortunately a reality of the Western
interpretations of success. Allowing for an expansion on the concept
of identity, I have yet to encounter any futures theorist who
acknowledges the *identity* of the non-human world; when we
desecrate and exploit the natural world, we affect billions of other lives
in detrimental and horrific repercussions. Why is this agonising reality
negated throughout futures literature?

David Selby (1995) delivers a humane/futures coalescing
paradigm that does in fact acknowledge our responsibility of caring
for the planet, the environment and non-human animals as these
entities are deserving of a future whereby nature – not humans –
dictates their destiny. Further, Selby emphasises humane values as
predicating a vision of a preferred future (Ibid.). Our *other-than-
human* neighbours possess identities; they are members of families,
communities, and life systems — thus, our lack of concern for such
overwhelming suffering reflects on our lack of moral responsibility
and our failure to recognise our connections with other species.
Moreover, we fail to fully understand our connection with nature, with
the natural entities of the biosphere, as eloquently deliberated by
David Suzuki (2002):

Human beings depend on Earth and its life-forms for every
aspect of their survival and life. It is impossible to draw lines
that delineate separate categories of air, water, soil and life.
You and I don't end at our fingertips or skin—we are
connected through air, water and soil; we are animated by the
same energy from the same source in the sky above. We *are*

> quite literally air, water, soil, energy and other living
> creatures (p. 130).

Accordingly, a working definition for a preferred future encompasses a futures vision whereby humane values are confirmed as egalitarian, morally equitable, and all-inclusive across all species boundaries. Achievement of such humane and eco-affirmative values cannot be realised without also recognising our inter-penetration with nature (Capra, 1996; Suzuki, 2002), the inherent value of the natural world, and the life-sustaining properties of the very entities that promote and maintain all beings: air, water, soil, and all natural elements that contribute to the earth community. When I address futures issues, I refer to preferable futures for the whole biosphere: humans, non-humans, the environment, and the cosmos (if you will allow me a holistic vision).

9.4.5 Futures Education Prompted by Eco-Feminist Philosophy

We need to be specific in the cognitive changes required in order to attain a humane transformation; further, in addition to cognitive change, emotional, psychological and spiritual change will cohesively contribute to this massive altering of social norms, systemic oppressions and inequities, and habitual ways of relating, knowing and living. This position serves as a springboard for my assertions for a humane and thriving world.

Eco-feminism urges us to critically reflect upon our relationship with Earth. The systemic oppressions and inequities that pervade society can only exacerbate social, political, and environmental issues. By expanding the feminist criterion for equity and equality to include the other-than-human, we arrive at a win-win situation. The needless pain and suffering of billions of living beings can be minimised and eventually halted and society can choose to embrace other species as community members and family. The strength of eco-feminism is the core message that we ought to treat others as we would want to be treated; literally, women and men are permitted to endure equitable opportunities regardless of gender; gays and lesbians are entitled to the same privileges as their heterosexual counterparts; we do not instigate pain and suffering unto non-human animals that we would find intolerable to cause towards humans.

9.4.6 Vegan Ethics as a Compelling Force for a Humane Future

In rendering a definition of what constitutes a preferable future, I am specifically and intentionally referring to a *humane non-anthropocentric future* – a future of diminished violence, suffering and needless killing. As academics will confess, it is almost impossible to render one's philosophies without conjuring subjective bias; it is virtually impossible to approach any topic of academic inquiry with complete and unfettered objectivity (Spring 2002, personal communication with David Selby). Realistically, I am painfully aware that we as the human species will in all likelihood not come to consensus as to the specific requirements, entitlements and laws that will govern a preferred future discourse. Hence, I can only relate my biased philosophy for what I believe conjures, mandates and ultimately creates a preferable future society. Obviously, my perspective is biased towards animal liberationist discourse with vegan ethics at the fore – a position that I feel is justified rationally, emotionally and morally as I divulge within this book and throughout all aspects of my life. My bias inevitably crosses over into my teaching; specifically, when I am teaching for social justice and for what I believe is needed for a preferable humane future, I infuse the values aligned with animal liberationist ideology throughout the curricula.

Teaching for social justice continues to thrive as a highly dynamic and encouraging paradigm for propagating a preferable future. Throughout academia, however, the confines of social justice adhere for the most part to a human-centred foundation. Discourse on social justice and equity predominantly pertains to racial, cultural, national and international, linguistic, gender, sexual orientation and socio-economic class differences. Without question, regarding equitable and just treatment and inclusiveness of rights, desires and needs, humans potentially benefit from such discourse. But what about other species; what about nature's interests? Should we include non-human animals and the natural environment within the protective framework of social justice?

The context of social justice need not be exclusively a human-centred paradigm – nor should it be restricted toward the benefit of humankind. A time of consciousness has arisen whereby connections between social and ecological justice are intertwined and interrelated to a point of planetary survival (Goldstein & Selby, 2000; Heller, 1999; Suzuki, 2002). Working towards social justice is a forward-thinking discourse – one that needs to infuse futures education complimenting humane environmental education and anti-oppression pedagogy and ontology. How can we teach about preferable futures scenarios without addressing ongoing peripheral oppression of others – human and non-human alike? Correspondingly, how can we invoke social justice without engaging in a futures orientation? The two are linked and interconnected in a dependent and circular relationship. For those who desire a preferable future of social justice, teaching and learning about oppression and ways to protest and avert such oppressive states result in a curriculum of anti-oppression/humane discourse.

Consequently and adhering to my philosophical assertion of *anti-speciesist egalitarian social justice*, I propose an alternative framework for planning our future – *our*, referring to all earthlings – human and otherwise. Ideally, we would treat other species in ways that we would accept as treatment towards members of our own species – not as food products, resources for clothing and manufacturing, scientific tools for research, or throw-away objects shut-up in shelters without proper care, companionship, and love, but as equal members of society in need of protection, respect, basic essentials of medical care, food, water, and a safe place to call home, and recognition as fellow living beings capable of experiencing pain and suffering (Regan, 1983). Admittedly, a social transformation forged by vegan ethics and animal liberationist values would entail a substantial altering of our relationship with nature and with other species. Such a transformation would serve as groundwork for shaping a future directed by humane non-anthropocentric environmental education.

9.4.6.1 Choosing Our Direction for the Future

In the discourse of futures education, discussion about directionality is central – specifically and concretely, the direction for which we choose to channel our energy and efforts in the hope of creating and sustaining a preferable future. Are we headed towards a probable future whereby the target has been set and it is too late to change course? Or do we have opportunity for social, political, economic and moral change – hence, transformation considering possible futures given an altering of present-day action? And the most crucial question – and a central component to futures thinking – can we choose to direct our society – locally, nationally, bio-regionally, internationally and globally – towards a preferable future? If so, how do we define preferable future?

Upon delving into futures discourse, it is important that we, as a society, invoke and emerge common frameworks for what we wish to compose as a preferable future. For example, a common desire for a less violent society legitimates a starting point for further discussion of anti-violence education. From this common notion streams many multi-faceted threads for further inquiry: origins of violence, repercussions from violence, precautions against violence, advocacy for non-violent alternatives of relating and solving conflicts, and infusing anti-violence curricula throughout scholastic and academic environments.

Educators need to begin, if they have not already done so, to analyse concerns and issues for a humane sustainable future from a holistic perspective – quite literally addressing the full spectrum of their students' lives insofar as acknowledging the multiple ways in which each entity and event of life connects and affects every other entity and event of the individual. More specifically, and stemming from a non-speciesist perspective, we need to acknowledge the anthropocentrism and economic greed that biases education towards increased technology and big business – we need to teach our students that their future entails a great deal more than merely 'making a living'.

"Fundamental relearning cannot occur [until] people become aware of the need for change" (Milbrath, 1996, p. 195). People maintain a society whereby the monetary system controls their lives, that the idea of eliminating the monetary system seems impossible. Unfortunately, as long as we sustain our current priorities of money, power and control, there will always be the *haves* and *have-nots* of society. Most people are caught in the trap of *having to work for a living*. They do not find passion or fulfilment in their work – they work because they need to make money to sustain a roof over their heads, clothes on their backs, and food in their stomachs. Milbrath's point of not working for a living, but working for something that matters, something that one feels is really important, renders a positive and even spiritual perspective for what constitutes *work* (Ibid.) – I am fully aware of this concept resounding as utopian; however, it remains a humane ideal and something to possibly strive for in future generations. Extending this confirmation, it *is* possible for one to work in an area of personal passion and contentment.

One major problem and obstacle to altering society towards a preferable future is breaking people of their routine, *have-to* lives. Such stagnation of thinking and believing begins with education and the messages conveyed to students.   Traditional curricula do not permit an entrée for futures education – futures education does not enjoy the credence awarded to 'hard' sciences, 'soft' sciences, humanities, or even applied sciences (Dator, 1996). Because students are not exposed to futures education, most of them are not aware of the vast array of opportunities and choices available for creating, sustaining and thriving in alternative, humane, and compassionate lifestyles nor are they allotted the opportunity for contemplating their own future – they are disabled from acting in a *futures-thinking and planning mode*; young learners are deprived of the essentiality of planning a life whereby they can live their values, while refusing to compromise their integrity or core beliefs for how they wish to contribute to the world around them.

9.4.6.2 Contrasting Futures

Fien and Gerber (1986) and Cox (1986) suggest that students need to explore values in order to actively assist in creating a preferable future. These theorists, like Smith and Carson (1998), approach futures education – the forming of a preferable future – from a human-centred relatedness to nature and the natural world. **Figure 9-2** indicates the dual ideologies for contrasting paradigms regarding values. One need be careful upon examining the dualities, however – what seems obvious may contain hidden exclusions. For example, the ideal of social justice is highly complex and multi-levelled. Are we referring to social justice within the human species exclusively; are non-human animals embraced by the confines of social justice? After all, non-human animals are members of our society. The term *society* need not be exclusively human in usage, although often excludes the non-human in its intent – communities of non-human animals make up societies (e.g., elephants are extremely family oriented and conscious of fellow community members; hence, elephants do form societies).

As specified in **Figure 9-2**, the dualism of *desecration of the earth vs. caring and stewardship* is fuzzy in meaning. Desecrating the earth and inhabitants thereof is obvious: destroying topsoil, water tables, air, plant life and animal life are some of the primary concerns for earth advocates. However, *caring and stewardship* remains open for interpretation. Does caring and stewardship refer to sustaining the planet for human use; hence, *sustainability* over *exhaustion* of natural resources for human use? Or does caring and stewardship refer to affirming *all* life forms so as to act in ways that nurture life and the planet? Animal liberationists and bio-centric environmentalists would tend to adhere to the latter while mainstream environmentalists would be biased towards the former. Deciphering interpretation and intent is central to the critical thought processing that mandates interpretation for caring and stewardship.

Contrasting Ideals/Discourses for Values/Futures Education
Desecration of the earth ↔ Caring and stewardship
Wastefulness ↔ Conservation
Exhaustion ↔ Sustainability
Social inequity ↔ Social justice

Figure 9-2: Value alternatives for futures education discourse. Adapted from Smith and Carson (1998), p. 96.

Likewise, sustainability is a problematic term. Is the aim to sustain current status quo? Or are we to transform environmental status and relationships between humans and other life forms insofar as sustaining a newly formed and altered paradigm of existence? Sustainability is one of those red flags that need not go unattended to in the process of securing values, invoking peace and planning for preferable futures that rely upon the recognition of interconnectedness among all living beings. If we focus the sustainability of all earthlings, then we need to alter our current exploitation and exhaustion of natural resources in major ways. From a non-anthropocentric environmental ethic perspective, and for the goal of a humane future, we are responsible to sustain all natural resources and the planet for the benefit of *all* earthlings: human and non-human. The concepts of conservation and wastefulness tie in with sustainability and exhaustion. By conserving natural resources (e.g. water), we are in turn sustaining a supply of that resource. The wasting of any resource results in eventual exhaustion of it. Hosing down driveways with hundreds of gallons of water, leaving the tap water run continuously while brushing one's teeth, and allowing leaky water pipes to go unchecked are examples of wasting and exhausting natural resources. Teaching about wastefulness versus conservation, exhaustion versus sustainability, social inequity versus social justice, and desecration of the Earth versus caring and stewardship are all concepts that can be integrated throughout humane environmental education curricula.

9.4.6.3 Working towards a Future of Humane Environmentalism

The realisation and recognition of humane ethics are difficult to ignore. If educators want to effect positive change in an effort to invoke a more humane and less violent society, we can no longer affirm the prescribed curriculum that negates humane values. A central theme to humane values requires an empathic and caring (Gilligan, 1982) attitude towards all life – towards a thriving planet. "Education devoted to ecological literacy may be the best fight against global warming, habitat destruction and the loss of biodiversity" (Karlan, 2000, p. 18). Students need to be made aware of other species as having inherent value (Ralston, 2001; Selby, 1995) and as deserving of needs and rights (Regan, 1983; Rowlands, 2002; Singer, 1990; P. Taylor, 1998) – a paradigm of parallel existence for humans and non-human animals requires deliberate illustration via educators (Weil, 1991), curricula (Selby, 1995) and overall learning throughout the community. Students need to recognise a global system of living organisms beyond their own backyard, their own species, and their own lives (Fujii, 2000).

A truly radical transformation requires (will require) monumental and comprehensive altering of our current ways of surviving; in fact, survival no longer serves as sufficient for the continuance of a thriving planet – mere survival may permit us and other species to continue our journey for a few more years, a few more decades, maybe even a few more centuries; heretofore, we need revitalisation of life and planet. Brown, Flavin, and Postel (2001) poignantly express a global need for creating a "new set of values" (p. 551). They suggest that sustainability of life and planet will require co-operative evaluation and restoration for the common good of all earthlings.

One thrusting message of futures education is the fact that students have choices about and for their futures. They have ample opportunity to transform their behaviours, goals and lifestyles so as to alter the current diminishing state of the global community. Young people need to know that by acting locally, with regard to their choices for consumption, recycling, dietary choices[19] and attitudes towards other living beings, the repercussions and rewards for such choices can reach global levels – each and every individual can make a positive difference and contribution to a cleaner environment, a more compassionate society, and a healthier planet.

9.4.7 Affirming the Need for Bio-Centricity through Eco-Spiritual Environmentalism

Speciesism is a root cause of enormous suffering in the world. No different than racism, sexism, or heterosexism, speciesism creates divisions of *us* and *them*, of the oppressor and the oppressed (see chapter 5), of a crime against nature and for those who believe in a higher power (i.e., God or Big Bang Theory), of an atrocity against evolution or creationism of life.

We, as one species living among millions of other species on Earth, need to critically question our place in this vast globe; the principles of bio-centricity acknowledge both the individuality of each living being as well as the interactive and integrative relationships of multiple living beings that comprise communities. Perhaps we need to scrutinise our apathy for indoctrinating actions that bring about severe pain and suffering to so many fellow living beings. In cases of utilising non-human animals for medical research, toxicity testing in the development of products, and the massive global use of animals as

---

[19] The vegan diet ultimately protects and harmonises the environment and all its inhabitants. Humans consume a healthier diet, non-human animals are saved from suffering and death inherent of the factory farming industries, and planetary degradation is significantly diminished through diminished agricultural gases emitted into the atmosphere by adapting veganism as a truly humane lifestyle.

food for human consumption, we need to ask if the means justify the ends, especially when the ends translate to the torturing and killing of millions of innocent animals who, not unlike us, have families, feelings, emotions, capacity for experiencing physical and psychological torment, and an inherent right to thrive in the world. This very inquiry is the thrust of experiencing the essence of eco-spirituality; I am emphasising a sense of spiritual awareness that reveres nature and all the creatures of the biosphere. If we relate to an animal, say a rabbit, from a spiritual essence, we are able to feel compassion, empathy, and even love for the rabbit. We may observe the rabbit as nature's creation or a valuable life put forth by the universe or for those who adhere to religion, one of God's creatures.

The example of the rabbit also serves as an excellent introduction to the principles and philosophy of bio-centricity or bio-centric environmentalism. A teacher may begin a lesson with her class by introducing the species 'lagomorphs' or rabbits. A conversation can endure as to the characteristics of the rabbit, where s/he may live, what s/he may eat, how s/he may relate to other rabbits or other critters. Students are given a glimpse into the life of one creature: a rabbit. To further the bio-centric oriented curriculum, the teacher may then discuss the family and community ties of rabbits, the fact that rabbits are social animals that thrive much better with other members of the species rather than alone, and the interdependency within rabbit colonies. At this juncture, the individuality of the rabbit and the communal relations of the rabbit have been employed. Next, the crucial point of the lesson arises whereby the teacher discusses the rabbit in relation to the rest of the biosphere including humans. Inquiries (on the part of the teacher or the students) may prompt critical thinking for how and why we relate to rabbits – an excellent tone set forth to engage the principles and philosophy of bio-centricity: *Why do people take rabbits into their homes as pets? Why do some people eat rabbits? Why do some people hunt rabbits? How might a rabbit feel if s/he lives alone in a cage without any interaction with other rabbits or anyone else? Are there behaviours that would indicate that the rabbit is unhappy? How can we live peaceably with rabbits? What can we do to improve the lives of rabbits?* The questions may be unlimited and contribute to a wide variety of curricula including writing about rabbits, reading stories about rabbits, speaking orally about rabbits, conducting further research about rabbits, and on and on.

We are able to view the rabbit or any other species as a multidimensional being with desires and needs not much different from our own. The more we find that we have in common with other species, the greater the plausibility that we may acquire an expanded sense for viewing other species as our fellow earthlings – a highly eco-spiritual position for propagating humane non-anthropocentric environmental awareness.

It is my assertion that if people were to attend to their evolutionary embeddedness within nature rather than view nature as separate from their life force, the human race would evolve towards a more eco-spiritual essence of awareness and existence, realising that we humans *are* nature – we are a small yet integrating *part* of the macro-organism known as Gaia (Margulis, 1998). We would recognise the value of our home (Earth) and all who abide herein – human and non-human alike. Subsequently, we would need to acknowledge and celebrate the rich kaleidoscope of all life within Gaia. We *are* related to whales, apes, zebras, dogs, rabbits, birds, fish, dragonflies, and every other living organism on the planet.

Fox (1990) examines transpersonal ecologists' views of evolutionary processes. According to the Big Bang Theory, every living being today is a descendant of the very first micro-organism(s) or cells that initiated the universe (Margulis, 1998; Suzuki, 2002).

> The evolution of plants and animals out of the microcosm
> proceeded through a succession of symbioses, in which the
> bacterial inventions from the previous two billion years were
> combined in endless expressions of creativity until viable
> forms were selected to survive. This evolutionary process is
> [characterised] by increasing [specialisation]—from the
> organelles in the first eukaryotes to the highly [specialised]
> cells in animals (Capra, 1996, p. 245).

It is perhaps a giant leap of faith for many people to comprehend the notion of all living beings having common ancestry. Such a cosmologically based identification (Fox, 1990) challenges anthropocentric habituation of hierarchical ordering in the universe; hence, placing humans in a superior position to all other life forms as opposed to the cosmology that all living beings are enfolded and embedded with one another (Ibid.).

We are not as significant as we may think in the survival and the continuance of the planet. In fact, Earth would more than likely thrive and flourish in a much healthier condition were we humans to vanish from existence (Taylor, 1999).[20]

9.4.8 Eco-Feminists' and Eco-Spiritualists' Shared Perspective

Eco-feminism is about celebrating the essence of the unique individual; eco-spirituality is about celebrating the essence of one's connection with nature, with the universe, with creation. Eco-feminists advocate for equitable desert regardless of gender, race, sexual orientation, socio-economic status, physical ability, and so forth; eco-spiritualists advocate for all diversity of the biosphere regardless of species, geographical locale, or topography categorisation. Eco-feminism is a philosophy of social, political, and cultural foundations; eco-spirituality stems from one's beliefs, one's sense of connectivity with the natural environment, and one's adherence to the acknowledgment and/or faith of a higher power. Nevertheless, eco-feminism and eco-spirituality are not incompatible; rather, it may be asserted that the two 'schools' raise awareness in one another. The primary shared objective of eco-feminists and eco-spiritualists is their sense of positive regard, respect, and passion for the planet, for nature, and for environmental defence. Eco-feminists often view nature as an *oppressed other* being exploited by humanocentric and more so by androcentric domination (Plumwood, 1998; Warren, 1998, 2001). Eco-spiritualists view nature as a 'place' and series of events to be revered and upheld as an essential core of creationism; simultaneously, many eco-spiritualists position themselves as embedded in nature; hence they do not see themselves as separate from nature, but rather an integral component of the grand scheme of nature (Bloom, 2000; Conn, 1995; Dwivedi, 2001). As a general rule, eco-feminists and eco-spiritualists do not find the need to

---

[20] Taylor (1999) indicates that wild animals and plants would thrive at a better rate with less catastrophic repercussions in the absence of humans; however, he does not allow for domesticated animals (i.e., dogs, cats, some birds, rabbits, hamsters, etc.) that have lived their entire lives in captivity and possess no capacity of survival skills in the wild—this latter group of animals depends upon the caring and nurturing of humans.

compartmentalise nature or their experience of nature, but instead, perceive nature and the environment as events of continuous flow, change, and rebirth.

9.4.9 Vegan Ethics and Eco-spirituality: Advancing Animal Liberationism to the Fore of Social Consciousness

Eco-spirituality embraces a cosmological view for environmental ethics that subsumes God within all living beings (Fox, 1998)—plants, animals, humans, earth, rocks, water — God in Nature, Nature in God. Therefore, based on a theological/cosmological orientation to environmental integrity, systemic degradation of environment, other living beings, entities of the biosphere, lend to derogation of God her/himself – in Greek mythology, the rape of the goddess Gaia (Lovelock, 2000). One could take the aforementioned assertion one step further: not only is God in Nature and Nature in God, but endemic within humane discourse subsists the pronouncement that God *is* Nature, Nature *is* God.[21]

Eco-spirituality celebrates our connection with nature, not apart from nature. Likewise, we need to embrace a deeper spiritual kinship with other species (Tobias & Solisti-Mattelon, 1998) insofar as viewing them as our fellow earthlings. If we harm nature — animals, plants, the environment — we inflict harm unto ourselves; to that end, upon invoking pain and suffering onto the other-than-human, we ensure pain and suffering onto ourselves. The eco-spiritual perspective embraces a holistic life-affirming *Self*: the individual *self* as part of a larger community *Self*; this bio-centric paradigmatic epistemology denounces fragmentation and compartmentalisation of individuated lives, species, and interests therein. Specifically, each life

---

[21] I am using the term God as a contextual reference point for creationism. Personally, I do not adhere to any religious views and I remain agnostic as to whether a God almighty exists. Whether one believes in a higher power referred to as God or whether one adopts the Big Bang Theory of creationism is not significant for the purpose of my assertions that all living beings are interconnected. The philosophies and assertions I express throughout this book may be adaptable into any realm or belief system for creationism – an exception may be one who unrelentingly adheres to a religious fundamentalist mindset whereby it is believed that man was created to dominate all other life forms – I doubt, *a priori*, that an individual of such thinking would engage my work in the first place.

matters unto itself *and* all lives matter as members of an interconnected Earth community.

The eco-spiritual essence views the *whole* of the planet, the universe if you will, as a system of congruity, interconnectivity and intra-dependency; nevertheless, I strongly advocate the animal liberationist end of the spectrum of bio-spirituality in that each living being needs and deserves respect, compassion, empathy, and the right to thrive as a member of the natural world. I further emphasise the notion of a *both/and* inclusiveness: we need to recognise the import of *both* the whole biosphere *and* the individual lives contained within this massive orb. Exploiting any living being within the biosphere results in pain and suffering of the individual as well as degradation of the whole life form: Earth. The intentional killing of a snail, a cow, a butterfly or a rainforest evinces the killing of Gaia — a slow but certain death of us all.

When I think of eco-spirituality, the premises and values that come to mind include love, beauty, and belongingness within the biosphere by sheer fact of existence, and humane values of compassion, empathy, reverence for life, and of course, autonomy of self—i.e., each living being having a place and inherent value within the realm of Gaia. On a deeper spiritual connection among and between living beings, non-human animals are members of families, engaged in multiple relationships: parent, offspring (child), mate, friend – members of communities dependent upon one another and within the species – e.g., elephants, coyotes, wolves, dolphins, orang-utans – these animals are keenly aware of their relations, fellow community members, tribal leaders and those in need of greater protection from potential prey or environmental threats. Such conscious awareness cannot be regarded as conditioned responses or instinct; non-human species deliberately, intentionally, cognitively, psychologically, and lovingly engage each other through family and community – much the same as do humans.

When one discovers an eco-spiritual essence, a deep connection with nature and with other living species, that individual may also unmask the unique gift of love. *Love* serves as a valid foundation for egalitarian justice and respect for biotic diversity. Aside from complex and intricate argumentation of moral and ethical consideration, the sheer existence of love – and I emphasise the overwhelming strength and power that love effects – is adequate for developing and conveying not only bio-centric values and an all-species orientation towards biotic justice, but also acknowledgement, recognition and confirmation of animal liberationist paradigms that embrace and celebrate earthlings from all species. Experiencing passion, compassion, empathy and utmost respect for another living being supports a foundation of transformation towards a greater and more prevalent existence and flourishing of love.

Realising a spiritual connection with nature is profoundly liberating; such emancipating awareness induces emotional and psychological affinity with other living beings and with the Earth itself. It reminds us that there is something much more grand and spectacular than us; we become unfettered from humanocentric narcissism and allow ourselves to experience life as flowing particles of life within the massive waves of the cosmological dynamism known as the Universe. Through this realisation, we learn to appreciate life more, to fully take in all that nature has to offer: purity, congruity, beauty, sense of purpose and love.

9.5 Practise of Humane Non-Anthropocentric Environmental Education: The Educator's Perspective

Humane non-anthropocentric environmental education may be integrated and framed within any scholastic/academic subject area. Utilisation of this view is unlimited; hence, the educator need not worry about 'doing it right' or abiding by strict guidelines. Introducing and facilitating this stance is more about process and ways of relating to students and to environmental themes than it is about actual curricular content. With regard to process and relating to students, several principles and philosophies may serve as resources: eco-feminism, bio-centricity, futures education, and eco-spiritual environmental education are the focus for this particular framework.

The educator may wish to bear in mind the values of eco-feminism; in particular, s/he will want to relate to her/his students as unique individuals with unique talents and abilities. In other words, rather than expecting all students to fit a fixed mould for how they learn, the speed of which they learn, and their abilities for academic achievement, the educator acknowledges and recognises the individuality of each learner. This mode of relatedness parallels Howard Gardner's (1993) theory of multiple intelligences whereby we recognise and celebrate a broader array of abilities and talents: linguistic, logical / mathematical, musical, naturalist, spatial, bodily / kinaesthetic, intrapersonal, and/or interpersonal intelligences. Furthermore, keeping with the mindset of eco-feminist thought, and on an on-going basis, the educator needs to remain consciously aware of any biases that s/he may hold with regard to gender, ability, or any other differences among students and families of students.

When teaching any given subject, adhering to the principles of bio-centricity is easy. Whether engaging curriculum of geography, history, writing, or even mathematics, it is advised to utilise examples whereby the interests, feelings, and experiences of other species are considered. For example, when teaching geography, not only do we want to discuss the physical geographical areas as they may affect people, but we also want to consider how geography affects non-human animals: where they live, how they survive, and how and why humans have infringed upon the natural habitats of other species. As another example of integrating bio-centric relatedness, when writing a creative essay, the educator may have students write a story from two perspectives: the position of a human and the position of a non-human animal; the class can then contrast and compare the experiences of both species and locate similarities and differences.

Educators may wish to think outside of prescribed curriculum by conjuring real life experiences of their students. In particular, facilitating class discussions about students' future prospects transcends as a most interesting and eye-opening activity. Students may be given opportunity to contemplate their own futures: their hopes, their dreams, their fears, and their perceived realities for what their futures hold. Engaging a futures thinking mode of erudition may be integrated throughout the curricula in unlimited ways. Teachers need to be allowed to utilise their own creativity in designing lessons and activities for their students; futures education and the possibilities for facilitating students in thinking about their own futures can be developed into numerous activities that get young people to ponder their own lives and perhaps assist them in planning future events and goals they wish to achieve.

Outdoor education is quickly becoming widely used in schools and across grade levels. Meaningful teaching and learning can occur outside of the classroom. Educators, if they are able, need to be allowed to take their students out of the classroom and into nature. Whether a fieldtrip to a local beach, forest or wetland is available, or just sitting under a large tree near the school, educators can begin to get their students acquainted with nature: plants, animals, and the biosphere as a whole. Developing a sense of eco-spirituality is not something that can be forced or even taught; however, if students never get an opportunity to be in a natural setting, they lose out on environmental discovery. Environmental educators do not need to force this experience onto students; however, by staging an activity of environmental education within a natural setting, students are prompted to think and feel the environment in ways that do not happen by just reading a book or searching online. Discussions regarding the experiences of various animal species in the community may also prompt students to develop empathy and even compassion for these other living beings.

The synthesis of eco-feminist relatedness, bio-centric ethics, futures discourse, and prompting for the encouragement of eco-spiritual essences carry an abundance of potentially positive messages that allow students to grasp a broader sense of who they are and how they fit into the environment. Additionally, students may begin to assume a greater role in their own responsibility for environmental protection and integrity. The teacher, through facilitating humane environmental education throughout the curricula, prepares students to lead the world in ways more convivial with the environment and all of Earth's inhabitants.

9.6 Experiencing Humane Non-Anthropocentric Environmental Education: The Student's Perspective

The student who is fortunate enough to be privy to such humane erudition will encounter learning in non-traditional and more experiential ways. When the teacher integrates humane non-anthropocentric environmental education throughout the processes and curricula for her/his students, the whole teaching/learning experience evolves as transformative education – transformative in that the student is affected holistically: physically, cognitively, emotionally, and even spiritually. The mind-body-spirit connection becomes evident in how the student learns, what the student learns, and in the dynamic ways that the individual learner is positively enriched as a global citizen. The following narrative shows how this framework can integrate principles and philosophies inherent of humane education, eco-feminism, bio-centricity, eco-spirituality, vegan ethics, and futures education.

The student will enjoy a safe space and place for learning and thriving. The humane classroom is a place where all voices are heard (although in an orderly manner) and where students may view themselves as both learners and teachers. The essence of the humane classroom stems from a position that everyone is capable of teaching and everyone is capable of learning; the teacher chooses to surrender complete control over the workings of the classroom and allows students a democratic arena for assisting in managing and running the class on a day to day basis.

Students will also experience a sense of equity regardless of her/his family; students and their families are recognised from an eco-feminist stance whereby students can feel proud of their home life whether from a home with a mother and father, only one parent, two fathers or two mothers, foster parents, grandparents, or any other variety of family dynamics. Families are welcomed into the classroom as observers and participants – a humane classroom invites family and significant others of a student's life into the process, when appropriate.

Since learning methodology embraces a holistic delivery and practise, students are free to grow to unlimited potential. They are encouraged to tap into their emotional, psychological, and spiritual selves. They learn to see themselves as members of a far more expansive community of humans, non-human animals, and an abundance of natural environmental spaces. This learning journey prepares young learners as global citizens to the extent that students become aware of their potential responsibility for environmental protection and sustainability. They understand that their actions, behaviours, and attitudes carry repercussions not only locally, but globally. This global relatedness allows them to realise that a rainforest three thousand miles away still depends upon their lifestyle choices in their local community.

In their more immediate environment, students empathise with and have compassion for local wildlife. They know that if they step on an earthworm or crush a snail, they bring pain and suffering to the small creature and to the family and community of the one who they stepped on. A whole new respect and a sense of reverence for life evolves from a humane environmental venue in that students may find themselves viewing all living beings from a very different perspective: pigeons and squirrels are not seen as things to which one may throw objects, insects are not targets for stomping, and even domestic animals – pets – may benefit (indirectly from the students' engagement in humane environmental education) from more attentive caretakers as students begin to understand the very real needs and desires of these animals.

The foregoing paragraph sets a tone for an eco-spiritual essence for environmental integrity. Other species are regarded as fellow earthlings entitled to rights and privileges not previously recognised. Students may develop a deep spiritual connection to other species as they discover not only the many similarities between humans and non-human animals, but as they appreciate other species' dependency upon human kindness and care. Comprehension of species interdependency has the potential to instil empowerment in the student to view her/himself as a caretaker of nature and of animals – such acknowledgment may encourage more responsible behaviour and a greater level of maturity.

Through increased respect for other living beings, students begin to relate to other species in very different ways. Such awareness may launch discussion and consideration of vegan ethics. This does not translate to indoctrinating young people into becoming vegans; that is a decision that every individual needs to arrive at in their own time. Nevertheless, no harm is perpetrated through exposure to vegetarianism – what it is about, why people choose to be vegetarian, and what benefits stem from a vegetarian lifestyle; additionally, students are entitled to learn about veganism in order to provide choices for how they wish to live their lives. Young people deserve to know how extensively animals are used and exploited by humankind. At their own pace, students can decide whether or not they wish to contribute to these repercussions or alter their daily decision making to more informed and humane choices. This decision making leads directly into futures education discourse. Students can think about what their future will be like, how they wish to contribute positively to the global community, and what values they hold in their heart. A futures perspective assists students in weighing pros and cons over numerous choices as they compare probable and preferable future scenarios.

The advancement in learning from holistic experiences of both the teacher and the student are unlimited through a humane environmental education framework. The principles and philosophies of bio-centricity, eco-feminism, and vegan ethics and the humane environmental education curricula of anti-violence education, futures education, and eco-spiritual environmental education are only as limited as the creativity, the imagination, and the motivation of the teachers and learners that bring their own passion and vitality to these experiences.

9.7 Concluding Remarks

As we take a critical look at our educational systems and the curricula that shapes and influences millions of students, we must not ever become complacent with current erudition. All of us share a responsibility for preparing the next generation in their motivation and efforts of creating a better world. The future of Earth depends significantly upon the judgments, decisions, and actions we render today. If we desire a future that is more peaceful, less violent, kinder and more compassionate, then we must alter our current ways of humanocentric narcissism away from selfish exploitation of nature and of other species, and towards a more humane, non-speciesist, environmentally conscious realm of thriving with all fellow earthlings.

We do not have the luxury of waiting years or decades; Earth's inhabitants are suffering horrific pain at this very moment. The time has long past for us to re-prioritise our motivations for continued existence. We can no longer exist for the sole purpose of making a living to pay bills, planning retirement and waiting to die. There is so much more that the universe has to offer, but we need to take the initiative to embrace life and discover the magnificence of being an earthling. There is a world of splendour outside of our overpriced and under-sized apartments, our tiny work cubicles, our tattered and overcrowded classrooms and our temples of materialism also known as shopping malls. You and I owe it to ourselves – and to our fellow earthlings – to venture out into nature, to learn all we can about the natural world without impeding nature's residents, and to discover why we are so privileged to know this world. We have innumerable opportunities to contribute our efforts and our energy towards a prospering Earth community – I am not using the term 'prosper' in the economic sense, but with reference to the thriving community of nature, allowing animals to live their lives as nature intended, allowing rainforests and natural geographies to flourish – and as for us humans: we gain feelings of emotional elation and spiritual sensation at knowing that we are part of a miraculous sphere of consciousness.

10

Sustainability For a *Truly* Humane Society

10.1 Critical Analysis of Sustainability: Shifting to a Humane Paradigm

When I hear the term 'sustainability', I cringe at the thought of supporting, sustaining and protecting the status quo of current social, educational, and global norms; i.e., keeping things as they are without allowing for improvement or increased awareness towards a more humane way of living. *Teaching for sustainability* carries a wide array of interpretations for implementation of both theory and practise within formal and informal learning environments. Multiple perspectives exist as explications for sustainability and no clear decisive model stands out above others. Notions of sustainability are currently under construction — both within theory formulation and pragmatic application.

Since so many academicians, theorists, economists, educators, students, politicians and community leaders are struggling to envelop and foment a more concrete notion of sustainability, I wish to qualify my own version of what *humane sustainability* would look like within an educational framework — formal and informal — the actual curricular design is not the focus of my assertion; however, the overall philosophy for what I believe constitutes sustainability for a more humane society takes centre stage for purposes of this book.

Adhering to humane ethics — i.e., values of compassion, respect, empathy, kindness, love and reverence for life, just to name a few of the essential criteria — my proposal for implementing a common framework for sustainability ensues. My proposal does not conform to a structuralist or highly organised paradigm — such a discourse for promoting humane ethics as a foundation for common reference and end goals requires freedom, flexibility, reflection, continuous reworking and a sense of biospheric justice for all living beings; nature is not highly structuralist; neither should our educational processes adhere to limited structure of boundaries or boxed curricula. 'Humane sustainability' can only convey and expand subsequent to a *transformational shift* in social consciousness; I am referring to perhaps the most dramatic and evolutionary shift from status quo present-day systems to a new holistic realisation of egalitarian justice — a social/societal justice whereby speciesism retires as a foundation of relating and an all-species inclusion of moral consideration emerges.

Regardless of subject, topic or issue at hand, or any educational goal, *humane ethics* plays an integral role in deciphering and analysing a teaching/learning process from a perspective of non-violence. Specifically, curricula — formal or informal — need to communicate via a non-anthropocentric ethical and moral foundation. This major shift to non-speciesism requires critical analysis of current learning curricula; concretely, we, as educators, need to ask whether such components of learning comprise human-centred bias and/or whether elements of the classroom (or informal setting) accounts for and recognises bio-centricity, egalitarian social justice from a non-anthropocentric perspective and non-speciesist paradigms, ideologies and philosophies of life-affirming anti-violent association and integration.

Theories comprising a continuous building of humane curricula encompass multiple and diverse theories and philosophies: bio-centricity — acknowledging intrinsic value in all living beings (Ralston, 2001), doctrine of *ahimsa* — an Eastern religious paradigm of non-violence against animals and human beings alike (Dwivedi, 1998), vegan ethics — abstaining from utilising non-human animals in any exploitative means for human ends (Marcus, 1998), and radical ecofeminist ideology that acknowledges non-human animals in the equation of biospheric justice (Adams, 1998; Hessing, 1993). The foregoing list is not exhaustive; any ideology or philosophy securing theorisation and pragmatism for animal liberation and environmental inclusion — i.e., refraining from degradation, destruction or demise of living entities and/or ecosystems — encompasses and confirms humane ethics both in theory and practise. Radical ecofeminism, both directly and indirectly, refers to and includes the *other-than-human* within the realm of moral inclusion:

> Radical ecofeminists reject the patriarchal, large-scale, [centralised], hierarchical, mechanistic basis of contemporary society as unsustainable. They support alternatives that favour co-operative, non-hierarchical, organic and [decentralised] forms of social [organisation] (Hessing, 1993, p. 16).

Marcus (1998) bestows veganism as *a new ethics of eating* [and living] — refraining from ingesting animal flesh or animal by-products is more than dietary; it relays a lifestyle confirming the sanctity of life, of respect for other living beings:

> The typical American diet puts us at war with animals, the environment, even our own bodies. Whatever one's reason for becoming vegan, it is at bottom **an act of compassion** (author's emphasis), and compassion can become an act of deep transformation (Ibid. p. 191).

In order for society to transform itself towards humane ethics, a humane way to sustain the planet and all who reside here, innumerable *acts of compassion* are mandated. The deep transformation that I assert to be essential for non-violence and for what I propose towards humane sustainability can only transpire following a bringing to consciousness the multitudes of anthropocentric systems, institutions and reverberations of human-centredness — specifically, an overwhelming degree of habitual and socially accepted cruelty and apathy towards our non-human neighbours.

10.2 A New Paradigm for Anti-Violence Education

Anti-violence education, endemic within the humane education curricula, is a strand of global education that needs immediate attention, especially in these times of inter-national and intra-national violence and upheaval. Assuming that most people favour non-violent means of conflict resolution and sustaining a world whereby pain and suffering is curtailed to an utmost degree, the foregoing assertions and ideologies of bio-centricity, radical 'humane' transformation, and vegan ethics/morals demands the desire and praxis for non-violence — these postulates of humane ethics and moral regard can be transposed into epistemological axioms for educational transformation and delivery.

The successful delivery and adaptation of anti-violence education messages, in the truest sense of global and non-speciesist paradigms, simultaneously precedes and juxtaposes the concept of *post-transformational humane sustainability*, a realm of thought that proposes a more compassionate society and global community. The post-transformational metamorphosis encompasses biospheric justice, egalitarian moral consideration for all species, and the rights of non-human animals to be free from pain and suffering perpetrated by human-egoist desires; hence, non-anthropocentric ways of living, relating and knowing. Naturally, in order for such a monumental shift to come to fruition and integrate social consciousness, multiple transformations need occur at a conscious level; human society would have to rethink, re-evaluate, and re-identify their relationships with other species and the natural environment. Only following such cardinal changes could we then switch to a mode of sustainability, specifically Post-Transformational Humane Sustainability —i.e., sustaining the *new found humane, bio-centric, non-anthropocentric foundation of non-violence and an all-inclusive/all-species rendition of egalitarian social justice and moral consideration.*

What would this non-speciesist educational model look like? This ideal for liberation — for all species and the environment — comprises a world not of economics or human-centred desires, but a world built on a foundation of psychological, emotional, and physical well-being, compassion and empathy for fellow earthlings, recognition of other species having capacity for emotions as well as an ability to experience pain and suffering, respect for life and a need and hope for caring, kindness and love. This leading-edge model of humane education is, at present, so far removed from current mainstream thought of human-centred habitation (and human-centred curricula), that my critics may find themselves dumbfounded at my assertions and recommendations for a monumental revamping and restructuring of the entire educational system. Systemically, habitually, and as an accepted norm for social order, most people, whether academicians, students or others, are unable or unwilling to grasp the concept(s) of sustaining a society whereby non-human animals are deemed equally worthy and deserving of life and liberty as we humans. (Animal liberationists are incessantly viewed as social anarchists and antithetic to mainstream social thought regarding our relatedness towards other species). The utmost irony concerning this divergence between the animal liberationists and the majority of "non-liberationist" citizens is that the liberationists have nothing to gain except the liberation of non-human animals from cruel and oppressive systems that prevail – those opposing humane education as a foundation for moral regard unto the next generation may resist the very changes mandated by such a transformation of thought and inquiry due to multiple justifications such as selfish desires to continue their daily habits regardless of the detriment these habits bring to others, or opposition may simply find it incomprehensible to transform their lifestyle in radical ways that refrain from activities leading to exploitation of others. For example, most people may not see the possibility of refraining from using animals as food products, clothing materials, or scientific laboratory subjects. Hence, such resistance or inability to comprehend such a shift in thought and action sustains the wall of resistance that humane education endeavours to crumble.

The *normalised* and systematised ways of exploiting, torturing and killing other species has evolved as justified and globally accepted behaviours; these atrocities are sustained as *non-issues* to mainstream society's discourse and behavioural norms. For example, the majority of humans eat animal flesh — vegetarians and especially vegans[22] are the minority of human society; hence, the proclaimed vegan endures continuous inquisition as to her/his nonconformist lifestyle. Upon examining the literature on 'sustainability', one would *not* retrieve any

---

[22] Although I do acknowledge the humane lifestyle of both vegetarianism and veganism, I focus primarily on veganism as the end goals of a pure-plant-based diet including the elimination of all exploitation and cruelty of animals in the food production industries; for example, the dairy and egg industries invoke monumental pain and suffering of animals through horrific torture, alienation, mass murder, and complete disregard for any physical, emotional, or psychological torment forced upon the innocent victims of such industries.

indication that veganism is on the agenda for positive social transformation; I have yet to locate an academic article addressing the issues of sustainability that includes and/or subscribes to the notions of veganism as parcel to the needed transformative actions towards a more functional society.

10.3 What is the Question of Sustainability?

The critical question pervades: How do we sustain the world as it is without incurring further damage, degradation or destruction to environment, human populous, or endangered species (or any species for that matter)? I wish to amend the foregoing inquisition to, *Why should we sustain the world as it is, period — taking into consideration that our current ways of relating to the environment and non-human species permits and exacerbates the problematique of degradation of the natural environment and demise of countless species?* The inquisitor for sustainability, in the main, does not consider the whole of the planet in terms of 'sustainability', as this concept is rendered in the literature — s/he only ponders human (or what I deem humanocentric) sustainability, while negating the survival and quality of life for the other-than-human existence. Environmental protection, in its usual human-centred assessment, is only contemplated because of pervasive fear of the planet becoming uninhabitable for humans due to toxicity of the environment; hence, a persistent anxiety that no human will be able to survive on Earth.

Conceptualisation and identification of endangered species, I perceive, subsists as hypocrisy of human intervention. First, species are only endangered *because of* human intrusion — we exploit them, invade their place and space, and curtail their population to a fraction of what nature would have allowed. Second, and perhaps one of the most infuriating hypocrisies of human allegation, is the proclaimed concern for protecting selected species for survival — humans deciding the value of each species — and humans accrediting any given species with a ranked privilege for moral consideration and a right to thrive in *the human* world; i.e., the Bald Eagle is valued and must be protected, while the chicken receives no consideration as to any pain, suffering, torture or death bestowed upon her/him. When I hear people talk of endangered species, and their desire to ensure protection of said species, I find the whole notion laughable and hypocritical. Only the human ego, in its infamous 'god-like role,' renders rights to life and freedom from suffering based on irrational and human-centred/human-serving motives. The cow or the chicken is not endangered; therefore, we do not consider them worthy of protection — categorically, cows and chickens are deemed food resources for human consumption. The spotted owl is endangered; therefore, we make efforts to protect this species. Randomly, humans decide which species are in need of *our* version of sustainable protection and which are disposable and unworthy of moral consideration.

What about the pain and suffering endured by billions of innocent living beings for the sake of human egoist desires? These animals are not encompassed within the realm of consideration in the human equation and interpretation of social justice. Nevertheless, permitting the vision of a Post-Transformational Humane Sustainability, a social/societal model based on non-anthropocentric ways of thinking, feeling, and acting, we can endure whereby veganism evolves as the normal and acceptable way of sustenance. People no longer eat animals, wear the skins or fur of animals, experiment upon animals for science or medical research, exploit animals for entertainment, or force any animal to endure humiliation, suffering, exploitation, abandonment of love, companionship or family, or any of the current sustaining atrocities perpetrated upon non-human animals. Non-violence means exactly that — refraining from behaviours that invoke pain and suffering through acts of violence — furthermore, notions of peace, progress, sanity, compassion, respect, value and inherent worth embraces non-human beings and the natural environment.

Within this model of humane sustainability, the mighty dollar is no longer mighty, but rather meaningless. People live and exist as caretakers of each other, other species, the environment: land, fauna, flora, water, oceans, mountains, ecosystems. Motivations for acting stem from compassion, empathy and acknowledgement of the needs of others, including other species — i.e., humans recognise non-human animals' abilities and needs to form intimate relationships with fellow family members, community and their space and place in the biosphere. Agricultural industries no longer supply animals as food products; instead, vegetation comprises sustenance of a humane model of agribusiness. Medical research no longer utilises non-human animals for experimentation; only human subjects or computer animated research remains. Exploitative (so-called) entertainment such as circuses, marine parks and bullfights become non-existent. Non-human animals are no longer viewed as precepts to human egoism and cruelty; any act deemed an atrocity toward a human would also be deemed an equal atrocity toward a non-human animal — the justice system and courts would acknowledge laws protecting all species from acts of violence, terrorism, overt cruelty and systemic oppression.

10.4 Humane Education for a Humane Society: Formal and Informal Learning

Concretely, humane sustainability, in the post-transformational paradigm (that is, once achieved), centres humane values and non-violent ways of relating and knowing within curricula, formal and informal alike. Any subject, topic or learning objective can be achieved from a humane perspective; invoking humane ethics does not require a totalitarian revamping of curricula. Such a transformation entails introduction of additional perspectives into already existing curricula and perhaps, engaging in humane practise not currently in place. For example, given any subject within the formal school curriculum, alternative ways of relating can be implemented to render the humane perspective. Consider, for instance, mathematics. Word problems can include exponential degradation of the environment given a meat-eating society (i.e., erosion of topsoil due to cattle grazing), probability of contracting various health problems based on animal-based diets versus pure vegetarian diets (i.e., high blood pressure, coronary heart disease, cancer). Other formal subjects such as philosophy, writing composition and sociology can easily include critical discussions, debates and projects surrounding topics of humane ethics and moral consideration of non-human life forms.

School administrations, aside from curriculum content, also can adopt humane values as part of the dynamics for running schools: implementing policies prohibiting violent behaviour towards fellow students, teachers and any animals that may enter the campus (i.e., pigeons, squirrels, chipmunks, etc.); teacher training seminars providing introduction of humane ethics/values to conjure ideas for how teachers can introduce topics in class; avoiding use of toxic chemicals on school grounds that harm nature (i.e., pesticides);

utilising school materials not manufactured by companies that continue testing on animals; analysing texts for anthropocentric language and biases; acknowledging nature/non-human animals as members of the community and conveying an all-species/all-inclusive community message to students; avoiding school field trips that encourage exploitation, humiliation and inhumane control of non-human species (i.e., the zoo, marine animal park, circus); for schools providing food service (cafeterias), supplying vegan options with the intent of teaching humane alternatives to eating animal-derived food products.

Informal learning occurs everywhere throughout the community. As with formal learning, humane ethics and alternatives can be introduced within these environments. However, in cases of private industry, government and community-based programmes, it is up to managers, supervisors and leaders to bring humane ways of knowing into consciousness. A mindset of moral consideration for the other-than-human needs introduction. I am envisioning a society of the utmost humane degree (towards non-human animals); people would bring to consciousness a universal truth that non-human life forms are intrinsically good, worthy and deserving of moral consideration. Planetary laws (of a legal and moral sense) would ensue whereby the killing of a non-human animal would carry the same punishment and retribution as the killing of a fellow human being. Factory farms and slaughterhouses -- these death camps would be considered deplorable by their very existence and would close their doors forever; the meat industries (i.e., beef, poultry, pork, dairy and fish) would cease to exist as they would be deemed immoral and an atrocity to all that is decent. Sport hunting or intentional killing of any animal would receive the same condemnation as the killing of a fellow human. Society would enter a new era of humane existence — sustainability in its most literal sense; i.e., *sustaining and protecting life for the sake of life, both human and non-human life.*

10.5 A Bigger Picture for a Humane Society

I mention only a few examples here in order to demonstrate how humane education/ethics applies outside of formal schooling. For example, city planners and developers need to consider any potential harm to non-human animals and/or the natural geography when crafting new projects; *natural* areas need to exist even within city limits in order to provide a home environment for free-roaming animals. Induction of toxic chemicals, over-erosion of soil, contamination of water tables, and careless construction activities that harm and kill animals (i.e., via bulldozers, heavy machinery) need special attention; specifically, ecosystems, animal communities and the biosphere itself must be given moral consideration for their inherent value. Urban animals reside as integral to our city living. With this post-transformational humane model in place, inhumane activities such as poisoning pigeons or setting mousetraps transcends to intolerance by the whole of society. For the sake of parallel existence of humans and non-human animals in urban areas, humane measures need implementation to avoid conflicting interests among species; parks and natural sanctuaries are ideal places for establishing safe havens for urban wildlife (of course, the human community needs to acknowledge these places as homes for their non-human neighbours). Animal shelters as they now stand are transformed into animal sanctuaries — places with "no-kill" policies — safe refuge for injured or sick animals unable to fend for themselves in the wild.

Implementing humane policy evolves as a form of social learning — community education — in that humane ways of knowing become widely understood, and socially accepted; ultimately, such ways of knowing and living evolve as globally accepted. Not only do the planners, leaders, managers and politicians learn alternative and humane ways of running society, but they set precedents for influencing and encouraging community members to relate to our non-human neighbours in more sympathetic, kind-hearted and compassionate interactions. By invoking lesser human-egoist and more bio-centric values, people learn respect, compassion and life-affirming acknowledgement for other-than-human species as well as for fellow humans.

Essentially, this new paradigm for community education from a humane perspective entails a new mindset, eviscerating anthropocentric ways of knowing and replacing them with an all-species orientation of moral consideration. Hence, through acknowledgement and recognition of humane ideals, ethics, morals, and ways of knowing, relating and interacting, a truly humane model of sustainability can emerge.

10.6 Concluding Remarks

My model for a humane future, a future whereby all-species liberation is central to sustaining Gaia and all who reside upon the planet, humane ways of knowing need to be integrated and orientated within and throughout learning environments (Caine, 2002) — in formal schools and universities as well as informal community learning settings — so as to invoke, promote and encourage ethics and morality of compassion via non-anthropocentric relatedness into a normalised status of our (human) consciousness — acknowledging and respecting all living beings, all members of Gaia (Lovelock, 2000). Humanocentrism, or human egoism, has no place in the living system of multiple and diverse species — the living planet (Capra, 1996; Lovelock, 2000) — a place where all living beings exist in their own right; hence, shear existence connotes intrinsic value for and of each living being (Regan, 1983) and worth as well as deserving of life and freedom from humanocentric cruelty and human ambivalence toward the *other-than-human* needs (Caine, 2001, 2002). In this post-transformational model for a humane society, people learn that we do not condone exploitation and torture of animals for food, medical research, entertainment or any other cruel and inhumane operatives. They — non-human animals — are our fellow earthlings, our neighbours, our friends, our family and loved ones; they are part of us. If we are going to ponder any notion of sustainability, we must include all living beings within the realm of survival, not merely for the sake of the continuance of our species, but survival for all integral players and residents of our small planet. Forthwith, we need to eradicate current exploits and systemic suffering of our non-human counterparts; subsequently, we need to explore the real potential for a post-transformational *truly* humane sustainability.

Bibliography

Adams, C.J. (1995). "Caring about Suffering: A Feminist Exploration." In
   Donovan, J. & C. J. Adams (Eds.), *Beyond Animal Rights*. (1996). New York:
   Continuum. Pp. 170-196.

Adams, C.J. (1998). *The Sexual* Politics *of Meat*. New York: Continuum.

Adams, C.J. (2001). *Living Among* Meat *Eaters*. New York: Three Rivers Press.

American Humane Association. (1992). Kaufmann, M.E., (Ed.), *Progress in
   Humane Education*. Englewood, Colorado: The American Humane
   Association.

American Humane Association. (1992). In *Protecting Children and Animals:
   Agenda for a Non-Violent Future*, summary of the American Humane
   Association's conference, Sept. 14-15, 1992, Herndorn, Virginia. AHA, Pp. 10-
   31.

American Psychiatric Association. (1994). *Diagnostic and Statistical Manual of
   Mental Disorders*, 4th Ed., Washington, D.C.: APA.

Anderson, M. (2007). *The Rave Diet and Lifestyle*. US: Ravediet.com

Arkow, P. (1992). "The Rationale and Goals of Humane Education." In *Humane
   Education: Operational Guide For Animal Care and Control Agencies*. New
   York: American Society for the Prevention of Cruelty to Animals.

Arkow, P. (Winter, 1997). "The Relationship Between Animal Abuse and Other
   Forms of Family Violence." *The Latham Letter*, Vol. XVIII, No. 1. Stratford
   (NJ): Latham Foundation.

Ascione, F.R. (1993). "Children who are cruel to animals: A review of research
   and implications for developmental psychopathology." *Anthrozoos*, Vol. 6,
   No. 4, Pp. 226-247.

Barnard, N.D. (1995). *Eat Right Live Longer*. New York: Three Rivers Press.

Barnard, N.D. & Kaufman, S.R. (Feb., 1997). "Animal Research is Wasteful and
   Misleading." *Scientific American*, Pp. 80-82.

Barnard, N.D. (Oct. 27, 1998). "The New Approach to Prostate Problems."
   Washington D.C.: Physicians Committee for Responsible Medicine. Pp. 1-4.

Barnard, Neal. (May, 2000). "Power Up Vegan-Style: The Revolutionary Diet for
   a Powerful, Healthy Body." Washington D.C.: Physicians Committee for
   Responsible Medicine.

Beilin, L.J. (1994). "Vegetarian and Other Complex Diets, Fats, Fiber, and
   Hypertension." *American Journal of Clinical Nutrition*. No. 59 (Suppl): 1130-
   1135.

Bertron, P., Barnard, N.D. & Mills, M. (1999). "Racial Bias in Federal Nutrition Policy, Part 1: The Public Health Implications of Variations in Lactase Persistence." *Journal of National Medical Association*; Vol. 91, Pp. 151-7.

Bloom, W. (Ed.), (2000). *Holistic Revolution. The Essential New Age Reader*. Harmondsworth, Middlesex, England: Penguin Group.

Bowd, A.D. & Shapiro, K.J. (1993). "The Case Against Laboratory Animal Research in Psychology." *Journal of Social Issues*, Vol. 49, No. 1, Pp. 133-142.

Brown, L.R. "Ecopsychology and the Environmental Revolution." In Roszak, T., et al. (Eds.), 1995, *Ecopsychology*. San Francisco: Sierra Club Books. Pp. xiii-xvi.

Brown, L., Flavin, C., & Postel, S. (2001). "Vision of a Sustainable World." In Pojman, L.P. (Ed.), *Environmental Ethics. Readings in Theory and Application*, 3rd Ed. Belmont, (CA): Wadsworth. Pp. 545-551.

Caine, R.S.E. (Dec., 2000). "Humane Education for a Humane Future: Accessing Mainstream Curriculum." Major Research Paper for completion of Master's Degree in Education, University of Toronto.

Caine, R.S.E. (Dec., 2001). "The Struggle for Animal Advocacy within Animal Liberationist Theorisation: Reconstructing Fragmented Theories into Cohesive Ethics." *International Journal of Curriculum and Instruction*, Vol. 3, No. 2, Pp. 91-102.

Caine, R.S.E. (Summer, 2002). "Futures Education from a Non-Anthropocentric Perspective." *Futures Research Quarterly*, Vol. 18, No. 2, Pp. 57-66.

Caine, R.S.E. (Summer, 2003). "Eco-spirituality." *Encounter*, Vol. 16, No. 2, Pp. 48-51.

Callicott, J.B. (Fall, 1985). "Intrinsic Value, Quantum Theory, and Environmental Ethics." *Environmental Ethics*, Vol. 7, Pp. 257-275.

Cantor, D. (Oct., 1992). "Animals Don't Belong in School." *The American School Board Journal*, Vol. 179, Pp. 39-40.

Capra, F. (1996). *The Web of Life*. New York: Anchor Books.

Conn, S.A. (1995). "When the Earth Hurts, Who Responds?" In Roszak, T., et al., (Eds.), *Ecopsychology*. San Francisco: Sierra Club Books. Pp. 156-171.

Cox, B. (1986). "Reflections on Geography Teaching for a Better World." In Fien, J. & Gerber, R., *Teaching Geography for a Better World*. Brisbane, Australian Geography Teachers Association with the Jacaranda Press.

Cummings, S.R., Nevitt, M.C., Browner, W.S., et al., (1995). "Risk Factors for Hip Fracture in White Women." *New England Journal of Medicine*, 332: 767-73.

Curtin, D. (1991). "Toward an Ecological Ethic of Care." In Donovan, J. & C.J. Adams (Eds.), 1996, *Beyond Animal Rights*. New York: Continuum. Pp. 60-76.

Curtin, D. (2001). "Recognizing Women's Environmental Expertise." In Zimmerman, M.E., et al., (Eds.), 2001, *Environmental Philosophy. From Animal Rights to Radical Ecology*, 3rd Ed. Upper Saddle River (NJ): Prentice Hall. Pp. 305-321.

Dator, J. (1996). "Futures studies as applied knowledge." In R. Slaughter (Ed.), 1996, *New Thinking for a New Millennium*. New York: Routledge.

Denzin, N.K. & Lincoln, Y.S. (2000). *Handbook of Qualitative Research*, 2nd Ed. Thousand Oaks, CA: Sage Publications, Inc.

De Silva, L. (2001). "The Buddhist Attitude Towards Nature." In Pojman, L.P., (Ed.), 2001, *Environmental Ethics. Readings in Theory and Application.* Belmont (CA): Wadsworth. Pp. 256-259.

Devall, B. & Sessions, G. (2001). "Deep Ecology." In Pojman, L.P., (Ed.), 2001, *Environmental Ethics. Readings in Theory and Application.* Belmont (CA): Wadsworth. Pp. 157-161.

Dewey, J. (1997, [1938]). *Experience and Education.* New York: Touchstone.

Dombrowski, D. A. (1984). *The Philosophy of Vegetarianism.* Amherst: University of Massachusetts Press.

Donovan, J. (1990). "Animal Rights and Feminist Theory." In Donovan, J. & C.J. Adams (Eds.), 1996, *Beyond Animal Rights.* New York: Continuum. Pp. 34-59.

Donovan, J. (1994). "Attention to Suffering: Sympathy as a Basis for Ethical Treatment of Animals." In Donovan, J. & C.J. Adams (Eds.), 1996, *Beyond Animal Rights,* Pp. 147-169.

Donovan, J. & Adams, C.J. (1996). *Beyond Animal Rights.* New York: Continuum.

Dwivedi, O.P. (2001). "Satyagraha for Conservation: Awakening the Spirit of Hinduism." In Pojman, L.P., (Ed.), 2001, *Environmental Ethics. Readings in Theory and Application.* Belmont (CA): Wadsworth. Pp. 250-255.

Farb, J. (2000). *Compassionate Souls.* New York: Lantern Books.

Felthous, A.R. (1980). "Aggression against cats, dogs and people." *Child Psychiatry and Human Development,* Vol. 10, No. 3, Pp. 169-177.

Felthous, A.R. & Kellert, S.R. (1986). "Violence against animals and people: Is aggression against living creatures generalized?" *Bulletin of the American Academy of Psychiatry and Law,* Vol. 14, No. 1, Pp. 55-69.

Feskanich, D., Willet, W.C., Stampfer, M.J. & Colditz, G.A. (1997). "Milk, Dietary Calcium, and Bone Fractures in Women: A 12-Year Prospective Study." *American Journal of Public Health,* Vol. 87, Pp. 992-7.

Fien, J. & Gerber, R. (1986). *Teaching Geography for a Better World.* Brisbane, Australian Geography Teachers Association with the Jacaranda Press.

Fox, M. (1990). *Inhumane Society. The American Way of Exploiting Animals.* New York: St. Martin's Press.

Fox, M. "Creation Spirituality." (1998). In Botzler, R.G. & S.J. Armstrong (Eds.), 1998, *Environmental Ethics. Divergence and Convergence.* Boston: McGraw-Hill, Pp. 228-235.

Freire, P. (2002 [1970]). *Pedagogy of the Oppressed.* New York: Continuum.

Friel, J. & Friel, L. (1990). *An Adult Child's Guide to What's "Normal".* Deerfield Beach, FL: Health Communications, Inc.

Fujii, T. (Spring, 2000). "Sound Development of Human Society: Buddhism and the Environment." *Futures Research Quarterly,* Vol. 16, No. 1, Pp. 29-48.

Gaard, G. (1993). *Ecofeminism: Women, Animals, Nature.* Philadelphia: Temple University Press.

Gardner, H. (1993). *Frames of Mind: The Theory of Multiple Intelligences.* New York: Basic Books.

Gannon, J.P. (1989). *Soul Survivors.* New York: Simon & Schuster.

Geddes, V.C. (1977). "Enuresis, fire setting and animal cruelty, a follow-up study to review the hypothesis in reference to the prediction of violence." MS

Thesis, Department of Criminal Justice, California State University, Long Beach, CA.

Gever, M. (1990). "The Names We Give Ourselves." In Ferguson, R., Gever, M., Minh-ha, T.T., & West, C. (Eds.), 1990, *Out There. Marginalization and Contemporary Cultures*. New York: The New Museum of Contemporary Art. Pp. 191-202.

Gilligan, C. (1982). *In a Different Voice: Psychological Theory and Women's Development*. Cambridge: Harvard University Press.

Goldstein, T. & Selby, D. (Eds.), 2000. *Weaving Connections. Educating for Peace, Social and Environmental Justice*. Toronto, Ontario, Canada: Sumach Press.

Gredley, E. (Fall/Winter, 1998). "Humane Education and the Curriculum." *The Humane Educator*. p. 3.

Gredley, E. (Spring/Summer, 1999). "Violence Link Research and Humane Education." *The Humane Educator*. Pp. 1,3.

Harper, S. (1995). "The Way of Wilderness." In Roszak, T., et al., (Eds.), 1995, *Ecopsychology*. San Francisco: Sierra Club Books, Pp. 183-200.

Heller, C. (1999). *Ecology of Everyday Life: Rethinking the Desire for Nature*. New York: Black Rose Books.

Hellman, O.S. & Blackman, N. (1966). "Enuresis, Firesetting and Cruelty to Animals: A Triad Predictive of Adult Crime." *American Journal of Psychiatry*, Vol. 122, Pp. 1431-1435.

Hessing, M. (1993). "Women and Sustainability. Ecofeminist Perspectives." *Alternatives*, Vol. 19, No. 4, Pp. 14-21.

Hicks, D. & Holden, C. (1995). *Visions of the Future: Why We Need to Teach for Tomorrow*. Staffordshire, England: Trentham Books.

Hill, J. L. (1996). *The Case for Vegetarianism: Philosophy for a Small Planet*. Maryland: Rowman & Littlefield Publishers.

Hillman, J. (1995). "A Psyche the Size of the Earth." In Roszak, T., et al. (Eds.), 1995, *Ecopsychology*. San Francisco: Sierra Club Books, Pp. xvii-xxiii.

Holbrook, A. (1998). "Teachers and Postgraduate Futures Education." In Hicks, D. & Slaughter, R.A. (Eds.), 1998, *World Yearbook of Education: Futures Education*. London: Kogan Page. Pp. 149-161.

hooks, bell. (1990). "Marginality as site of resistance." In Ferguson, R., et al., (Eds.), 1990, *Out There. Marginalisation and Contemporary Cultures*. New York: The New Museum of Contemporary Art. Pp. 341-344.

Huang, Z., Himes, J.H. & McGovern, P.G. (1996). "Nutrition and Subsequent Hip Fracture Risk Among a National Cohort of White Women." *American Journal Epidemiol*, Vol. 144, Pp. 124-34.

Johnson, L.E. (1997). *A Morally Deep World: An Essay on Moral Significance and Environmental Ethics*. Cambridge (UK): Cambridge University Press.

Karlan, J.W. (Summer, 2000). "The Biosphere Challenge: Developing Ecological Literacy." *Green Teacher*, Vol. 62, Pp. 13-18.

Kellert, S.R. (1996). *The Value of Life*. Washington, D.C.: Island Press.

Kellert, S.R. & Felthous, A.R. (1985). "Childhood cruelty toward animals among criminals and noncriminals," *Human Relations*, Vol. 38, Pp. 1113-1129.

Kheel, M. (1985). "The Liberation of Nature: A Circular Affair." In Donovan, J. & Adams, C.J. (Eds.), 1996, *Beyond Animal Rights. A Feminist Caring Ethic for the Treatment of Animals*. New York: Continuum. Pp. 17-33.

Kowalski, G. (1999 [1991]). *The Souls of Animals*. Novato, CA: New World Library.

Langley, G.R. (1991). "Animals in science education—ethics and alternatives." *Journal of Biological Education,* Vol. 25, No. 4, Pp. 274-279.

Leopold, A. (1968, [1949]). *A Sand County Almanac*. Oxford University Press.

Lindahl, O., Lindwall, L., Spangberg, A., Stenram, A., Ockerman, P.A. (1984). "A vegan regimen with reduced medication in the treatment of hypertension." *Br. Journal of Nutrition,* Vol. 52, Pp. 11-20.

Linzey, A. (1998). *Animal Gospel*. Louisville (KY): Westminster John Knox Press.

Linzey, A. (2009). *Why Animal Suffering Matters*. New York: Oxford University Press.

Locke, J. (1905). *Some Thoughts Concerning Education*, 5th Ed. London, England.

Lovelock, J. (2000). *Gaia: A New Look at Life on Earth*. Oxford: Oxford University Press.

Luke, B. (1992). "Justice, Caring, and Animal Liberation." In Donovan, J. & C.J. Adams (Eds.), 1996, *Beyond Animal Rights. A Feminist Caring Ethic for the Treatment of Animals*. New York: Continuum. Pp. 77-102.

Lyman, H.F. (1998). *Mad Cowboy*. New York: Touchstone.

Macy, J. (1995). "Working Through Environmental Despair." In Roszak, T., et al., (Eds.), *Ecopsychology*. San Francisco: Sierra Club Books, Pp. 240-259.

Macy, J. (2000). "World as Lover, World as Self." In Bloom, W. (Ed.), 2000. *Holistic Revolution. The Essential New Age Reader*. Harmondsworth, Middlesex, England: Penguin Press. Pp. 133-137.

Malter, M., Schriever, G, Eilber, U. (1989). "Natural Killer Cells, Vitamins, and Other Blood Components of Vegetarian and Omnivorous Men." *Nutr Cancer*, Vol. 12, Pp. 271-8.

Manning, R.C. (1992). "Caring for Animals." In Donovan, J. & Adams, C. (Eds.), 1996, *Beyond Animal Rights. A Feminist Caring Ethic for the Treatment of Animals*. New York: Continuum. Pp. 103-125.

Marcus, E. (1998). *Vegan: The New Ethics of Eating*. New York: McBooks Press.

Margulis, L. (1998). *Symbiotic Planet: A New Look at Evolution*. Amherst (MA): Basic Books.

Marsh, R.F. (1993). "Bovine Spongiform Encephalopathy: A New Disease of Cattle?" *Arch Virol*, Vol. 7 (Suppl), Pp. 225-9.

Maslow, A. H. (1954). *Motivation and personality*. New York: Harper & Row.

Maslow, A. H. (1968). *Toward a psychology of being*, (2nd Ed.). New York: D. Van Nostrand.

Masson, J. M. & McCarthy, S. (1995). *When Elephants Weep: The Emotional Lives of Animals*. New York: Delacorte Press.

Mayer, V.J. & Hinton, N.K. (March, 1990). "Animals in the Classroom." *The Science Teacher*, Vol. 57, No. 3, Pp. 27-30.

McAdams, D.P. (1990). *The Person*. Orlando, Florida: Harcourt Brace Jovanovich.

McEwan, C. (1993). "Are We Raising Morally Illiterate Kids?" In Thacker, P. (Ed.), 1993, *Values*. Toronto: McGraw-Hill Ryerson. Pp. 114-119.

McGinn, C. (8 April, 1996). "Born Free." *The New Republic.*

McInerney, J.D. (May, 1993). "Animals in Education: Are We Prisoners of False Sentiment?" *The American Biology Teacher*, Vol. 55, No. 5, Pp. 276-280.

Merchant, C. (2001). "The Death of Nature." In Zimmerman, M.E. et al., (Eds.), 2001, *Environmental Philosophy. From Animal Rights to Radical Ecology.* Upper Saddle River (NJ): Prentice Hall. Pp. 273-286.

Messina, V. & Burke, K. (Nov., 1997). "Position of The American Dietetic Association: Vegetarian Diets." *Journal of the American Dietetic Association*, Vol. 97, No. 11, Pp. 1317-21.

Metzner, R. (1995). "The Psychopathology of the Human-Nature Relationship." In Roszak, T., et al., (Eds.), 1995, *Ecopsychology.* San Francisco: Sierra Club Books. Pp. 55-67.

Milbrath, L.W. (1996). "Envisioning a Sustainable Society." In Slaughter, R.A. (Ed.), 1996, *New Thinking for a New Millennium*, Pp. 185-197. London: Routledge.

Montgomery, C. (2000). *Blood Relations.* Toronto: Between The Lines Publishing.

Morrison, A.R. (Jan.-Jun., 1992). "What's Wrong with 'Animal Rights'". *The American School Board Journal*, Vol. 179, Pp. 20-23.

Munoz de Chavez, M. & Chavez, A. (1998). "Diet That Prevents Cancer: Recommendations from the American Institute for Cancer Research." *International Journal of Cancer* (Suppl), Vol. 11, Pp. 85-89.

Newkirk, I. (1992). *Free the Animals.* Chicago: The Noble Press, Inc.

Newman, J.H. (1868). "The Crucifixion (1842) Sermon X," *Parochial and Plain Sermons.* London: Rivingtons. Pp. 133-145.

O'Connor, T. (1995). "Therapy for a Dying Planet." In Roszak, T., et al., (Eds.), 1995, *Ecopsychology.* San Francisco: Sierra Club Books, Pp. 149-155.

Ontario Curriculum, Grades 1-8. (1998). *Health and Physical Education.* Ministry of Education and Training.

Ornish, D., Brown, S.E., Scherwitz, L.W., Billings, J.H., Armstrong, W.T. & Ports, T.A. (1990). "Can Lifestyle Changes Reverse Coronary Heart Disease?" *Lancet*, Vol. 336, Pp. 129-33.

Orr, D.W. (1994). *Earth in Mind. On Education, Environment, and the Human Prospect.* Washington, D.C.: Island Press.

O'Sullivan, E. (2001). *Transformative Learning. Educational Vision for the 21st Century.* Toronto: University of Toronto Press.

Outwater, J.L., Nicholson, A. & Barnard, N. (1997). "Dairy Products and Breast Cancer: The IGF-1, Estrogen, and bGH Hypothesis." *Medical Hypothesis*, Vol. 48, Pp. 453-61.

Pennington, J.A.T. (1998). *Bowes and Churches Food Values of Portions Commonly Used*, 17th edition, New York: Lippincott.

Phillips, R. L. (1975). "Role of Lifestyle and Dietary Habits in Risk of Cancer Among Seventh-Day Adventists." *Cancer Res* (Suppl), Vol. 35, Pp. 3513-22.

Physicians Committee for Responsible Medicine. (Nov. 16, 1998). "Mad Cow Disease: The Risk to the U.S." Washington D.C.

Physicians Committee for Responsible Medicine. (Nov. 18, 1998). "Foods for Cancer Prevention." Washington D.C. Pp. 1-2.

Physicians Committee for Responsible Medicine. (July 12, 1999). "The Protein Myth." Washington D.C. Pp. 1-2.

Physicians Committee for Responsible Medicine. (Dec. 4, 1998). "Vegetarian Diets for Children: Right from the Start." Washington, D.C. Pp. 1-3.

Physicians Committee for Responsible Medicine. (Dec. 10, 1998). "Vegetarian Foods: Powerful for Health." Washington, D.C. Pp.1-2.

Physicians Committee for Responsible Medicine. (Feb. 28, 2000). " What's Wrong with Dairy Products? " Washington D.C.

Physicians Committee for Responsible Medicine. (March 10, 2000). "Diet and Prostate Cancer." Washington D.C.

Pike, G. & Selby, D. (1999). *In The Global Classroom 1*. Toronto, Ontario, Canada: Pippin Publishing.

Pike, G. & Selby, D. (2000). *In The Global Classroom 2*. Toronto, Ontario, Canada: Pippin Publishing.

Pike, G. (2000). "A Tapestry in the Making: The Strands of Global Education." In T. Goldstein & D. Selby (Eds.), 2000, *Weaving Connections. Educating for Peace, Social and Environmental Justice*. Toronto: Sumach Press. Pp. 218-241.

Plumwood, V. (1998). "Nature, Self, and Gender: Feminism, Environmental Philosophy, and the Critique of Rationalism." In Zimmerman, M.E., et al., (Eds.), 1998. *Environmental Philosophy. From Animal Rights to Radical Ecology*. Upper Saddle River (NJ): Prentice Hall. Pp. 291-314.

Plumwood, V. (2000). "The environment." In Jaggar, A.M. & Young, I.M. (Eds.), 2000, *A Companion To Feminist Philosophy*. Oxford (UK): Blackwell Publishing Company Limited. Pp. 213-222.

Prusiner, S.B. (Jan., 1995). "The Prion Diseases." *Scientific American*, Pp. 48-57.

Ralston, H. (1998). "Yes, Value is Intrinsic in Nature." In Pojman, L. (Ed.), 1998, *Environmental Ethics. Readings in Theory and Application*. Belmont (CA): Wadsworth. Pp. 70-81.

Ralston, H. (2001). "Challenges in Environmental Ethics." In Zimmerman, M.E. et al., (Eds.), 2001, *Environmental Philosophy. From Animal Rights to Radical Ecology*. Upper Saddle River (NJ): Prentice Hall. Pp. 126-146.

Ralston, H. (2001). "Naturalizing Values: Organisms and Species." In Pojman, L.P., (Ed.), 2001, *Environmental Ethics. Readings in Theory and Application*. Belmont (CA): Wadsworth. Pp. 76-85.

Randour, M.L. (2000). *Animal Grace. Entering a Spiritual Relationship with Our Fellow Creatures*. Novato (CA): New World Library.

Rawls, J. (1971). *A Theory of Justice*. Oxford: Oxford University Press.

Regan, T. (1983). *The Case for Animal Rights*. Berkeley (CA): University of California Press.

Regan, T. (1998). "The Radical Egalitarian Case for Animal Rights." In Pojman, L.P., (Ed.), 1998, *Environmental Ethics: Readings in Theory and Application*. Belmont (CA): Wadsworth. Pp. 46-57.

Regan, T. (2001). "The Radical Egalitarian Case for Animal Rights." In Pojman, L.P., (Ed.), 2001, *Environmental Ethics. Readings in Theory and Application*. Belmont (CA): Wadsworth. Pp. 40-45.

Ressler, R.K., Burgess, A.W., & Douglas, J.E. (1988). *Sexual Homicide: Patterns and Motives.* Lexington (MA): Lexington Books.

Richmond, G., Engelmann, M. & Krupka, L.R. (Nov./Dec., 1990). "The Animal Research Controversy: Exploring Student Attitudes." *The American Biology Teacher*, Vol. 52, No. 8, Pp. 467-470.

Rigdon, J.D. & Tapia, F. (1977). "Children Who Are Cruel To Animals – A Follow-Up Study." *Journal of Operational Psychology*, Vol. 8, No. 1, Pp. 27-36.

Robbins, J. (1987). *Diet for a New America.* Walpole (NH): Stillpoint Publishers.

Robbins, J. (2001). *The Food Revolution.* Berkeley (CA): Conari Press.

Robertson, J. (1983). *The Sane Alternative. A Choice of Futures.* James Robertson, Shropshire, UK.

Rollin, B.E. (1990). *The Unheeded Cry: Animal Consciousness Animal Pain and Science.* Oxford: Oxford University Press.

Rollin, B.E. (1992). *Animal Rights & Human Morality.* New York: Prometheus Books.

Roszak, T. (1995). "Where Psyche Meets Gaia." In Roszak, T., et al., (Eds.), 1995, *Ecopsychology.* San Francisco: Sierra Club Books. Pp. 1-17.

Rouse, I.L. & Beilin, L.J. (1984). "Editorial Review: vegetarian diet and blood pressure. *J. Hypertens*, Vol. 2, Pp. 231-240.

Rowlands, M. (2002). *Animals Like Us.* London & New York: Verso.

Rubenstein, H.R. (Winter, 1999). "Ten Questions to Guide Future Studies at the Turn of the Century." *Futures Research Quarterly*, Vol. 15, No. 4, Pp. 65-67.

Ryder, R.D. (1983). *Victims of Science: The Use of Animals in Research.* 2nd Ed. London: National Anti-Vivisection Society.

Ryder, R.D. (1989). *Animal Revolution.* Oxford, UK: Basil Blackwell Ltd.

Ryder, R.D. (1998). *The Political Animal: The Conquest of Speciesism.* Jefferson (NC): McFarland & Company, Inc., Publishers.

Sagoff, M. (2001). "Animal Liberation and Environmental Ethics: Bad Marriage, Quick Divorce." In Zimmerman, M.E., et al., (Eds.), 2001, *Environmental Philosophy. From Animal Rights to Radical Ecology*, 3rd Ed. Upper Saddle River (NJ): Prentice Hall. Pp. 87-96.

Salt, H.S. (1980). *Animals' Rights Considered in Relation to Social Progress.* London: Centaur. Originally published (1892), London: George Bell & Son.

Sapp, J. (Winter, 2001). "Self-Knowing as Social Justice. The Impact of a Gay Professor on Ending Homophobia in Education." *Encounter*, Vol. 14, No. 4, Pp. 17-28.

Schlosser, E. (2002). *Fast Food Nation.* New York: Perennial.

Schweitzer, A. (2001). "Reverence for Life", In Pojman, L.P., (Ed.), 2001, *Environmental Ethics. Readings in Theory and Applications.* Belmont (CA): Wadsworth. Pp. 95-99.

Selby, D. (1995). *Earthkind.* Staffordshire, England: Trentham Books.

Selby, D. (Spring/Summer, 1998). "Humane Education: Challenging Anthropocentrism in the Curriculum." *The Humane Educator.*

Selby, D. (Summer, 1999). "Global Education: Towards a Quantum Model of Environmental Education." *Canadian Journal of Environmental Education*, No. 4, Pp. 125-141. Toronto: University of Toronto.

Selby, D. (Fall, 2000). "The Signature of the Whole: Radical Interconnectedness and its Implications for Global and Environmental Education." *Connections*, Vol. 25, No. 1. Pp. 16-25.

Selby, D. (Sept., 2000). "Global Education as Transformative Education." *ZEP*, 3. Pp. 2-10.

Shapiro, K. (1994). "The Caring Sleuth: Portrait of an Animal Rights Activist." In Donovan, J. & Adams, C.J., (Eds.), 1996, *Beyond Animal Rights. A Feminist Caring Ethic for the Treatment of Animals*. New York: Continuum. Pp. 126-146.

Shepard, P. Nature and Madness. (1995). In Roszak, T., Gomes, M.E., & Kanner, A.D., (Eds.). 1995. *Ecopsychology*. San Francisco: Sierra Club Books. Pp. 21-40.

Shostak, A.B. (Sept./Oct., 2000). "Teaching Utopia." *The Futurist*, Vol. 34, P. 68.

Singer, P. (1985). *In Defense of Animals*. New York: Harper & Row Publishers.

Singer, P. (1990). *Animal Liberation*. New York: Avon Books.

Singer, P. (1998). "All Animals Are Equal." In Zimmerman, M.E. et al., (Eds.), 1998, *Environmental Philosophy: From Animal Rights to Radical Ecology*, 3rd Ed. Upper Saddle River (NJ): Prentice Hall. Pp. 26-40.

Smith, D.C. & Carson, T.R. (1998). *Educating for a Peaceful Future*. Toronto: Kagan and Woo Limited.

Sorabji, R. (1993). *Animal Minds and Human Morals: The Origins of the Western Debate*. Ithaca, New York: Cornell University Press.

Spock, B. (May, 2000). "Good Nutrition for Kids." Reprinted from *Good Medicine* Spring/Summer 1998 by the Physicians Committee for Responsible Medicine.

Stone, C.D. (2001). "Should Trees Have Standing? Toward Legal Rights for Natural Objects." In Pojman, L.P. (Ed.), 2001, *Environmental Ethics. Readings in Theory and Application*. Belmont (CA): Wadsworth. Pp. 240-248.

Suzuki, D. (2002 [1997]). *The Sacred Balance*. Vancouver, BC: Greystone Books.

Tapia, F. (1971). "Children Who Are Cruel To Animals." *Child Psychology and Human Development*, Vol. 2, No. 2, Pp. 70-77.

Taylor, A. (1999). *Magpies, Monkeys, and Morals*. Peterborough, Ontario: Broadview Press.

Taylor, P.W. (1998). "The Ethics of Respect for Nature." In Zimmerman, M.E., et al., (Eds.), 1998, *Environmental Philosophy: From Animal Rights to Radical Ecology*, 3rd Ed. Upper Saddle River (NJ): Prentice Hall. Pp. 71-86.

Taylor, P.W. (2001). "Biocentric Egalitarianism." In Pojman, L.P., (Ed.), 2001, *Environmental Ethics. Readings in Theory and Applications*. Belmont (CA): Wadsworth. Pp. 100-111.

Taylor, P.W. (2001). "The Ethics of Respect for Nature." In Zimmerman, M.E., et al., (Eds.), 2001, *Environmental Philosophy. From Animal Rights to Radical Ecology*, 3rd Ed. Upper Saddle River (NJ): Prentice Hall. Pp. 71-86.

Tester, K. (1991). *Animals and Society: The Humanity of Animal Rights*. London/New York: Routledge.

Tobias, M. & Solisti-Mattelon, K. (Eds.), 1998. *Kinship with the Animals*. Hillsboro, Oregon: Beyond Words Publishing.

Trotter, A. (Jan.-Jun., 1992). "Animal rights groups target high school dissection." *The American School Board Journal*, Vol. 179, Pp. 22-23.

Vander Zanden, J. W. (1989). *Human Development.* (4th Ed). San Francisco: McGraw Hill.

VegetarianTimes.com. `Vegetarianism in America`, 2008.

Vockell, E. & Hodal, F. (1977). In Arkow, P. [article] "The Rationale and Goals of Humane Education" in *Humane Education, Operational Guide for Animal Care and Control Agencies*, American Humane Association, (undated), p. 1.

Vockell, E. & Hodal, F. (Winter, 1978). "Everything We Always Wanted To Know About Humane Education – But Never Bothered To Find Out." *Humane Education*, Pp. 4-5.

Walker, K.D., Hueston, W.D., Hurd, H.S. & Wilesmith, J.W. (1991). "Comparison of Bovine Spongiform Encephalopathy Risk Factors in the United States and Great Britain." *JAVMA*, Vol. 199, Pp. 1554-1561.

Warren, K.J. (1990). "The Promise and Power of Ecofeminism." *Environmental Ethics*, Vol. 12, No. 2, P. 126.

Warren, K.J. (1998). "The Power and the Promise of Ecological Feminism." In Zimmerman, M.E., et al., (Eds.), 1998, *Environmental Philosophy. From Animal Rights to Radical Ecology.* Upper Saddle River (NJ): Prentice Hall. Pp. 325-344.

Warren, K.J. (2001). "The Power and Promise of Ecological Feminism." In Pojman, L.P., (Ed.), 2001, *Environmental Ethics. Readings in Theory and Application.* Belmont (CA): Wadsworth. Pp. 189-198.

Wax, D.E. & Haddox, V.G. (1974). "Enuresis, Firesetting, and Animal Cruelty: A Useful Danger Signal in Predicting Vulnerability of Adolescent Males to Assaultive Behaviour." *Child Psychiatry and Human Development*, Vol. 4, No. 3, Pp. 151-156.

Weil, Z. (1991). *Animals in Society.* Jenkintown (PA): Animalearn.

Weil, Z. (Jun. 10, 1999). "Preventing Violence through Humane Education." *The Ellsworth American.*

Weil, Z. & Sikora, R. (Eds.), (1999). *Sowing Seeds Workbook: A Humane Education Primer.* Surry (ME): Center for Compassionate Living.

West, C. (1990). "The New Cultural Politics of Difference." In Ferguson, R., Gever, M., Minh-ha, T.T., & West, C., (Eds.), 1990, *Out There. Marginalization and Contemporary Cultures.* New York: The New Museum of Contemporary Art. Pp. 19-37.

Wittig, M. (1990). "The Straight Mind." In Ferguson, R., Gever, M., Minh-ha, T.T., & West, C., (Eds.), 1990, *Out There. Marginalization and Contemporary Cultures.* New York: The New Museum of Contemporary Art. Pp. 51-57.

Woititz, J.G. & Garner, A. (1990). *Life-Skills for Adult Children.* Deerfield Beach, FL.: Health Communications, Inc.

Zimmerman, M.E. (Spring, 1988). "Quantum Theory, Intrinsic Value, and Panentheism." *Environmental Ethics*, Vol. 10, Pp. 3-30.

Appendix: Classroom Activities

The following activities are designed as transformative learning tools for students to reflect upon their own attitudes, beliefs, and interactions with non-human species. Stemming from the field of Humane Education, these interactive learning models serve as part of a foundation for critical analysis and thought provoking exchange regarding our human relationship with other-than-human fellow earthlings. Here is an opportunity for participants to explore their own biases and deeply ingrained feelings that were most likely embedded in their daily living since early childhood. But even more critical is the potential for learners to rethink their relatedness towards other species and optimally, evolve towards a more compassionate and empathic mode of viewing and interacting with others.

Each activity prescribes an age/grade level recommendation for classroom engagement; however, it is at the discretion of the instructor/facilitator, based on the maturity and ability levels of her/his students/participants, to decipher whether any given activity will serve learners in positive and productive ways. For example, Activity 1 recommends a starting level of grade 10 students; however, this activity can be successfully achieved with younger students depending on their unique abilities and openness for learning new perspectives.

Although specific procedures are provided for each activity, the instructor may insert her/his own creativity as long as key components remain intact. For example, in Activity 5, of the four different animal pictures used, at least one must be of a common domestic "pet" such as a dog or a cat and at least one picture must be of an animal that most people usually eat such as a cow or a pig.

Regarding time frames, a guideline is provided for how much time is needed to successfully complete each activity; however, most of the activities can easily be extended as long-term group projects. Further, instructors may add additional components to activities such as on-going research papers for various animal species or species' habitats, behaviours, and characteristics.

The main objective is to engage learners throughout these activities in a fun, non-threatening manner whereby they will enjoy learning new ways of thinking about and relating to other species. Humane education is an essential extension of and compliment to anti-violence education; more than ever, we need to plan some of our curricular time focussing on the very critical discourse of peace, conflict resolution, and compassionate living.

It is my hope, as the author, that this book will reach many educators and animal lovers alike and that the activities contained herein will provide a rich and life-altering learning experience for the many students (and educators) who are privy to participation in these transformative, eye-opening, and much needed lessons focussed at encouraging and facilitating a more humane society.

Activity 1: Where Do We Draw The Line?

(Portions of this activity adapted from Pike & Selby (2000)).

Participants: Grade 10 and up

Materials Needed: (1) Sets of statement cards (see below); one set per group; (2) coloured markers; (3) tape or glue sticks; (4) large poster/chart paper (one sheet per group); (5) a large open space for groups to comfortably spread out and work.

Time Needed: 60 to 70 minutes

Procedure: Divide participants into small groups of 5 or 6 people. Distribute a copy of the list of activities/actions (**Table A-1**), one copy per group, along with the other supplies. Instruct participants to order the listed items from "not acceptable at all" to "very acceptable." Groups will place (tape/glue) the cards along a continuum based on their cooperative decisions. If there are any cards that groups cannot come to consensus on, these cards are placed in the section marked "undecided" (See **Figure A-1**).

After allowing ten to fifteen minutes for groups to complete their card placements, regroup as one large discussion arena and have a spokesperson from each group share their findings with the whole class. Post the charts on the walls around the room.

A debriefing discussion, the most significant segment of this activity, is now facilitated by the instructor. It is important to allow participants the opportunity to share their ideas and explain their rationale for their responses, without any bias coming from the facilitator. The whole class needs to discuss the issues at hand in a respectful, orderly manner whereby everyone gets a chance to contribute her/his opinions.

Using animals for scientific experiments to test whether cosmetics and toiletries are safe for human use.	Using animals for military experiments to test the effects of new weapons of chemical, gas, and biological warfare.	Using specially bred and freshly killed animals for dissection purposes in school biology lessons.	Meat will no longer be sold at grocery stores or markets. Anyone who desires to eat meat will be required to kill the animal themselves for this purpose.
The killing of non-human animals should carry the same legal punishments as the killing of human beings.	Using animal organs for transplanting into humans.	Eating meat is acceptable as long as the animals are raised in a free-range environment.	Choosing to adapt a vegan lifestyle for the reason of not contributing to the suffering of farm animals.
Keeping wild animals in zoos, aquaria and aviaries for purposes of amusement and education.	Using specifically bred and purpose-trained dogs to assist disabled people.	Using animals in television commercials as a means of promoting products.	People should be allowed to have their deceased pet(s) buried with them if they so desire.
High school students should be taught the truths and realities about factory farming, medical research using animals and other forms of animal exploitation.	Tougher laws are needed in order to punish people guilty of animal abuse to the point whereby a court sentence for animal cruelty could match a similar sentence for similar crimes committed against people.	Hunting animals for pleasure -- the thrill of the chase and catch.	Wearing fur, leather, suede or wool even though animals are subjected to cruel agony in the manufacturing of these products.

Table A-1: Activities/Actions Statements

Potential Benefits: Hopefully, participants will acquire a new found perspective for thinking about how animals are treated in our society as well as ponder the extent to which their daily activities may contribute to the plight, pain and suffering of so many living beings. This activity really gives participants an opportunity to reflect upon their own contribution to animal suffering through routine daily activities; additionally, participants have the prospect of rethinking their perspective regarding animals and the potential to alter their habits towards more humane ones.

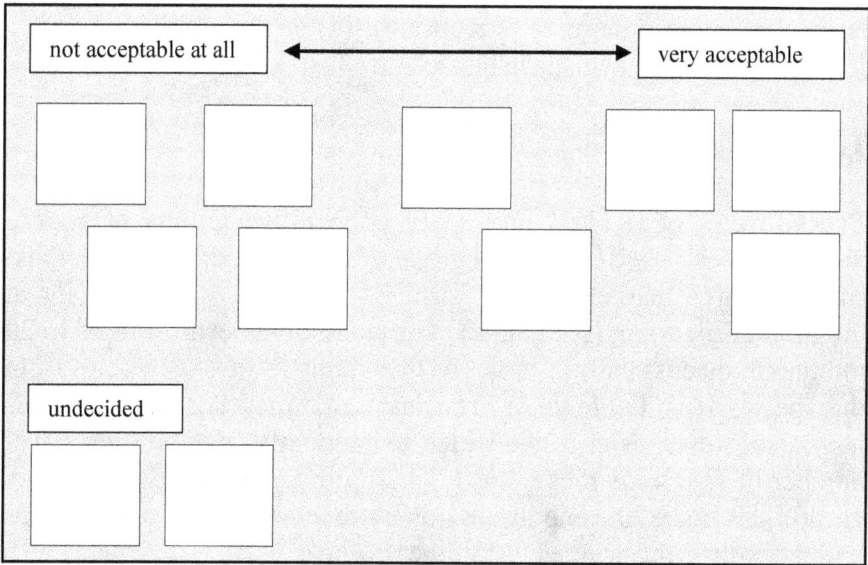

Figure A-1: Completed chart with all statement cards attached as agreed upon by group members.

Activity 2: What Do We Have In Common?

Participants: Grade 4 and up

Materials Needed: (1) Large white board; (2) coloured markers; (3) large chart paper (one piece per group); (4) sub-topics list posted in front of room; (5) open space classroom

Time Needed: 60 to 70 minutes

Procedure: Divide class into small cooperative groups of 5 or 6 members each. Give each small group a large piece of chart paper and some coloured markers. Have participants refer to sub-topics list at the front of the room (see below). Groups should be allowed 15 to 20 minutes to discuss the sub-topics as they apply to various species from the species list (**Table A-2**). The instructor may add other species names; however, it is a good idea to randomly distribute an equal number of species names to each small group (i.e., 4 - 6 species per group); this makes the end discussion more interesting as some groups will have differing species from other groups.

Groups should create a continuum (e.g., 1 to 5, 1 = strongly disagree; 5 = strongly agree; continuum example: see **Figure A-2**) for each species as to whether group members believe that said species carries the ability/capacity for each sub-topic item. Using their own creativity, groups compose a chart, graph, list, or storyboard representation of their findings; allow students to use their creativity to create their final product.

Finally, all groups rejoin the class as a whole and share and discuss and compare their findings/opinions/beliefs. A debriefing completes this activity as the facilitator (instructor) highlights commonalities/differences and wraps up activity with final remarks. Note: Always encourage students to explain their rationale.

Potential Benefits: Students are given an opportunity to discover how their classmates feel about various animal species; they also may learn their own biases/prejudices towards certain animal species. Further, participants may expand their sense of humane values by tapping into empathy and compassion they may possess for our non-human fellow earthlings.

Sub-topics	Species
Ability to feel pain	Humans
Ability to feel joy	Dogs
Capacity for experiencing hunger	Cows
Capacity for forming relationships with fellow community members	Pigs
	Chickens
Ability to experience fear, terror	Earthworms
Capacity to love others	Pigeons
Desire to live, thrive	Donkeys
Capacity for feeling lonely	Horses
Capacity for feeling depressed	Ducks
Ability to feel anger	Cockatiels
Mourns when a loved one dies	Rabbits
Ability to experience boredom	Snails

Table A-2: Sub-Topics/Experiences and Species' Names

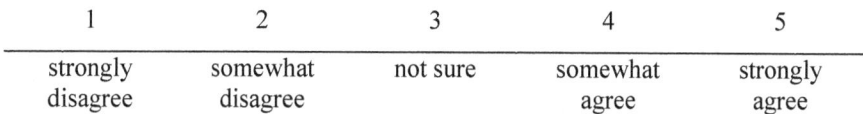

1	2	3	4	5
strongly disagree	somewhat disagree	not sure	somewhat agree	strongly agree

Figure A-2: Example of Continuum

Activity 3: My Best Friend

Participants: Grade 3 and up (Note: although this activity may be conducted with young students, it is also very powerful when implemented in an adult learning setting).

Materials Needed: (1) one sheet of writing paper per person; (2) pens/pencils; (3) large white board; (4) coloured white board markers

Time Needed: 60 to 70 minutes

Procedure: Participants are to work independently and quietly. Instruct all participants to think about someone whom they consider their best friend; they are to brainstorm all the qualities and characteristics of their best friend (e.g., very giving, kind, compassionate -- the instructor may offer a few examples, but allow participants to do the brainstorming work on their own). Each person will compose their own list for the qualities and characteristics of their best friend (allow about 15 minutes for this segment of the activity).

The whole group comes together and individuals offer to share some of the items from their lists. This is an opportunity for the group to compare their lists and see if common themes emerge, for example, are there common qualities or characteristics that many participants seek in a best friend? If there are several common responses, they may be written on the white board for further discussion.

To help facilitate discussion and critical thinking for what constitutes friendship, write the following questions on the white board or on a chart to display in the classroom; proffer the questions, one at a time, and invoke responses to continue the discussion:

Questions:

(1) What is the one most important quality you look for in a best friend? Why?

(2) Do you believe that you possess the same or similar qualities as your best friend? If so, what are they?

(3) Without naming names, think about someone who you prefer *not* to keep company with; what qualities does this person have that you do not like?

(4) Do you think that *you* possess any of the qualities of the person whom you do *not* like to spend time with?

(5) Is it possible for you to have a best friend who is a non-human animal? If so, would her/his qualities vary from a human friend? If so, how would they vary?

(6) Can a friendship with a non-human animal carry as much strength (i.e., trust, compassion, love) as a friendship with a fellow human? Explain.

Potential Benefits: This activity allows participants to tap into their feelings and thoughts about what constitutes friendship. Further, it helps to understand the concepts of empathy and compassion and hopefully, participants are able to make the connection of shared qualities between humans and non-human animals as a way of developing deeper respect and empathy for animals' experiences and how they may feel or what they may think in various life events. Ultimately, this activity permits an opportunity for students to ponder the concept of friendship and their unique role and contribution to those they relate to throughout their lives.

Activity 4: Needs or Desires?

(Inspired by activity in Pike & Selby (1999))

Participants: Grade 7 and up

Materials Needed: (1) strips of paper, large enough to read if posted on the wall (e.g., 3 inches by 10 inches); 10 strips per student (have extra strips just in case students have more than 10 responses); (2) coloured markers; (3) white board/bulletin board divided into two sections labelled "needs" and "desires" (not to be posted until *after* students brainstorm their lists)

Time Needed: 60 minutes

Procedure: Instruct participants to work alone and quietly as they brainstorm and list as many answers as they can to the question, "What will make me happy in my life?" Each participant should attempt to conjure up at least ten answers.

Only after students have completed their lists, and still working independently, participants are now instructed to separate their list into two categories: "needs" and "desires." When they have completed separating their list into the two categories, participants write the answers, one per each strip of paper. Then, have all participants post their answer strips under the appropriate category at the front of the room (i.e., either under the heading "needs" or the heading "desires").

A plenary discussion follows whereby the instructor facilitates a discussion as to motivations and/or rationale for categorisation of a "need" or a "desire." The instructor may refer to the questions provided as well as conjure additional questions pertinent to this activity.

Some key questions to facilitate discussion are as follows:

(1) What is the difference between a "need" and a "desire?"

(2) How much of what you purchase do you consider needs? Offer a percentage.

(3) Name some things that you have purchased in the past year that you thought you *needed*, but afterwards realised that you did not *need* the item, but that you only *desired* the item.

(4) Why do you think people purchase things that they truly do not *need*?

(5) Do you get pleasure from shopping/purchasing clothing, electronics, media, etc.? If so, could you describe that pleasure?

(6) Can you name any needs that we humans have in common with non-human animals?

(7) Do you think that non-human animals have both needs *and* desires? What might be some of their desires?

(8) Do you think that the quality of your life would change if you cut back on purchasing non-necessary items? If so, how? If not, why?

Potential Benefits: This activity gives students an opportunity to view others' desires as well as what their classmates consider needs in surviving and thriving throughout their lives. Further, students have an opportunity to ponder whether their perceived *needs* are truly needs or simply *desires*. For more mature students, this is an opportunity for re-prioritising what they perceive as needs versus desires and potentially altering their worldview for what will make them feel happy and complete in their lives.

Activity 5: Why Love One and Eat the Other?

Participants: Grade 7 and up

Materials Needed: (1) pictures/posters of at least four different animals (e.g., cow, dog, pig, elephant) posted at the front of the room; (2) large sheets of chart paper (one sheet per small group); (3) coloured markers; (4) tape

Time Needed: 60 to 80 minutes (or continuous over several days)

Procedure: Post at least four separate pictures/posters of four different animals at the front of the room; the pictures need to include at least one "pet" type animal (e.g., dog or cat) and at least one animal used in the agricultural industry for food production (e.g., pig or cow). Divide the class into small groups of 4 or 5; distribute one piece of chart paper and several markers to each group.

Instruct participants to focus on each of the animals pictured on the wall and think about the following:[23]

> (1) How do you relate to each animal? As a pet? As a companion? As food?
>
> (2) What do the different animals have in common? Feelings? Physical abilities? Ability to form relationships? Ability to have a family? Ability to love?

---

[23] Note: Different cultures around the world relate to animals in varying ways; in some cultures, dogs are common family pets while in other cultures dogs are considered as food products. The instructor may wish to discuss this issue as a way of getting students to critically think about how they were raised to think with regards to various types of animals.

(3) How do the animals differ one from another? Feelings? Physical abilities? Ability to form relationships? Ability to have a family? Ability to love?

(4) If you are not a vegetarian or vegan, why do think that it is acceptable to eat some animals while embracing other animals into your home, your family, and your life?

Instruct participants to create a chart or diagram explaining their findings based on their small group discussion. Allow them to be as creative as they wish. Once group charts are complete, regroup the entire class, post all charts on the wall as a walking gallery, and allow students to survey the gallery for several minutes. Then, reform into one large group and begin the discussion of the following (the following questions may be written on the white board):

(1) How did your group begin your discussion?

(2) Were you easily able to find *differences* between and among the various animals? -- What particular differences did you agree to?

(3) Were you easily able to find *similarities* between and among the various animals? -- What particular similarities did you agree to?

(4) Regarding question #4 from above, what rationale, explanations or justifications did your group reach in terms of why you may choose to eat one type of animal but not another?

Following large group discussion, facilitate a debriefing session whereby the instructor and the participants are able to talk further about how they felt while engaging this activity; for example, the instructor may ask, "Does anyone feel differently now about any given animal as compared to how you may have felt about that animal prior to this activity?" The instructor needs to maintain as much objectivity as possible so as not to influence students in their thinking, but to allow students to ponder and critically think about these issues at their own pace.

Follow-Up Activity: Writing composition/persuasive writing. This follow-up activity will be completed more successfully if students have been taught how to write a persuasive essay prior to beginning this essay. Students are to write a persuasive essay on one of the following statements (arguing *for* or *against* any given statement with sound persuasive points):

> (1) Some animals make excellent pets while other animals are for humans to eat.
>
> (2) All animals deserve the same respect, compassion, empathy, and love; they are not ours to use for our own selfish desires.
>
> (3) As long as we raise animals in humane/kind ways, it is acceptable for us to eat them.
>
> (4) There is no such thing as "humane" killing and therefore, we do not have a right to eat animals.
>
> (5) Historically, humans have eaten animals for centuries; therefore, we should continue to do so.

[Note: The instructor may conjure other statements that are related to the topic at hand. The above statements are only supplied as a starting point. Also, it is at the discretion of the instructor to ensure that each student writes a truly persuasive essay that provides strong arguments of their position].

Potential Benefits: Activity 5, along with the follow-up persuasive essay, is designed to get students to critically think about an issue that most of them have probably never thought about before. This activity allows the opportunity for comparing one species to another species and deciphering any similarities/differences that may affect the way(s) people relate to various types of animals. This activity also serves as a springboard for further discussions on kindness to animals, organisational and institutional cruelty towards animals, vegetarianism and veganism, the hypocrisy of treating some animals with respect and love while torturing and killing other animals, noting that both types of animals carry the capacity for pain and suffering, joy and love, companionship and forming bonds with others. The optimal outcome, of course, is to increase and develop a greater sense of compassion and empathy for suffering animals.

Activity 6: Your Daily Interaction with Animals

Participants: Grade 7 and up

Materials Needed: (1) writing paper and pen for each student; (2) large open classroom where students may either sit on the floor or in chairs, but in pairs; (3) white board and markers

Preparatory Note: The instructor needs to have some knowledge about common products used daily by most people that contain animal derived ingredients and/or are tested on animals. For example, many shampoos and soaps are manufactured by companies that test chemicals and product ingredients on laboratory animals. It is essential that the instructor has as much of this knowledge as possible in order to facilitate students on the truth behind the development of products used on a regular basis.

Before engaging your students in this activity, visit web sites such as the following in order to educate yourself about how animals are used throughout the research and development process of testing, creating, and marketing products:

www.thevegetariansite.com/ethics_test.htm,

www.navs.org/science/animals-in-product-testing,

www.peta.org,

www.leapingbunny.org,

www.uncaged.co.uk/animaltesting.htm, or

veganrabbit.com/list-of-companies-that-do-test-on-animals.

Examples of what to look for: many soaps and candles are made from animal tallow (e.g., chicken fat, whale blubber); many cosmetic/personal hygiene products are tested on animals in laboratories and/or contain animal derived ingredients (see lists like the one provided at veganrabbit.com); clothing such as leather or suede jackets are made from the skins of cows killed in slaughterhouses; etc.

Time Needed: 45 to 60 minutes

Procedure: Divide students into dyads/pairs; each dyad should have a couple pieces of paper and a pen or pencil. Give the following instructions to your students:

"Think about your daily routines, what you do from the time you first wake up in the morning until the time you go to bed at night. Begin with your morning routine of showering, brushing your teeth, washing your face, applying make-up (if applicable, based on age group), the clothes you put on for the day, what you eat for breakfast, how you get to school or work, any activities you do at school or work, what you eat for lunch, how you spend your afternoon, how you get home from school or work, what you eat for dinner, your evening activities, your bedtime preparations (e.g., showering, brushing teeth, etc.), as well as any products and/or services you use on a daily or regular basis. List all the items you use throughout your day; each participant should compile her/his own list. After your lists are complete to the best of your ability, exchange your list with your partner. Quietly read your partner's list and next to each item, write the name of any animal species that may have something to do with that item. For example, if your partner eats eggs for breakfast, you will write "chicken" next to that item. If your partner uses a brand of soap that you know is made from animal tallow, write the name of the animal(s) you believe that tallow may derive from."

After all dyads have completed the above activity, re-group the entire class into one large assembly. One dyad at a time, quickly go around the room and have students read the items *and* animal species related to those items.

> Example: This is what one student might say, "Johnny eats eggs for breakfast: chicken; he shampoos his hair: his shampoo is not labelled as "cruelty free" so it may have been tested on a rabbit (if the product is one tested on laboratory animals); he put on his leather jacket: leather is the skin of a cow; after school, he plays piano: piano keys are usually made from ivory which comes from elephants, etc., etc.

The instructor or an assigned student may write down the names of all the animals mentioned on the white board at the front of the room.

Finally, the class engages a discussion about how much their lives are impacted by the lives of animals. Some key questions for the instructor to pose are:

> (1) Were you aware of how many animals' lives you impacted on a daily basis prior to this activity?;

> (2) How do you feel about the impact your activities have on animals?;

> (3) Are you satisfied with your current habits that impact animals' lives or would you prefer to alter your habits to minimise your negative impact on animals?;

> (4) If you decide to live a more compassionate lifestyle, what changes could you make?;

> (5) What would be the most challenging changes for you to make to evolve towards a more humane and compassionate lifestyle?;

> (6) What would be the easiest lifestyle changes you could make to minimise your negative impact on the lives of animals?

Potential Benefits: This activity truly brings the negative impact that people's lives have on other species to the forefront of social consciousness. It gives students an opportunity to critically ponder how their daily/regular activities affect the lives of others. Further, this activity serves as a springboard for participants evolving towards a more humane, more compassionate, lifestyle that not only has potential for saving animals' lives, but also has the capacity for encouraging more humane living that purports the values of compassion, empathy, kindness, respect, reverence for life, integrity, and love.

Activity 7: Humans Hurt Me By...

Participants: Grade 6 and up

Materials Needed: (1) large white board; (2) white board markers; (3) template phrase as shown below; (4) list of species

Time Needed: 60 to 75 minutes

Procedure: The instructor posts the template phrase (see below) on the white board at the front of the classroom. Each student chooses a species name from the list provided; species names may be written on small pieces of paper, placed in a hat, and students can randomly choose their species name to work with. Students work independently; allow about 8 to 10 minutes for students to brainstorm their answers.[24] The whole class may be seated in a large circle for optimal interaction.

<u>Template Statement</u>: Write the following statement on the white board:

> "I am a [species name], and humans hurt me by [action/behaviour/belief/habit of humans that causes harm to this particular species]. People could show their compassion, kindness, empathy, and love for me by [an action/behaviour/belief/newly formed habit of humans that demonstrates humane values towards this particular species]."

---

[24] If your students have not been received any lessons in various species (i.e., biology, zoology), you may wish to have them spend a few days researching a variety of species to learn about their characteristics as well as how animals are treated in factory farms and slaughterhouses; this research project has potential for long term learning of research methods, the writing process, and enlightenment of how humans relate to other species.

Example: A response from a student might look like the following:

> "I am a [pig], and humans hurt me by [imprisoning me in a slaughterhouse, killing my babies at the young age of only 6 months, and then killing me for human consumption]. People could show their compassion, kindness, empathy, and love for me by [adopting a vegan diet and refraining from eating pigs]."[25]

Once all students have had an opportunity to share their species' experiences and desires, a debriefing discussion may ensue whereby everyone should be encouraged to discuss their feelings and thoughts that emerged from this activity.

List of Species:

cow	pig	dog	horse	elephant	lion	trout
chicken	goat	rabbit	duck	raccoon	bull	deer
mouse	rat	snake	shark	whale	parrot	donkey
llama	turtle	dove	rhino	jaguar	mink	squirrel
pigeon	fox	ostrich	turkey	wild boar	lynx	moose

Potential Benefits: Bringing the pain and suffering we humans force upon other species to the forefront of our conscience is at the core of this activity. This activity has powerful potential in that students are strongly encouraged to think of the many ways that humans abuse, exploit, and kill other species. It is only through a conscientious effort of brainstorming and discussion that there will be any chance of our society evolving towards a more humane existence and coexisting with other species in a peaceful and non-anthropocentric world.

---

[25] Do not expect students to conjure such lengthy and expanded answers; this example simply provides more expansive information about how pigs are treated in the pork industry.

Activity 8: Writing for Compassion

Participants: Grade 4 and up

Materials Needed: (1) computer/writing paper; (2) pens; (3) a quiet space to think

Time Needed: this activity may be completed over a period of several days

Note: It is highly recommended that lessons/activities in humane education covering the topics of humane values towards animals be delivered prior to assigning this essay. This will help your writers produce more in-depth essays of clear and well-thought-out assertions and action plans. Before commencing the writing process, the whole class could engage in a brainstorming session to highlight and review some of the key issues and philosophies of the field (e.g., veganism, speciesism, ways in which humans harm animals, creating a more humane society, etc.).

Procedure: Throughout most composition classes, the topics relating to humane education and kindness towards animals rarely emerges as a writing topic. Treat this activity as a comprehensive essay assignment; however, the focus remains within the confines of humane values (i.e., compassion, empathy, kindness, respect, reverence for life, love) towards animals and the multiple ways that we can alter our lifestyles towards a more compassionate way of thinking, of behaving, of living.

Potential Benefits: There are many potential benefits that may stem from this essay assignment. Hopefully, students have had ample opportunity to reflect on their own ways of relating to various animal species. After several class discussions, and any other activities that students have experienced as part of the humane education discourse, it is the hope that participants have reconsidered how they think about non-human species and have evolved towards a more humane lifestyle. Naturally, we cannot expect every person to give up eating animals and animal products, nor can we expect everyone to stop wearing leather and fur, nor can we expect everyone to immediately cease buying products manufactured by cruel companies that engage in animal testing; however, humane education is about planting seeds of compassion. It is the hope of all humane educators, animal liberationists, and animal compassionists that our students will move, at their own pace, towards a more humane, kinder, and more compassionate lifestyle.

ABOUT THE AUTHOR

Dr. Robert S. E. Caine, Ph.D. earned his Doctorate of Philosophy from the University of Toronto. He focussed his studies in the areas of Humane Education, Environmental Education and Ethics, Animal Liberationist Philosophy, and Vegan Nutrition/Ethics; his Master's Degree of Education focussed within the same areas of study. His teaching experience ranges from elementary education to college level courses. Dr. Caine has also published academic articles addressing topics of animal liberation, teaching compassion, and creating a humane future through moral regard for our non-human counterparts. Having lived extensively in both California and Ontario, Canada, Dr. Caine has contributed his efforts within several animal rights advocacy organisations including In Defence of Animals, Toronto Pig/Cow/Chicken Save, People for the Ethical Treatment of Animals, Toronto Vegetarian Association, as well as several farm animal sanctuaries and humane societies and animal shelters; he also served as the keynote speaker for Toronto's first March to Close All Slaughterhouses. He is whole-heartedly dedicated to liberating animals from current oppressive environments and he has adopted over a dozen companion animals from shelters, rescue organisations, and dire situations. Dr. Caine currently resides with his companion animals: Sonoma, Berkeley, and Forest.

9 780099 393824